Profiles In Passion

Volume One :
Artists & Artisans

Buz Swerkstrom

Full Court Press

© Copyright 2014
by Buz Swerkstrom

Full **C**ourt **P**ress
Atlas, Wisconsin

**Other Books
By Buz Swerkstrom :**

Polk County Places: Impressions And
   Explorations of Polk County, Wisconsin

In The Time of Twelve (a sequel to
   Lewis Carroll's two Alice stories)

Born To Coast And Other Stories (humor)

Infinity On Trial: Essays About The Essential,
   The Elemental & The Easily Mocked

Sgt. Pepper's Inner Groove   (novel)

Golfing With Grace (novel)

Contents

Preface   7

Wood

Super Cooper   *John Giacalone, barrel maker*   9
Carousel Creations   *Ron Helstern, woodcarver*   22
Winging It   *Keith Davidson, woodcarver*   30
How Sweet The Shape   *Dan Jahr, folk harp builder*   34
Tune In, Turn On, Turn Out   *Rus Hurt, wood turner*   39
Patience In A Bottle   *John Fox, model ship builder*   43

Metal

A Business In Bronze   *Wally Shoop, bronze sculptor*   47
Metal Evolution   *Jack Route, metal artist (and son Mike, metalsmith)*   54
From Scrap To Sculpture   *Dennis O'Donnell, junque sculptor*   63
Math + Metal = Geometric Sculpture   *John Ganske, abstract sculptor*   67
Riding High   *Mike Polodna, high-wheel bicycle builder*   70
Fancy Framework   *Tim Paterek, bicycle frame builder*   76

Ceramics

Feats Of Clay   *Marty Pearson, potter*   79
Accent Artists   *Wendy Penta, Laura McCaul & Mark Tomlinson, tile makers*   84
Diane Keeler's Small World   *Diane Keeler, collectible doll maker*   91

Glass

Shades Of Grace *Mike Bloyer, stained glass artisan* 96
Dancing With Heat *Jim Engebretson, glassblower* 101
Splendor In The Glass *Nancy Potek, beadmaker* 105

Textiles

Extra Texture *Julie Crabtree, embroidery artist* 108
Rug Bug *Margaret Miller, weaver* 113
Intimate Curtains *Mary Jackelen, quilt artist* 117
Millions Of Stitches In Time *Jean Judd, quilt artist* 123
Sheer Artistry *Marge Lindemann, silk art artist* 129
A Sewer Of Sails, A Catcher Of Wind *Judy Tepley, sailmaker* 133
Subterranean Simplicity *Don Karsky, weaver* 139

Film

A Lens Of Place *Bob Olsgard, photographer* 145
Guided By The Light *Dianne Bryant, photographer* 148
Blind Intention *Bill Kinney, wildlife photographer* 152

Paint

Visions Of Francene *Fran Hart, watercolor artist* 156
Calendar Man *Louis Raymer, wildlife artist* 160
Portraits Of Americana *Christine Mount Kapp, portrait artist* 163
Expressions Of Love For The Land *Gregg Rochester, landscape artist* 167
Three Directions At Once *Al Servoss, watercolor artist* 172
Frame Of Mind *Jeff Hile, painter, potter, sculptor* 177
Ornamental Art *Eugene Kraskiewitz, ornament artist* 181
Leaves Of Class *Laurie Paulson, leaf painter* 186
Becoming Mary Pettis *Mary Pettis, landscape artist* 190

Miscellaneous Mediums

Eggtraordinarily Eggacting *Ernie Spinks, eggshell carver* 230
Atavistically Haunting *Glen Riddle, found-object constructionist* 233
Don't Spare The Rod *Tom Lovick, John Fox & Lewi May, fishing rod builders* 236
Taking Note Of Anita Beck *Anita Beck, greeting and note card designer* 245
Come Out And Play *Suzanne Vadnais Monson, collage and jewelry artist, painter and writer* 249
A Person Of Characters *Terry Scott, cartoonist* 256
Shelf Life *Mark Wardean, mushroom carver* 259
The Bird Knows The Words *David DeMattia, animatronics designer* 263
The Light Stuff *Cork Marcheschi, light artist* 267
Computer Clash *Don Miller, computer art artist* 278

Preface

Existentialist philosopher Jean-Paul Sartre caused quite a stir in intellectual circles in the 1940s when he opined humans are but bundles of useless passions. While I don't know the context of that comment, I would take issue with it on its face. Like fire, or atoms, or any number of other entities, passion can be either beneficial or harmful, energizing or virulent. Johann W. von Goethe hit the nail on the head when he wrote: "Passions are vices or virtues in their highest powers." They "are good servants but bad masters," Sir Roger L'Estrange observed. The same could be said of fire and water. To Alexander Pope, passion was "the gale" that allowed humans to sail "on life's vast ocean diversely."

Passion is when your soul is on fire for something. It is the essence of a stimulating life. The lifelessness Bob Dylan decried as a sin in "Desolation Row" can be traced to a lack of passion, or ennui.

Between the late 1970s and the early 1990s I had the good fortune, as a freelance writer, to write hundreds of feature stories about interesting people, places and events for several regional and statewide [Wisconsin] newspapers, as well as a far fewer number of articles for magazines. I interviewed hundreds of people about their passions, venturing around much of Wisconsin, and even occasionally into Minnesota, gathering stories about people who did interesting and unusual things, or who had outstanding talent. A large percentage of them possessed a remarkable level of eloquence—sometimes plainspoken eloquence—for describing and explaining their passions. Most of these passionate individuals were independent; they either worked independently or pursued an avocation in their own time in their own way. People who worked independently were almost invariably more enthusiastic and eloquent about what they did than were people who worked for companies. Their passion seemed to promote a freer sort of thinking and expression. Or perhaps their freedom fed their passion.

I tape recorded all of my interviews, which allowed me to stuff most of my stories with relatively long direct quotes, largely telling people's stories in their own words. Still, there were length limitations to contend with, which left a lot of expressive, eloquent statements stuck in the interview transcripts with nowhere else to go, until now. While the profiles in this book remain snapshots in time and have not been updated, most have been expanded to include larger chunks of verbatim quotations than the restrictive newspaper and magazine formats allowed. That gives many of the profiles even a stronger flavor of oral history. Indeed, in a couple of instances the material is presented as pure oral history.

More than a few of those I interviewed remarked that I must have had an interesting job, talking to all sorts of different people about what they loved to do and learning about different things. And it was interesting, if not as fulfilling as writing novels, essays and humor pieces. Evidence of how interesting I found many of those profiled in this book is the number of them I interviewed more than once—generally once for a newspaper feature and a second time for a magazine article.

As it turned out, I got in on the last phase of the golden age for freelance writers, as far as newspapers are concerned. All five of the newspapers for which I wrote stopped buying freelance material in the late 1980s and early 1990s, mainly without explanation. The market for magazine articles left me producing fewer pieces in a year than I did in a month during the newspaper years.

I hope this volume of profiles, about artists and artisans, is the first of at least three such volumes. My filing cabinets and cardboard boxes of files have enough material for more than three volumes, so the number is undetermined at this point.

Super Cooper

John Giacalone ... barrel maker

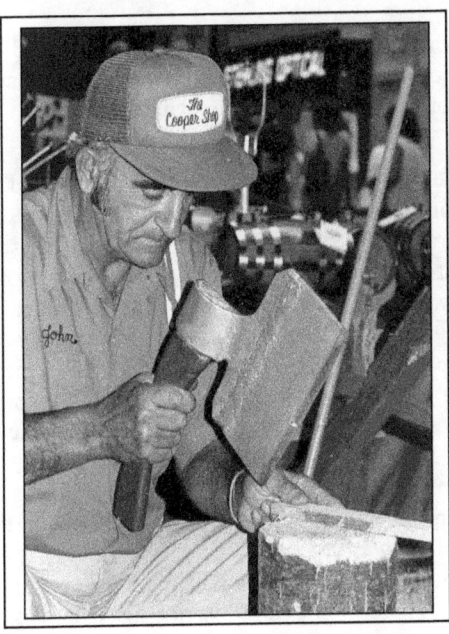

He works with wood and metal—with solid, substantial substances—and yet there is as much magic in what John Giacalone does as if he were conjuring creations from thin air with flashes of gossamer silk and flaming bursts of fire. You can watch him demonstrate each intricate step of the ancient craft of coopering, or barrel making, and still not understand how he manages to make every barrel perfectly round and watertight without the use of any geometric devices or gauges, nails or glue.

Take, for example, the man who approached Giacalone after a demonstration in Madison, Wisconsin—the third one in two days he had observed. "I don't understand," the man said, shaking his head in wonder. Giacalone asked what he didn't understand. "How in the hell do you get 360 degrees without a measure, without gadgets, without anything?" the man said, like some hopelessly confused soul driven to the edge of insanity by his inability to solve a mind-boggling puzzle. Giacalone asked what he did for a living. The man said he was an engineer. Giacalone thought to himself that he spoke like one. "Believe me," the man went on, "nowadays we have many sophisticated gauges and still many times we are a millimeter off. Yesterday I spent four hours watching you. This morning I spent another two hours watching. And I still don't understand how in the hell you get the 360 degrees."

"Do you know what, sir?" Giacalone said. "Honestly and sincerely, I have no explanation. The only thing I can tell you is my hands and my eyes. That's the only thing. I have no explanation."

When someone begins learning a craft at the tender age of nine, when he spends nine long years learning a craft so that every required skill becomes as natural as breathing, he develops some mystical ability even he does not fully comprehend and cannot fully explain. One could as easily explain romantic love as a master cooper's handcraft artistry at beveling staves so that they fit together as tightly as machine-made blocks. The osmotic skill is so deeply ingrained in the craftsman, so much a part of his being, that he does not lose the ability, does not lose the magic, even after more than 20 years away from the trade.

John Giacalone (pronounced Jack-a-lone) is proof of that. Emigrating from his native Italy at age 27 to start life anew following the death of his fiancée, Giacalone was unable to find work as a cooper in Windsor, Canada, so he drove a truck and worked on highway construction crews to make a living. There he met and married his wife, Josie. In 1964 they and their five sons moved to Milwaukee. Not happy living in a crowded city, they bought a dairy farm in central Wisconsin about nine miles southwest of the small town of Amherst and settled there in February of 1966, even though Giacalone had only a passing acquaintance with cows—literally; he had never been closer to them than driving past and seeing them grazing in pastures. By then they had a sixth child, a daughter. "I never knew how to work the land—to prepare the land and so forth," he says. "It took a lot of guts. But if you have the ambition and the willingness to work, no matter what you're doing, you'll make it. You cannot expect gold overnight, but you'll survive."

He "didn't touch" his cooper tools for 23 years. Then in the mid-1970s he started making a few small barrels in his spare time. "From there on," he relates, "some people saw them and people started coming, wanting to know when they could buy barrels, if they could order a barrel. And then the television stations started coming from all over the state, and before you know it I was forced to sell all my livestock and concentrate on the shop because the orders were coming in so often, and it takes quite a long time to produce one of those beautiful barrels. So in the spring of 1977 I sold them all—78 head of cattle. From there on I've been concentrating two-thirds of my time in the shop and one-third of my time on the farm, because I've got the land, I've gotta pay the [property] tax. That's the only reason I do a little bit of farming. [He raises corn, oats and hay.] But otherwise most of my work is concentrated in the shop."

Josie and John agonized over the decision to sell off all of the cattle. "Sure, he was getting a lot of publicity—fine and dandy," Josie says. "But, who was going to buy them [the barrels]? Would there be enough sales? But, we have a lot of faith in God, and we work hard, and we've made our own paths."

Dr. William Hanford, dean of fine arts at the University of Wisconsin—Stevens Point, 17 miles away, was instrumental in persuading Giacalone to become a full-time barrel maker again. Hanford told him he was wasting his talent farming. "Try it," he encouraged. "I don't think you're going to be sorry."

Josie calls what has happened since "an incredible phenomenon." It perhaps isn't really all that incredible, though, when you consider that Giacalone is one of a very few—a *very* few—coopers in the United States still capable of making barrels by hand, without the aid of machines. In fact, he is probably the only one doing so commercially.

Even in Marsala, Sicily, where Giacalone grew up, barrels are now made by machine. The 130 wineries in that port city of 100,000 people made it the coopering capitol of the world when Giacalone was young.

"There was, in the '40s and before that, about 6,000 coopers in that city," says Giacalone, now 60. "And I understand now, because the young men don't want to do such hard work, they went to machines. There's no more handcraft; it's all machine. Because the production has got to be made the same, you see, and young men don't want to spend 10 or 12 years—depending on how their brains work—to learn this craft. Today the world spins so fast that there is. . . 'I've gotta make money now.' That's the way the world is today. In my day it was different. And now I understand there's only 450 men left that do the coopering. So you, as the owner of a shop, have no choice, you've gotta go into machinery. In the last 20 years everything is done by machine.

"But me—no," Giacalone continues, his voice changing tone from a nostalgic sadness to a fierce Old World pride. "I'll die with that. I learned the handcraft and that's the way I'm going to stay all the way through until I retire, which will be a few years from now. It will be handcraft, no machine. I don't want any machine whatsoever in my shop. I have a drill; that's the only machine I have. Otherwise, no machines. I can buy any machine, but I don't want any. If they gave me a machine free and paid me a good amount of money to take it I wouldn't. No way. In our country, in America, people are starving of craft people. The country went too far and neglected any kind of craft—not just mine; I'm talking any kind of craftperson's. And so now, finally, I guess we are coming back and appreciating such handcraft."

Cardboard boxes and bags are modern inventions. The barrel was Mankind's basic package for centuries. It wasn't all that long ago, of course, when large barrels full of all sorts of items were common in country stores. Giacalone likens the importance of coopers in the 19th century, and previous centuries, to mechanics today. "Every house had some cooper vessels around—a bucket and tub and so on and so forth," he says.

Giacalone became fascinated with barrel making at age six or seven, when he passed a cooper's shop on his short walks between home and school every day.

"I liked the way the people were pounding, firing and so on and so forth," he says. ". . . Pretty often I was stopping after school. School was from eight to one at that time—five hours. And pretty often I said to my sister, 'You go home and tell Mama I'll watch here.' So I was in the door looking at how they were doing their jobs."

When he was not quite nine years old his father told him it was time for him to decide what he wanted to do with his life, if he wanted to learn a trade or continue going to school. "I'd like to become a cooper," he told his father. And so he began looking for a job while still going to school. A master cooper with the same last name, but not related, lived but a half-block away. A son of that cooper, two years younger, was one of Giacalone's playmates. Giacalone asked the man for a job. "It happened to be my luck that at that time, when I went to ask, he said yes," Giacalone says. "He usually had half a dozen men, and two or three teenagers [as apprentices], and a couple of children—young boys—who did some sweeping and moved stuff and stuff like that in the shop. He said, 'Yes. But only for one week. If I see potential in you that you will make a good cooper, then you can stay as long as you want. That's the way I usually hire young boys. Some go and some stay. It depends what I see in this boy. I'll take a chance.' That week lasted 11 years, and I left him because I went to open my own shop. And he was very cooperative. To him I was like his own son because, you know, he kind of saw me grow in the same street when I was playing with his son and so on and so forth.

"Now, as a young boy I didn't know the capacity of this man—I didn't know the capacity of this master cooper. After a while, when I became a young man, I found out that he happened to be the best in town, the best in the country, and the best in all Europe. People from Germany, France, Spain, Romania, Hungary, Yugoslavia, and many other countries came to grab this five-foot-two-inch man to build or restore those five-, six-, eight-thousand-gallon barrels. So, actually, I was lucky to have such a master to teach me the trade. So you realize I had a great ambition to learn this trade, and the quality of this person."

Giacalone apprenticed for nine years, learning the many different skills required in barrel-making, repeating each of them many times until they were set in his mind. When he was 18 the master cooper finally allowed him to build a barrel by himself.

"There's the wood. Start," the master instructed.

"Well," Giacalone says, "I built a barrel—a 50-gallon barrel. It wasn't perfect. It was watertight, yes, but ship-wise, no. He had pretty good eyes and could see little defects here and there. But he says, 'I think for a beginner that's beautiful, as you can see yourself. Come here and take a look.' So you look in the barrel. 'See any little--?' 'Yeah, there is a little bit here.' You know, little things like that. But he was very encouraging to me and says, 'You are okay now. From now on you master all those things by doing them.'"

At age 20 Giacalone became his own master by opening his own shop in Marsala.

"**O**ne of the big things in coopering that makes it so extraordinary a craft," Josie contributes, "is that there's hardly any measuring, so that's why it takes so long to master all the skills, like beveling, or angling, each stave to form 360 degrees. They don't use any geometric device.

That has to be mastered over years and years of practice. . . . Coopering is one of the most difficult crafts man has ever devised. I'm quoting from books about coopering. So that's why it's so difficult, it's so rare. When you get a good cooper he's in a class all by himself. There are the wet coopers and the dry coopers. He's a wet cooper because his barrels hold beverages. [Barrels built by] dry coopers hold nails, dry goods, flour. . ."

A cooper makes only two measurements when constructing a barrel, for height and circumference. Those two measurements determine the barrel's capacity. "The rest you've gotta judge with your eyes, for the shape, for the depth of the lid—like where the groove has to go—and so on and so forth," Giacalone says.

As evidence of the skill that Ludovico Giacalone possessed—and that John Giacalone possesses—consider this: Of the 6,000 coopers in Marsala, only five could make small oval barrels—Ludovico Giacalone, one of his brothers, John Giacalone and two other apprentices of Lucovico Giacalone. The four others are either deceased or have stopped making barrels, leaving John Giacalone as the only one carrying on that tradition of virtuosity.

Oval barrels are particularly difficult to make, he explains, because a cooper must first make a round barrel, then disassemble it so the staves can be re-beveled. It takes Giacalone eight to 10 hours to make a conventional round barrel and more on the order of a week to create an oval-shaped barrel.

Whereas wineries in Sicily wanted large barrels, today Giacalone makes only small barrels—about 120 each year. Most hold one to two gallons of liquid; about a dozen of them are five-gallon-capacity barrels. People want small barrels that can be set almost anywhere, even in a refrigerator.

Giacalone works with white and red oak that has been aged at least 18 months, preferably two years. He also uses black walnut in more expensive barrels, which have alternate black walnut and white oak staves. Because of his disdain for machines, he has a neighbor cut stave-size boards with a table saw. He uses a cooper's axe (a hatchet, actually) to rough-cut the staves, then a plane for the more delicate beveling, or angling. This is all done without the aid of any measuring tool.

"Now, you can ask me how I know how much bevel to give each stave, because the staves are not all the same," he says. "Some are a little narrower and some a little wider. And you know that I have no answer for that. I have no answer. The only thing I can tell you is my hands and my eyes."

After a cooper has beveled the right number of staves he places metal rings around one end of them as he stands them up. The a-borning barrel is then set inside a windlass loop over a fire fueled by the wood shavings produced by the beveling process. As the wood warms it becomes slightly pliable. Then more rings are hammered on with a metal driver and the windlass is cranked to draw in the bottom. The cooper then takes the bulging barrel from the windlass and pounds on more metal rings to further shape the barrel. This squeezing and pounding takes about a half hour. Next the barrel is set in an X-shaped stand so the stave ends can be planed level, the grooves for the lids cut with a special toothed tool and the outside of the barrel cleaned with a concave planer. At this point the forming rings are replaced with permanent rings of "milder" metal that will hold the staves to their proper shape without digging into the wood.

The lids, too, are handmade, shaped with a cooper's axe and a draw knife, and beveled so that they fit tightly in the grooves. The first lid is pounded into place with the end of a hammer handle. The trick of fitting the other lid into its groove, which appears as if it would be as difficult as getting a model ship inside a bottle, is accomplished with the aid of a wire. Giacalone's barrels have both wood and glass lids.

Holes are drilled for the spigot on one end of the barrel and for the bung, or stopper, on the top. The inside of the barrel is coated with pitch to seal it and prevent an under-taste when the contents of the barrel are changed. Finally, the outside is stained and varnished.

Giacalone's barrels range in price from $60 for the simplest one to $750 for a two-compartment, glass-lidded model. About half of the buyers use them for decorative purposes and half for functional reasons. He does his best business during the Christmas season.

Many middlemen wannabes have approached the Giacalones, wanting to serve as John's business agent. In order to price the barrels at a more affordable cost, they prefer to sell the barrels themselves, from their home shop, at craft fairs, and at places where Giacalone demonstrates his craft, such as fairs, colleges, shopping malls and conventions.

"With our product you never can tell how many you're going to sell," Giacalone says. "You'll be surprised. You might sell a few or you might sell much more than a few; you never know. It depends on how many interested people you find."

At the Wisconsin State Fair three days passed during which they didn't sell a single barrel, and they sold only 18 during the fair's 11-day run. At tiny Cadott, Wisconsin, on the other hand, customers besieged them. "We said, 'Cadott? What going to happen in Cadott?'" Josie recalls. "Things happened in Cadott! Things were terrific in Cadott. You cannot tell how far a frog jumps by looking at it. That's my favorite saying." Another occasion when they were pleasantly surprised was at a convention of the National Homemakers of America in Stevens Point. They nearly ran out of barrels that evening, selling more than 20. "These women were buying barrels as if they were doughnuts," Josie says. "And they [the barrels] went all over the country. There were representatives there from 35 different states. Oh, what an audience they were! They were just fantastic."

Shopping mall executives in Houston, New York, Phoenix and other cities have tried to hire Giacalone to demonstrate the craft of barrel-making in their cities. Giacalone has turned down all such distant offers. "My time is limited, plus I'm getting older," he says. "I hate to drive long by myself, because my wife doesn't drive at all, you see. So that's about the size of it."

Giacalone also had to pass on the opportunity to sell large quantities of barrels to two California wineries. After a sales executive at the Christian Brothers winery saw a national TV commercial for Wausau Insurance featuring Giacalone he called and requested to see some barrels. John and Josie flew out to California with two sample barrels—one round one and one oval one. They say the winery executive was awestruck when they showed him the barrels. He was speechless for about 30 seconds, then simply said, "Wow!" He thought they were beautiful and wanted to order 1,000. Giacalone had to explain he could not fill such an order because his focus is on quality, not quantity.

It was a similar story at the Englenook winery, where company officials wanted to place an initial order for 500 barrels.

After John resumed barrel-making 10 years ago Josie encouraged him to write to his old master, Lucovico Giacalone, to let him know about the development, thinking he would be pleased to hear about it. A correspondence developed. The two coopers exchange five or six letters a year. In an aside to Josie in one of the letters the old master, once the finest cooper in all Europe, confided to her that he felt his former apprentice has surpassed the master.

***

The interview for the preceding profile was conducted June 6, 1984. John and Josie liked the profile I wrote well enough to invite me to write a follow-up piece about seven special one-of-a-kind barrels John crafted over the years. Aside from family members and a few close friends, I was the first person permitted to see the special barrels when I again interviewed Giacalone on July 5, 1991, which happened to be his 67th birthday. He had suffered a heart attack 16 months previously and was looking to retire from barrel-making by the end of the year. After some preliminary discussion about their health and retirement plans, I asked John when he made his first odd-shaped barrel.

The first one was 1977.

So, that was just sort of a challenge for yourself?

Yes, yes. I made some of those conventional barrels, and then I had some time sometimes. It came into my mind that I wanted to make that two-compartment oval with the glasses [glass lids]—three glasses, one inside and two on the outside. And I made that. In the meantime, I kept working with the regular work and so forth, and sometimes I had a little time, so I thought, "Heck, I'm going to try to make something that has never been built in the world." I'm challenging the world right now. To do such things I got to put all those things—what I'm going to do, and the way I'm going to do it—in my mind. Once I got it straight in my mind, step by step, then I do it.

So I started, and off and on, because sometimes I had some orders to finish and so forth. It took about five, six months, and I finished that triangular barrel. I finished it with glass lids and chrome rings.

Then time goes by, and I think the other one was that diamond shape. I'm not going to tell you the difficulty and the frustration to make those two. . . and now I'm going to challenge myself to more frustration. But, you see, it was maybe 30 years back, I don't think I could do it because my temper is bad, and once you get mad you better quit and go. But now because of my age I guess my nerves are a little bit settled, and so I keep fighting and fighting and fighting, and I made a diamond shape, with glass lids.

How long did that one take?

About six months or more. . . . Anyway, I accomplished that. Then I decided to make a hexagon shape. Now, mind you, I've been doing coopering—learning and working at it—57 years, and I had never saw this shape or done it myself. But because I'm the kind of person who likes a challenge. . . The frustration to make the forms, it's. . . The time involved. If anybody should pay (for) the time involved, and the frustration and everything else, I don't think there's money that can buy this barrel. . . . All right: I accomplished that.

Then. . . I decided, well if I made a six [-sided barrel] I'm going to make an octagon now. An octagon was a little easier because I already had the idea and the tricks that were used in the hexagon. But it was still very difficult. . . . Now we are at 1983.

[His five sons played football in the yard, so he decided to make a football-shaped barrel, to the exact measurements of an official-size football.]

In the evening, before I fall asleep, when I have such difficult jobs I work with my mind, and I saw a very difficult job (to) produce this thing. I saw right away that the problem was (that the ends are so small). I think it's an inch and a half—just enough to put a spigot. I saw that the rings on the ends wouldn't stay. I couldn't figure that out. But still I thought: *I think I'll do it*. . . . The other ones were difficult and frustrating, but this was super frustrating and super difficult. I think three times I got so frustrated that I grabbed the barrel with both my hands and I slammed it right on the concrete. . . . My family, especially my wife, they could not talk with me at all when I was in such worry, in such a frustrated (state of) mind. So, anyway, I put it away maybe a month or two. And then. . . You see, my nature is, I'm fighting until I can't fight. I don't give up very easy. I'm very stubborn. . . . I compared myself with the barrel, and it's winning and I'm losing. "No way! You're not going to win! I'm going to fight again!" So I grabbed the barrel and started working again, a little bit here, a little bit there. Now I got this football already made (and) I gotta put the lids, the covers, because you can use it for liquid.

[Eventually he managed to insert two lids and proceeded with the task of trying to place rings on each side of the football-shaped barrel.]

I slowly, carefully pounded it, and it bounced back because the shape was too sharp. We have tricks for this thing here. Whenever the ring bounces we use a chalk inside. So I chalked this little ring very well and put it back slowly and carefully and kept pounding around. I was nearly there and it bounced again. Many times you get mad, but time flies and you get mad. So I chalked again, and—uh uh—it bounced. I could not do it. This was steel, this metal. So I thought: *No; I'm going to use copper.* Copper is a substance that could give while I pound. Maybe I'm going to try it that way. So, I tried copper, I tried aluminum, I tried brass, stainless steel. Nothing worked. These two rings drove me nuts. The barrel was complete, but I could not finish it because I had to tighten the ends, otherwise it would leak.

[He shelved that unfinished project, and about a year passed, during which time he practically forgot about it.]

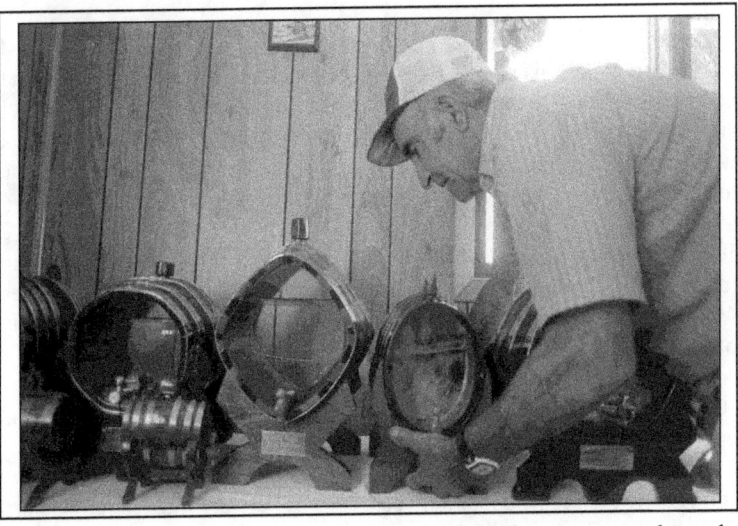

Then one day—I guess the Lord told me, "I think you are ready to do it." So that morning I went into the shop and it came to my mind, that barrel. *I think I'm going to get it.* So I get the barrel and bring it in the shop and figure out a few things. I look and see it and so forth. I get the rings and say, "Now I'm going to start with regular steel—ring steel." So I used the steel and promise very good, but was bouncing and bouncing and bouncing—I would say two hours. . . . But I was calm. I guess the Lord said, "You're going to do it." Finally, carefully, by chalking and pounding slowly and around and around, finally I got it where I wanted it, straight with the staves. I didn't want to put it down, the barrel under my arm. I get the drill and made a little hole in the ring about an eighth of an inch and just touched the wood, and then I found a small quarter-of-an-inch screw. So I put the screw in one side and turned it to the other side and said, "Now I'm happy because you won't come out anymore from there, and you've been giving me too much trouble and too much frustration. You almost drove me nuts. Now I got you."

Now, this is one side. I've gotta have the other. And so the other took about the same time—a good couple of hours or so. But, anyway—luckily—I did it. . . .

[His next challenge was a heart-shaped barrel. That proved to be "a super troublemaker." Even though he had thought about the project for four or five years before he began the actual work, that barrel perplexed and frustrated him for about two-and-a-half years before he again achieved success, finishing that one two years ago.]

I thought: *Well, I've gotta make another shape before I die.* So I decided to make this shape. Oh, my goodness! I shouldn't have. That and the football I should not have dared to do. Yes, I did it, but once I started them I got very nervous and very mad inside of myself while I was just talking about them. . . . People don't know the torment, the torture that I went through with some of these.

JOSIE: I can tell you, as his wife. He would be at the table eating (and) all of a sudden he would stop dead, and the look in his eyes would be so terrifying. I don't know how to explain it. He was way off. I would say, "John! John!" He would say, "Leave me alone."

JOHN: I was working in my mind, and sometimes even when I was eating I would stop.

JOSIE: It was scary, absolutely scary. . . . There are musicians who are temperamental, or some people that do some type of work, they really go off kind of on a tangent or whatever. I experienced that with him. . . There were times when he would come in and I would look at him and I knew I wasn't even to talk because his mind was far away.

Did you ever doubt that he would complete any of them?

JOSIE: Yeah, I never thought he would make the heart one—never. I saw obstacles all the way.

JOHN: Many times she said, "Why do you have to frustrate yourself? Let it go." No way, Jose!

JOSIE: It just seemed right at the onset it was an impossibility. I said, "Why are you doing this? Why are you torturing not only yourself, but me and the rest of us that are here?" There were times when I was very upset. *[At the same time, she understood John was driven to do it. John explains there also was another motivating force.]*

JOHN: This country has been very good to me and my family, and I like to share the talent and the ability that the Lord gave to me (with) the country. I like to show the country what I did.

[Since they primarily are barrels, the odd-shaped barrels still have contours rather than sharp edges and angles.

[Giacalone says a National Football League team owner offered $25,000 for the football-shaped barrel after a friend sent photos of the barrel to the man. Giacalone didn't think that was sufficient recompense. He had intended to let his children sell the barrels after he passes away, figuring the barrels probably would increase in value after his death. His children encouraged him to sell the barrels now, though, so Giacalone decided he would, and divide the profits among his children. Josie thinks it would make sense for a winery to buy all seven to showcase them in one place.]

We are dealing with one thing in the world. Not in America or Canada or France or whatever. In the world. . . . If I find the right buyers I'll sell them, otherwise the children will take care of them later on.

[The two-compartment oval barrel is priced at $25,000, the football-shaped barrel at $35,000, the hexagon- and octagon-shaped barrels at $40,000 each, the diamond- and heart-shaped barrels at $50,000 each, and the triangle-shaped barrel at $100,000.]

I want to have some satisfaction to sell them and see my children happy when I hand them their share (of the money). That's my wish.

☼

Carousel Creations

Ron Helstern ... woodcarver

I first interviewed Ron Helstern on June 27, 1990. Later that same year, Oct. 31, I conducted another very short interview with him. I interviewed him a third time on June 22, 1994 while gathering material for an article about "bubbling, beguiling Barronett." I interviewed him about his cradle beds on August 27, 1997, then for a fifth and final time July 22, 1998.

Is there anyone who doesn't like carousel horses? Their grand garishness and frozen-in-time galloping poses make them as irresistible as a fireworks display. Nearly everyone has happy memories of youthful merry-go-round rides, for with their enticing lights, swirling calliope music and contrapuntal motion (up and down as well as around), merry-go-rounds introduced us to carnival excitement when we were too young to go on more dangerous, hair-raising rides. As a North Lake, Wisconsin, antique restorer told an Associated Press reporter 20 years ago, for many people carousel horses are "the ultimate in nostalgia."

Woodcarver Ron Helstern nurtures that nostalgia by handcrafting wooden carousel horses and restoring antique survivors of the breed in a Barronett, Wisconsin, workshop, keeping alive an almost-lost art whose golden era ended more than 60 years ago.

Since the mid-1930s most merry-go-round horses [merry-go-round and carousel are synonymous] have been mass-produced out of fiberglass, aluminum and plastic. While some wooden carousel horses are still in use, many are now prized as art objects, owned by well-heeled collectors who treasure and care for their painted ponies as they would a valuable oil painting.

"It is part of our heritage that a few of us have been trying to bring back," says Helstern. ". . . There are more carvers turning their talents

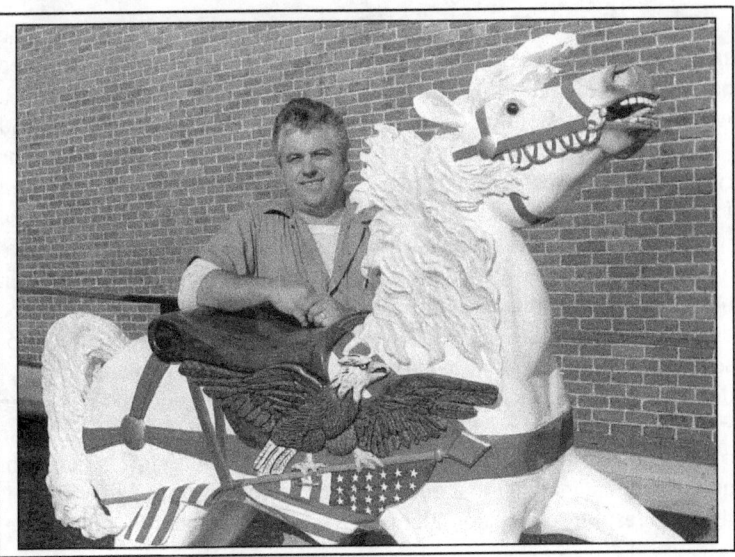

into carving carousel animals every year, but as far as a figure I would probably still venture to say that a dozen, or a few more, would probably be pretty close—carving them to the extent as what you're seeing here. There are carvers out there that are trying their hand at maybe just one carousel horse for their grandchild or something like that, but as far as the extent of the carving, what you see here, I don't think there are too many out there that are doing it. Maybe there are more than what I'm thinking; I don't know. . . . There are people out there that want that quality and not the plastic, and that's what we strive to do. And we stay busy doing that because there is quality here to be had. I really strive for that."

Helstern, who carves everything from wall-hangable relief carvings to fireplace mantel faces to human figures, has carved more than 20 carousel and rocking horses in the past decade at his Carousel Creations shop in Barronett, an unincorporated community along busy State Highway 63 midway between Cumberland and Shell Lake. He and his wife, Sue, who paints most of the carousel horses, also operate a custom sign business in the same space. In addition to his original carvings, Helstern has restored more than 20 collectible wooden carousel and hobby horses, some dating to the 19th Century.

"I have just as much fun restoring an old one as I do carving a new one," he says, "because you're working on something that was made so many years ago and you get a lot of satisfaction to make them look new again. One lady brought me a toy horse that was on a glider platform.

I would guess it was probably made about the turn of the century. She said, 'Somebody was going to throw it away and I knew you restored horses, so I brought it to you to see if you could do anything with it.' It wasn't even six months before that I restored one exactly like it, so I knew just what it was. So I restored it. I had to replace some legs. The two right legs were missing, and a little part of an ear was missing. But I can replace new wood wherever that's missing, and I don't use any wood fillers. When I replaced this wood, then I carved the horse like he was made originally, and it turned out nice. She almost had a tear in her eye when she picked him up. She said, 'I didn't think it could be done.' Well, there are a lot of things that can be done. I've carved for so many years that I find it fairly simple, but very time-consuming. I don't struggle with it because I know what has to be done. But I also know that it takes an awful lot of time and patience to put some of these old ones back in brand new condition. . . . Most of this stuff is heirloom quality. It's something that people have had for years, and they bring it to me to restore so they don't have to trash it."

The oldest carousel horses on his restoration resume were from the 1890s.

"I've had them in the shop where people brought them in in baskets," says Helstern, a woodcarver since 1982. "I've restored so many of them that I can take a look and just about tell when it was carved, and sometimes what company carved it. If it's a carousel horse I can usually tell if it's a Parker. Most of the carvers at the turn of the century had their own styles."

Most of the turn of the century master carvers were German, Russian, Italitan, and other European immigrants.

"Most of them were furniture carvers," Helstern explains. "Then along came the carousel horses, and that's where they made their money. . . . Every carver had a little different style, and something that he put on it to make it different than the rest. Some [of the carved horses] had really wild and flamboyant manes that stuck up about a foot off the neck. . . . Now that I'm carving them I really take an interest in looking at the art of the carousels. When you're carving something like that you can appreciate the factories that carved them out for a living. Some of those things had a hundred horses on them. You just think about how much carving that would take."

Helstern says the immigrant artisans "thought so much of the United States and what the United States had to offer that they showed their appreciation by putting something patriotic on [many of] their horses. . Usually at least one horse on the carousel had something patriotic on it." Favorite symbols included bald eagles and American flags.

"The unique part of a carousel horse is how it's put together," says Helstern. "A lot of people think that it's a solid block of wood, and a lot of people think that they're all plastic and that they weren't made of wood at all, because after they're painted they do take on kind of a plastic look."

Like the old-time carvers, Helstern carves his horses out of laminated basswood and uses about three-dozen dowels to join the different parts of a horse. The legs, head, neck, chest and tail are solid; the body is hollow. Even so, a large Coney Island or Philadelphia style carousel horse can weigh more than 250 pounds. The Philadelphia style horse was carved to look as much like a real horse as possible. In contrast, Coney Island style horses were caricatures of a sort, with wild manes and vivid, eye-candy colors that made them as flamboyant as Las Vegas showgirls. "They were a beautiful horse," Helstern says of the Coney Island style. "They looked in some aspects like a real horse; the face and everything was carved pretty well. It's just that they added all these bright colors, and sometimes even jewelry, on them." At approximately six feet in length, both Philadelphia and Coney Island style horses were created for permanent carousels. Smaller [three- to four-foot-long] county fair style carousel horses, on the other hand, were moved from town to town week after week.

"The ones that came to Cumberland were the county fair size," Helstern says. "At that time I thought they were plastic. But they weren't; they were wood. But when I was a kid I didn't realize that the things were wood. I loved to ride on a carousel. But those are the only ones that I ever rode on, the smaller ones."

Even some smaller horses had "some pretty nice trappings," Helstern says—trappings being adornments—"but not a lot of detail on them because they put up with a lot of abuse [with the carousel] being taken apart every week."

Helstern found more than two pounds of rusty nails in one horse he restored. "You could see what they did to get their nickel a ride," he notes. "Every time a leg would fall off they kept nailing it back on."

The carvers whose names became legend owned their own companies. "They would go out and have their men set up a carousel," Helstern says. "They would carve all the horses and put them on. But some of the carousels had three or four different carvers' work aboard. You can just imagine the abuse that carousel horses took through the years, so if one busted and they couldn't get one from the original carver they would find one from another carver and put it aboard that carousel, as long as it was about the same size of horse. That's why some carousels wound up with different carvers' styles on them."

Large carousels carried dozens of horses, so workshops turned out horses in assembly line fashion to meet the demand. According to a 1978 Associated Press newspaper feature, one large company built 92 merry-go-rounds, each with 48 to 64 wooden horses. Horses made for the outside row—those most visible to fairgoers and amusement park patrons—were most elaborately detailed. "The second row had a lot of the elaborate stuff on, but not as much as the first row," Helstern says. "The third row had even less, and the fourth row even less yet." Since only one side of a carousel horse showed to the public, that "romance side" received most of the trappings.

"**I**'ve loved art ever since I can remember," Helstern says. ". . . As much as I've loved art, it's hard just to go into something like that and make a living at it. We're doing very well now because it's taken me a long time for my name to get out there, and people like my work. But for the artist that's just starting out it can be a real struggle. I was an insurance investigator for about 12 years. My wife was a sign painter. We both loved art, so we kind of thought: Well, let's get into the sign business. I was doing carving part-time. And then all of a sudden people started liking the work, and then it just kept getting busier. I know darn well there are a lot of people out there that have talents they don't know they've got until they try it. I know it because I'm one of them.

"I loved art, but woodcarving, that's a whole 'nother thing. You've gotta be somewhat of a sculptor and artist at the same time. I never thought I could do it. I'm a self-taught carver. But I picked up the chisels at one time and tried it, and I liked it, and it turned out pretty good. My oldest daughter has my first carving; it was a relief carving of a moose. Then I started getting into the bigger carvings."

The wooden carousel horse era lasted from approximately the last third of the 19th Century through the first third of the 20th Century. Beginning in 1937, the mass production of less-detailed fiberglass and cast-aluminum carousel horses "put the master carver right out of a job," as Helstern puts it.

"That's why I like to carve the old style, because it is kind of a thing of the past. . . . .I can take a picture of an old carousel horse, study it, and make my pattern off of that picture and reproduce it right from that picture. I'll get them pretty close. You'll never get them exact, but no two artists are alike anyway."

Helstern carves most carousel horses on commission. The price "depends on the size of the horse and what trappings go on the horse. Depending on how intricate some of these carvings get, there's a big variable there, just for the fact that it takes you a lot longer to carve." Suffice it to say that a Helstern original is worth several thousand dollars.

That could still be considered a relative bargain compared to the prices paid for some antique carousel horses and other carousel animals. Individual carousel horses have exchanged hands for as much as $100,000. A carousel rooster Gustav Dentzel carved in 1895 sold for nearly $150,000 in 1989. Helstern carved a reproduction of that 50-inch-high Dentzel rooster for his small showroom, which also features a carousel lion and a carousel tiger in addition to a couple of carousel horses and a number of other carvings.

Helstern has considered creating a museum for his carvings. If that idea ever comes to fruition it may feature seven very large "holiday" horses celebrating Christmas, Valentine's Day, St. Patrick's Day, Easter, the Fourth of July, Halloween and Thanksgiving. That ambitious project is on hold at present. After finishing the Valentine's Day and Christmas horses, which are on large rockers, Helstern has not been able to find the time to work on any others. In fact, he will have to carve another Valentine's Day horse because a Boulder, Colorado, woman persuaded him to part with the first one. "I didn't want to sell it, but she talked me out of it," he says. "She wouldn't take no for an answer. You've gotta pay your bills too."

A big reason Helstern hasn't had time to work on his holiday horse series for several years is that he has been busy transforming his lakeside log home into a showplace of his carving talent. Seven relief-carved panels, all featuring a Western frontier theme, form the outside wall of a sunken living room. Two carved bald eagles nest in an elk-horn chandelier. A banister post is carved with cattails, with baby owls atop that post (the mother owl perches on a different post). There are reproductions of an 1860s English-style glider horse and a turn-of-the-century German-style rocking horse on display, a carved mantelpiece with an attached swan, a howling wolf atop a rock pile (the rocks are carved from wood as well) at the edge of a loft, and even stylized duck carvings on window boxes and shutters.

There also is a queen-size cradle bed in the master bedroom. This original Helstern creation, which he came up with about five years ago, has carved head- and footboards that rock from side to side. His large Christmas rocking horse inspired the design. "I see a cradle bed in this thing," he said to Sue one day. Even as Sue laughed, Ron said, "I think I'm going to try it."

"I could visualize this cradle bed," he says. "She couldn't really understand what I was talking about at first. One thing led to another. I had to figure out how to get the frame all welded together, which is not a big thing. But it had to be bolted together because it has to be heavy and strong to withstand the weight of this thing. . . . The way it's balanced on the rockers, it'll rock if you want it to rock; if you're lying in bed normal it won't move at all. But you can make it rock. Or if you sit on the side of it, putting your shoes on or whatever, it will rock to let you in and out. . . . If it does rock if you roll over at night or something it's just a little tiny bit, just to let you know it's a cradle. It comes right back to a stationary bed." Wedges can be placed under the headboard to prevent the bed from rocking.

"It's comfortable," Sue attests. "It sleeps great."

Helstern has sold a half-dozen customized cradle beds, which are priced at $4,500. "The people that have bought them come up with kind of their own theme," he says. "And then usually they will trust me to lay it out the way that I think is the best way that's going to fit. It's just what I do for a living—I lay that stuff out and I carve it the way that makes the best picture. . . . The way we've advertised this in brochures is that we can carve them from sailing scenes in Florida to grizzly bears in Alaska, or horse ranches in Tennessee. It can be anybody's theme, and it personalizes their feelings in their home."

For a cradle bed to rock smoothly, the headboard and footboard rockers must have synchronized movements. "I laminate the big headboard," Helstern explains, "and then lay the one that's done on top of the other one and trace around it, and then I'll be real careful how I cut it out and sand it. Then they wind up to be just exactly alike."

To Helstern, woodcarving is such pleasure that he is one of the lucky people who finds it fun going to work in the morning. "A lot of days you can't wait to get here, and there are days you don't want to leave. You've gotta have your fishing time and hunting time and private time too, but at least when I do come to work I have a lot of fun doing it."

While he obviously enjoys all the various types of woodcarving he does, one senses he takes special pride in his carousel creations, in the carousel and toy horses he carves and restores.

He laments that these days "kids wake up to a plastic Christmas. But years ago they had toys they could pass on to their grandkids. It's not that way anymore. That's why we try to bring back a tradition that's kind of been lost in the shuffle. We're trying to make the new horses that we make exactly like the old ones were made so people again can pass them down as heirlooms."

Whether reproducing a classic carousel horse or creating a self-designed one, Helstern attaches a red wooden heart inside the body of each carousel horse he carves as a signature touch. For a woodcarver who puts so much heart into his craft, that seems symbolically appropriate.

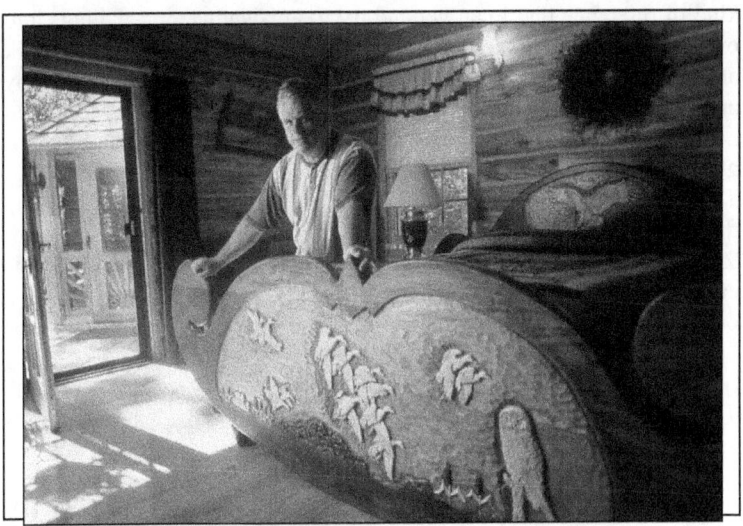

☼

Winging It

Keith Davidson ... woodcarver

Interviews from September 10, 1980 and September 14, 1983 served as the basis for this profile.

A common criticism of carved birds is that many are mere copies of mounts and photographs. Woodcarver Keith Davidson of Falun, Wisconsin, a Burnett County hamlet between Grantsburg and Siren, pays particular attention to making his creations unique, one-of-a-kind works of art.

"You see some of these carvings," he says, "and you look at them, and you think: 'Gee, haven't I seen that somewhere before?' And you can find some excellent photograph that this person has used for reference and built the whole thing around that one photo. To me, it's far better if you can take a number of different sources of material. . . . I use any kind of reference that I can get and try to amalgamate these things into one bird rather than take one pose, or one mounted bird, and just walk around and copy it. . . . I don't think a carving should be just a copy anymore than a painting should be. If you paint something it should not just be a copy. Of course, some people do work right off photographs, and then it's a matter of making a photograph into a painting. There's still kind of some copy work involved there. The less copying the better. Each should be an original thing. As far as I'm concerned, to find an eagle that's in that posture [the posture of one of his carvings] you've just gotta go out and find one, and it better be a live one because otherwise I don't think it's possible that it could be duplicated."

To Davidson, this is all in the service of trying to make his carved birds as life-like and naturalistic as possible.

In the 10 years he has been carving he has turned out more than 180 wooden birds, nearly all from basswood and nearly all life-size.

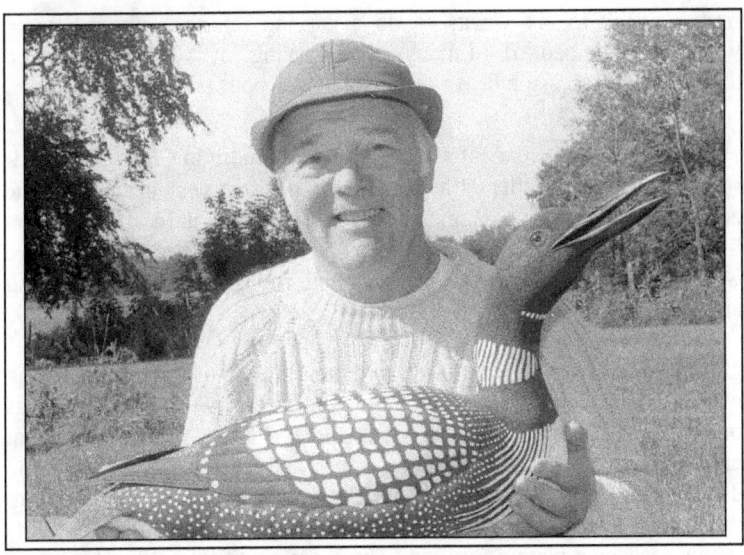

Species include ducks, geese, osprey, grouse, pheasant, woodcock, loon, bobwhite, cardinal, sandpiper and robin.

"Personally," he says, "I'd rather do game birds and maybe birds of prey if I had the choice, but my favorite bird is the bird I'm working on at the moment, because I get that interested. . . . Everything I do is one-of-a-kind; that's the basic thought. Sometimes it's variations. . . . I don't retain anything to copy or work from, so it makes it a little more difficult, but there's a little more originality in each effort then too."

His most ambitious project was a life-size bald eagle that was displayed at the Minnesota Science Museum in St. Paul for six months to celebrate the 200th anniversary of the bald eagle being named our national bird. The eagle is 20 inches wide, 35 inches long, and has a small-mouth bass gripped in its talons. The fish, which Davidson also carved, has a life-like suppleness surpassing most mounts. The work, which took six months, was done on commission for a couple who paid $10,000 for it.

Most of his carvings sell for several hundred dollars, a few for as much as $2,500 to $3,500. Considering the time it takes him to complete a carving, most people would agree Davidson is far from overpaid. While he has never kept track of how many hours he spends on an average project, other carvers who have say they make about half of what auto plant workers do. Depending on the complexity of the design and the number of hours he puts in, it takes Davidson anywhere from a week to six weeks to do a carving. Since only relatively wealthy people can afford many of his carvings, it is somewhat ironic that the 1974 recession drove Davidson into woodcarving.

After spending 28 years at a commercial art studio in Chicago, Davidson found himself reduced to part-time work that year because of the economic conditions. Rather than go into debt until the situation improved, Davidson and his wife decided to move to her parents' place west of Siren. They felt they had had enough of suburban living anyway.

"I tried to get work in Minneapolis in the same field, and nothing came of it," Davidson relates. "Everyone who interviewed me, nine times out of ten, would say, 'Well, what are you doing now?' And that embarrassed me, so I took along some color prints of some of the decoys that I had carved as a hobby, 'cause that's what I was doing, rather than just standing around like a dummy. So on a number of different occasions people told me 'Those are beautiful. Why don't you keep doing that?' There was no work forthcoming, so eventually it got to a situation where that's what happened. It wasn't so much a decision on my part as just the way things worked out."

For the first few years more than half of his carvings were ornamental decoys. Bing Crosby purchased one. The percentage of decoys has dropped drastically as his carving skill and knowledge of birds have improved. He now carves more full-bodied birds, complete with feet, which are made of wire and auto body putty.

Davidson thought he would pick up the pace as his experience expanded, but that hasn't happened.

"I wish I could work faster," he says, "but it seems that the more carving I do the more involved I get with detail and the idea of trying to make it better. I've gotten so I can do some things faster, but because I'm trying to do more it works against me. I wind up going slower than I like."

He believes the care he takes with his carving will pay off in personal satisfaction as well as in the value of his works. A few of his carvings are sold through wildlife art galleries and exclusive sporting goods companies, but most are ordered directly from Davidson. He has had carvings displayed at the annual Bird Art Exhibition at the Leigh Yawkey Woodson Art Museum in Wausau, Wisconsin, four times.

That show is generally regarded as the most prestigious such exhibit in the country. Only about 20 carvings are on display there each year.

Davidson is constantly striving to improve his carving skill. He casts severe judgment on his previous efforts, seeing flaws and areas for improvement where most people wouldn't. Taking out a photo of the first pheasant he carved, he notes that the body now looks a little long, and he isn't pleased with the way he handled the head. "All you've gotta do is take a photograph of something, and if it's at all stiff or dead-looking it shows up in a photo; it really emphasizes it," he says.

Generally, he likes to have several projects in progress.

"For a while there," he says, "I was trying to work on three birds at once. That way I had a variety of work. Like, if you've been working on a head for a while, it's nice to back away from it and pick up a new piece of wood where you can just kind of hack away, or do something different. Otherwise you get kind of intense, and it's not too enjoyable sometimes that way. Of course, there are times when in order to finish an item you have to bear down and don't have the opportunity of choice."

Davidson begins by making numerous drawings, not only of the complete bird but of individual parts such as wings as well. Using basswood that has been aged for two years to prevent splitting or warping, he then roughs out the shape of the bird with a band-saw. He further refines the shape with rasps, chisels, gouges, knives and sandpaper, and produces a feathered texture and the barbules of individual feathers with a wood-burning tool. The final step is painting, which Davidson considers his strongest skill.

The finished carving is mounted on either a piece of driftwood or a varnished wood base.

A simple decorative decoy has two parts—head and body—joined with a dowel. A carving of a bird in flight may consist of five separate pieces—head, body, two wings, and a fan of tail feathers. Some of his carved birds are perched so precariously on one claw that they appear to balance as much by magic as anything else.

Davidson's ultimate goal is to not have a piece look like either a mount or a carving. "You want to try and make it look like a bird," he says.

☼

How Sweet The Shape

Dan Jahr ... folk harp builder

For Dan Jahr, it was love at first sound, an emotional seduction of soothing strings. In his words, he "flipped out." His initial reaction to hearing a folk harp played is far from uncommon. "Most people really are grabbed like that by it too," he believes.

When a professional harpist asked if he would build her a small folk harp Jahr jumped at the opportunity. He went on to build several hundred folk harps and is about to hit the market with seven new models he spent the past several years developing.

The Star Prairie, Wisconsin, area resident has been handcrafting wooden folk harps for about 15 years, which makes him one of America's most experienced folk harp builders. Few other harp builders have as much training, practical experience and knowledge-through-study as he has. He acquired most of his harp building skills the hard way, through the learn-as-you-proceed approach. Harp building was not his first love, however. Study of piano rebuilding and violin restoration at technical colleges in the mid-1970s led to a job doing violin restoration in Chicago. A gristly, apparently random murder of a next-door neighbor prompted him to flee that big city. "It could just as easily have been me," he says of the chilling murder. So he moved to Oshkosh, Wisconsin and opened his own violin shop there. At that point he was starting to become more interested in building than restoring instruments. "The business sort of was evolving," he says. "I wasn't sure what it was that I wanted to do. A lot of violin makers... do half repair work and half building in order to get by. At that point I wasn't interested in it [repair work]; I wanted to build. So when the opportunity came along to make some harps and I got involved in the harp community I saw my chance for just building."

Concert and performing harpist Kim Robertson, of California, requested Jahr build her a folk harp, then encouraged him to build more.

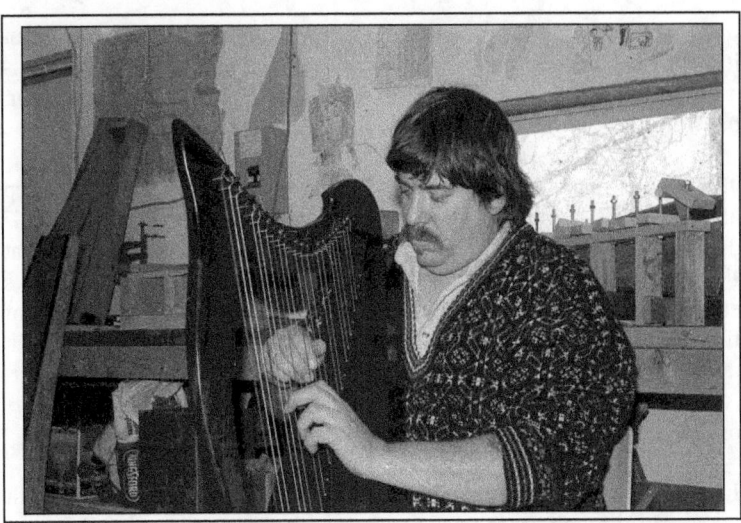

"I've always been involved in country music and folk music, and rock 'n' roll, when I was a teenager and in my early 20s," Jahr says. "I've been an avid listener to orchestral music; I love it. As a matter of fact, it's my favorite type of music, along with folk music. When the harp came along I was very happy because people get the idea that when they hear a harp. . . angelic music, and soulful, classical music, or something like this. What I'm involved in is folk music; it's Irish folk music. And nowadays it's any kind of folk music, really. The harp has a long tradition. It was part of the culture of the Celtic people. The orchestral harp really is new on the scene. The kind of harps I'm building, the folk harps, can be traced back about 25 centuries. The popularity kind of goes up and down. It's going up right now. They're very popular, and they're getting to be a lot more popular. . . .

"There's quite an amount of learning that goes into undertaking the first instrument (you build), unless you work from a pattern or something. But me being the person I am, I can't understand even a small part of something until I understand all of it. I have to take it in pieces and understand every piece, and then I can understand the whole thing. Well, there isn't a great deal of literature out there on building harps, so I had to kind of learn as I went. It involved a lot of math skills that I didn't have."

He had never even seen a folk harp before he built his first one. "At that time it was quite unusual for me to run into somebody playing a harp," he says. "I was flabbergasted. . . . I knew harps because I had lived in Chicago, where the biggest harp factory in the world is. But it's classical, concert harps. Here was somebody playing a folk harp—a little harp that somebody built of wood. The music that was coming out of it just. . . I just flipped out. I thought it was fantastic. . . .

"Playing as many instruments as I do [violin, guitar, banjo, folk harp and others], I know how difficult instruments are to learn—which is difficult and which isn't. The [folk] harp probably is the easiest that I've ever attempted to play. It's not as easy to get very good at it; it's easy to play and (make it) sound good. And it's easy to have a lot of fun on it. But it's not easy to be an expert musician on the harp; it takes a lot of work. But that's true with any instrument. The easy part is getting into it, which is not true of the violin. It's definitely not true of the guitar."

Jahr was in Oshkosh about eight years. Many of the folk harps he built were sold through other music stores, with the Washington, DC, area being a particularly good market for less expensive "student models." He moved to the Star Prairie area five years ago. Since that move he has constructed a workshop, designed and perfected new folk harp models, wrote a book-length manuscript about harps he hopes to have published, and tried to re-gear his business to selective direct marketing.

"It's tough to go into business," he says. "It's almost like everybody is lined up against you. I would like to sell my cassette tapes and books through the mail. . . . Well, in order to make a business like that go you have to be able to let people purchase with their credit cards. You try and get one of those imprinting machines!" He laughs and paraphrases the type of response he has received. " 'No, no, no. We have quite a few people in business doing that already. I don't think we're just going to open the door and let you walk through. Here's a hoop; jump through the hoop.' I'm going to have to be in business a year before they'll allow me to do credit card purchases. Well, who can stay in business a year [without a credit card imprinter] if your business is selling through the mail?"

Jahr builds both student and professional model folk harps. The price depends on his time, the cost of materials, and other factors.

"People know me," he says. "It's not a very big world, the harp world. People know me, and I know the market too. The prices are really high for harps. My plan, with this new design, was to make something that I could build at a reasonable price that a student could afford, starting at about $300 and going up to about $500 for student instruments. . . . The harps that teachers are looking at right now are quite expensive. I'm offering a line of, in most cases, higher quality instruments, because most of the people building them don't have the training (and) haven't been at it as long as I have, for one thing. Also, I've traveled a lot. I've visited many factories and talked to a lot of people who are involved in production. So I've really paid my dues."

While a concert harp has 46 strings, and mechanical components, folk harps have between 22 and 36 strings. Jahr says he can produce his least expensive student model, with mahogany and spruce, "very fast" while still turning out a good-quality instrument. Some better wood and more handcrafting goes into the more expensive professional models, which cost as much as $2,200.

"Teachers are going to love this," he says of the student model. "What's available at the price range that I'm talking about is really pathetic instruments. This is a brand new thing for the harp community, to be faced with good instruments at low prices. I'm not sure what's going to happen, but I'm fairly confident that I can make my own way."

"There's been a resurgence of harp playing in the United States," he says. "What I've seen happen is that we've gone from copying Irish harps, which were common a hundred years ago, and 50 years ago, to a whole new genre of harps that has been developed in the United States. Even now it's evolving. It's fantastic to see a new instrument. It's like back when the violin was first invented. It didn't suddenly appear; it evolved from another form. The harps that you see here are harps that have evolved from another form, which was the Irish harp, I guess you could say. They had round backs. The earlier harps had square backs—the harps from the 14th, 15th centuries. And the harps that are being built now, in America, are kind of a hybrid of those two.

"I did see a disturbing trend, and that was that the people who were building them (were) kind of ignoring the rules of acoustics and using heavy planks of wood to build harps. . . . A lot of people aren't real familiar with the physics of musical instruments."

Jahr wrote an article for *Folk Harp Journal* exhorting harp builders to look at guitars and other boxes that project musical sound and notice how they are made of thinner wood.

"People have taken it to heart somewhat," he says, "because I recently read that the newer designs are lighter designs."

Jarh also is disturbed that some harp builders seem more concerned about aesthetics than acoustics.

"People have been building harps from any pretty wood," he says. "And that's fine. But when you get back to the acoustics, some woods are better than others. The idea has been: Let's make it pretty. Well, that's fine, but use an acoustically superior wood. I use mahogany [for the soundbox, spruce for the soundboard]. If you go into a music store looking for guitars, that's what you're going to see—mahogany and spruce. The reason for that is because it's acoustically superior. There are a couple of other good woods. Maple is probably okay. But mahogany really is the thing to use, as far as I'm concerned, for harps."

Given that, Jahr still finds it exciting that "the form is evolving right here in America. The harps that we're building are American harps. The world is going to recognize it as a form of instrument 200 years from now, that it evolved in America at this period of time."

The growth in the number of recordings of harp music also energizes Jahr.

"When I started building harps there were a couple of recordings available," he says. "Right now. . . there are well over a hundred recordings available, and the number is growing by leaps and bounds. The more people who are exposed to it, the faster it grows. I would encourage anybody who wishes to get into instrument building to build harps because the more harps there are the more people are going to want them. This is not a competitive market; it's wide open. Have at it! You'll have customers if you build harps."

Jahr believes the folk harp is "the easiest road into the world of performing musically" because it is easy to play. "I know a lot of people wish they could perform, but they look at it as a daunting task. You can't just sit and play; you have to go through all of these things first [with most instruments]. That's not true with the harp. You can just pick it up and play it. That's what's so remarkable about it."

- *February 4, 1993*

☼

Tune In, Turn On, Turn Out

Rus Hurt ... wood turner

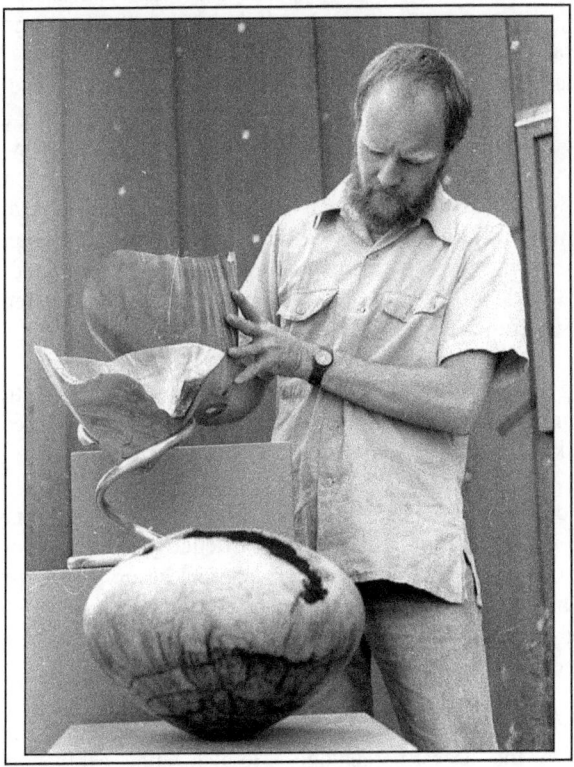

This profile is based on an interview from August 24, 1989.

Just as it takes training to read music and translate notes into pleasant songs, it takes a special eye to "read" a piece of wood and turn something deformed and gnarly into something beautiful. Rus Hurt has that sort of special eye. Hurt, 38, is a wood turner who lives a few miles south of Lake Superior, near unincorporated Port Wing, Wisconsin, approximately midway between Bayfield and Superior.

He turns out both functional and decorative bowls, and various other types of vessels, on a lathe in his workshop. Generally speaking, the more misshapen and abnormal a hunk of wood looks the more artistic the bowl, with natural flaws, decay and other features giving it ornamental qualities.

"What most people look at and consider unusual or unsplitable to go into the stove someone else who has maybe the machinery and the interest and the technical skill with their hands and can combine that with the artisticness of one's eye can come up with something that suddenly is valuable to somebody who once thought that same piece of wood was a nuisance," Hurt says. "So these unsuspecting chunks of wood can really be things that are quite beautiful when handled properly. And that's where all the technical stuff of woodturning comes in. You need to know certain things like how to deal with wet wood, how to deal with medium dry wood. There are different techniques for dealing with all that kind of stuff. Once you gain that broad knowledge of how wood is and how it moves and that kind of thing, then you can experiment with those parameters in mind and start to do kind of untraditional things with wood. Sometimes you succeed and sometimes you don't. Sometimes things sell really well, sometimes they don't."

Working almost entirely with wood from native Midwestern trees, Hurt creates many of his bowls from what are called burls, the cancerous-looking knots found on some trees.

"Occasionally I'll do a piece of exotic wood, but rarely," he says. "I'm just not into exotic woods. I don't particularly want to contribute to using exotics. I think there's enough inherent beauty in the wood that's around here that if you have your sense of design together, and your sense of shape and form, you can produce beautiful articles out of the abundance of wood that is in Minnesota and Wisconsin."

Woodturning is not the sole source of Hurt's income, but it does account for the largest percentage. He also builds cabinets and furniture from time to time, is caretaker to a couple of cabins, and does other odd wood-related jobs. His woodturning is divided into three areas: architectural work, functional items and sculptural pieces.

Architectural work includes such items as newel posts for porches and stairways, and table legs for other furniture makers.

"Maybe the largest third" of his woodturning business is functional bowls—bowls people use for popcorn, nuts, salads, fruit, or whatever else.

Then there is the "artistic stuff" that drew him to woodturning in the first place, eight years ago. He teases these artistic creations from what he calls "neat wood" because the most common reaction to them is: "Wow, that's really neat!"

"Unfortunately," he says, "that sometimes is the hardest stuff to sell because people admire it for its beauty but say, 'What do you do with it?' Some of this is all a function of where you live too, and how far you're willing to go. I could strictly do art work—neat bowls with holes in them, and narrow little tops, and that kind of thing, but I may have to go to the East Coast or the West Coast, or south—out of my area—to sell them, and at this point in my life, when we've got kids around and we're still trying to get our house finished and get a bathroom put in the house after 13 years, I don't want to go that far. So that means that some of my working time has to be with stuff that I can sell in this area. That sometimes is more functional—things that people can afford and identify with."

Hurt and his wife, Cindy, were part of the back to the land movement of the 1970s. "Like a lot of young people looking for a place to start, you don't really realize what it takes to live out in the country," he says. After gradually getting into carpentry work, he found out that was not exactly what he wanted to do and looked for a different path. "I ended up painting a house and trading part of my labor for an old lathe that was out in the garage," he relates. "So I took that route. Once I decided that this could work, I said, 'Well, maybe I better go learn how to turn wood.' So we got a decent vehicle and headed out to Utah, and I spent some time with Dale Nish, one of the master turners in the country, and Rude Osolnik [in Kentucky] a year or so later." Through magazines and brochures, he knew those master wood turners ran summer workshops. "Once you go to one," he says, "then you almost set up a network, sort of, of other people who were there, and you communicate through the mail and phone calls. After you gain a certain amount of expertise and confidence, then it gets kind of repetitious going to some of those, so then you kind of just go your own way. You don't go to those things expecting to learn a whole lot. You may start to develop more of a style rather than (learn) how to hold a tool or that kind of thing." His first such classes were in 1981 and 1982.

"I like to do things that are really simplistic, in many ways—the design is very elementary, very basic," Hurt says. "But it's very solid. I like to use that with as much of the organic elements—natural design—that's already there. I don't really have to do anything to it; it's there, I just bring it out. . . . Basically once it's on the lathe it's all done with lathe tools, which I hand-hold."

The cause of burls, also known as excretions, is not fully understood. "Some people theorize it could be frost damage," Hurt says. "Some people theorize insects cause them. Some people figure it could be all of those things. Some people feel the trees are genetically predisposed at certain points in their growth to start producing what looks like bud growth upon bud growth. It just keeps going, almost like a cancer. It just keeps getting bigger and bigger and bigger." One burl Hurt acquired was so large that only half of it yielded six turned pieces.

Hurt says the secret of avoiding "dry cracking" is knowing how to deal with different types of wood and different degrees of moisture content. "Dealing with green wood, you've got to turn a little faster," he explains. "With dry wood you can afford to work more slowly because it's not going to warp as quickly." Sometimes it is necessary to adjust and use different turning techniques on different sections of the same hunk of wood.

Hurt currently sells his wood-turned items through "six or eight" shops throughout a five-state area. Some customers buy directly from him, at his shop. "I've put together a nice brochure, and people tend to just find me," he says. "I think that part of the enchantment of purchasing work from various artists is to kind of get into their realm, into their world, by finding out where they live and tracking them down and buying right off their doorstep."

Art fairs are not his bag, to borrow a word from the 1960s. "I am not the kind that likes to go to the uptown and fight with 500 artists and 100,000 people come streaming by," he says. "I feel like a monkey in a cage or something. I don't like that. I don't want to do it, and I don't have to do it. . . . I could do the American Craft Council fairs. . . . But I have just decided to go a different route. I know the quality of my work is right up there; it's good work. I just don't want to go that route. . . . I want to do my thing. My thing is on a different plateau. Plus, a lot of it relates to the fact of me being kind of a homebody. I like being home. I don't want to have to figure out how to ship all my stuff to New York or San Francisco. I just don't want to do it." ☼

Patience In A Bottle

John Fox ... model ship builder

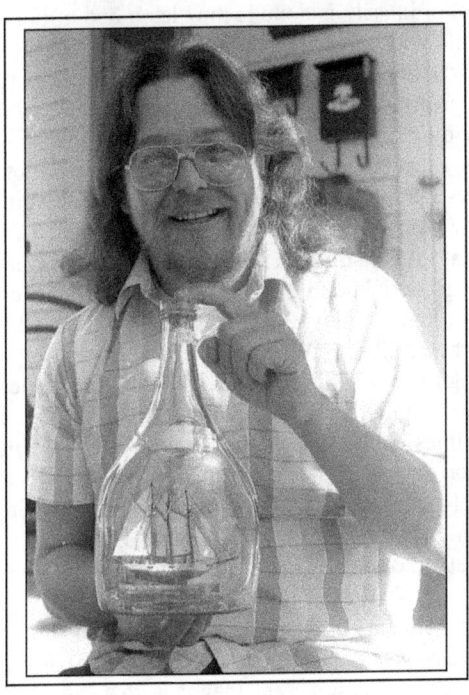

I interviewed John Fox about his ships-in-bottles creations October 9, 1986. He also is featured in the Miscellaneous Mediums section for his custom fishing rods.

A common wish is that pleasant experiences could be bottled, to be saved and savored many more times. John Fox, of Rice Lake, Wisconsin, is trying his best to fulfill that desire by building small-scale, bottled models of all 19 Class A sailing ships he saw at the Parade of Tall Ships in New York on the Fourth of July.

Fox, 35, has a passion for sailing ships, especially those of the Revolutionary War period.

He began assembling ship model kits 15 years ago, graduated to building all of his own pieces from wood, moved on to the detailed plank-on-frame construction method, and started building ships-in-bottles three years ago. His ships-in-bottles are unique creations.

"I haven't found anyone, anywhere, yet who does ships-in-a-bottle the way I do, with the entire hull and then a little stand," he says. "Maybe there is someone, but I don't know about him, and I get trade magazines—magazines for people who are crazy like me and build miniature ships. What ordinarily is done is they lay a bed of blue clay in the bottom of a bottle and only build the model ship from the white line, which is the water line, up. With the blue clay in there representing water, they just press that part a little bit down into the clay and it looks like the ship is riding on water. It gives you lots of advantages because on a lot of ships, especially fully rigged ships, there are a lot more lines than just the ones that go through the bowsprit; there are quite a few of them that go down through the bottom of the hull itself. When you're working with clay like that, when you put it in and press it down, you pull some of the lines tight and then you can just cut off the excess line and bury it down into the clay and then smooth it over a little bit, and nobody knows they're there. When I started doing the full hulls I had to find something to do with those lines." His solution: place a piece of plastic between the hull's two parts, with a small channel carved into the top half for lines, then route the lines up through the "house hole," where the anchor rope comes out, cutting off excess line with special utensils. "I really like the idea of having the whole hull in the bottle, rather than having that messy clay. As far as I know, it's something unique to my method of building ships-in-a-bottle."

Amazingly, since it seems impossible to slip a model ship into a bottle with a small neck, a ship is fully assembled before it's placed in a bottle. The secret of this apparent magic is that "the bottom of the masts have little hinges on them, so they fold back," Fox explains. "You very carefully slip the whole works in a bottle." The rigging lines are as much as three feet too long so that it is easy to pull them from outside the bottle. The lines are pulled in a certain sequence to pull the masts and sails back into place. Fox learned that secret from a book.

"Anytime you have rigging like this there's a certain amount of tension involved," he says, "and the yards and masts are so small and slender that if you pull a line too hard or pull the wrong lines they would just snap, which will kill you. . . . The precision and delicacy of the whole thing is just. . . Most people really don't think that you put it together with tweezers through the neck of the bottle."

Most of the ships-in-bottles Fox makes are only four or five inches long, so it is extremely delicate work, particularly since he likes to include as much detail as possible. The larger plank-on-frame models he builds, which are placed in glass display cases, require time-consuming delicacy and patience as well. The plank-on-frame method, he explains, is "where you build it literally exactly the way the real ship was built, by laying a keel and then putting ribs up, and planking with individual planks all the way up the outside of the hull and everything. That really sold me. You can't do ships-in-bottles quite that way." The planks on one of his model ships are $1/16^{th}$ of an inch wide. "That got to be so fascinating," he enthuses. "That's just about the only way I do larger ship models like that. It's just absolutely fantastic."

He took on the ships-in-bottles challenge because it intrigued him.

"Usually, if I can get them, I work from actual blueprints of the ships," he says. "I have a whole file of blueprints. There are companies that collect them and send them out. . . . After I get an idea what my next ship is going to be I try and find plans, then I Xerox [photocopy] them and reduce them down to the size that I think is about right. And being a draftsman, what I'll do is sit down and draw a set of plans where I calculate where every line is going to go through the hull, where I'm going to carve the little channels for the lines to go through. All of that stuff has to be figured. Then I do what I call a prototype. I do one to see if everything that I've planned is going to work out when I try and put it in a bottle. Once that works, then I ink up the plans and put them in a special file and save them. If I ever need to build that ship again I have the plans, and I'll do three of them at a time instead of one at a time. It's just as easy to do the carving and everything else with three at a time instead of one at a time."

Fox uses various types of wood—mainly basswood for hulls, black walnut for stands, masts and spars, and an exotic Brazilian wood for the deck boards. "I haven't been in the wooden model building long enough to learn the advantages of each different type of wood yet," he says. "But I'm always telling people that if they have a black walnut tree or a hickory tree or something and they cut it down to save me at least a chunk of it. Then I dry it and cut it up into small enough pieces to use. Wherever I can, I try to incorporate more and more woods into each different model. So far just about every one, as I do a new one, I've got some different kind of wood and I do experiments."

He also relies on others to keep him supplied with glass bottles.

"I've got some real old bottles, but I haven't really got the technique yet of how to clean them up decent," he says, "so I'm still stuck with using kind of modern-day glass bottles."

Fox has been selling some of his model ship creations at art shows for more than five years. "It wouldn't matter whether I was selling them or not," he says. "I'd do it anyway, I just love doing it so much."

The Upper Midwest "isn't what you call a real hot area for ship art," he says. "While we were out East I got quite a few contacts. That's why I'm working on the series of ships of Operation Sail '86 that we saw out there, because I got a few people who actually asked me to send them pictures of my work when they found out what I did, like the U.S.S. Constitution gift shop and the Scrimsaw Shop in Boston, which made a real point to say, 'Hey, we'd definitely like to see some of your work here. Send us a catalog or something.' Well, first of all I don't have a catalog, and second of all I don't have enough of a supply yet. What I'd like to do is get at least three or four of each of the different models I do before I send out a catalog. . . . But I'm real hopeful that something like that will work out, because I'd much rather spend my time here building the ships than doing what I usually do in the summer—going around to art shows all summer. The only time I can really work on these things is in the wintertime."

Model ships he saw out East were priced at least four times higher than what Fox asks for. Most of the model schooners he puts in bottles sell for $75. Fully rigged ships are priced at $125. Larger plank-on-frame models are priced as high as $500.

"It takes me five weeks to build three of them, so I'm only making about $75 a week," he points out. "And I work, on average, three-and-a-half to five hours a day, seven days a week, to build something like that. It comes out to something like two or three dollars an hour or something. But it's like I say: even when I was working for a living I was still doing that kind of stuff just because I love it so much."

☼

A Business In Bronze

Wally Shoop ... bronze sculptor

Interviews from July 31, 1984, at Shoop's foundry in Hudson, Wisconsin, and October 25, 1984, at his home north of Stillwater, Minnesota, went into the creation of this profile. He later moved his foundry to Osceola, Wisconsin, where I interviewed him for another newspaper feature story early in 1993.

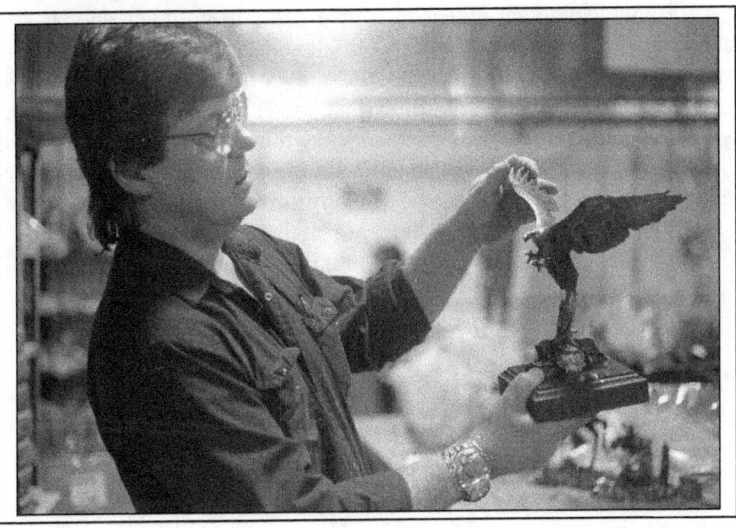

He follows an ancient creative process and uses modern marketing methods. He is both a head-in-the-clouds artist and a down-to-earth businessman. Dichotomous might be a good word with which to characterize Wally Shoop, an internationally known bronze sculptor who found his place in the world through lost wax.

Shoop, who lives near Stillwater, Minnesota, and fashions realistic bronze sculptures that he hopes will uplift and inspire others, is one of the few sculptors in the United States with his own foundry. About 20 full-time employees produce an average of 200 to 300 bronzes a week at that Hudson, Wisconsin, facility. Business has consistently doubled each year. Shoop's creations are found in many private and corporate collections. More than 300 of the Fortune 500 companies have commissioned pieces from him, largely for awards and incentives programs.

To Shoop, large corporations are to modern artists what The Church was to artists several centuries ago. "Michelangelo and Leonardo da Vinci were supported by the Catholic Church four or five hundred years ago," he points out. "Well, now the money and the power is in corporate America, and that's where we go."

He is perplexed that most artists resist using modern marketing strategies to reap rewards in fertile corporate fields.

"I'm surprised at how other artists that I know reject change," he says. ". . . I know some very talented people that still go down and sit in a shopping mall and watch the ladies all day push the kids by in the strollers. They still do the one-man shows in galleries. They resist change in marketing. You'd think that artists would be the most innovative and imaginative and ready for anything new and different and interesting. . . . Everything's in an evolution. People are buying differently now than they ever have. The downtown doesn't exist anymore, so people are going to the shopping malls. The small Ma and Pa grocery store is gone. If you went into the business and set up a small Ma and Pa grocery store in a neighborhood they'd all think you were crazy. Well, why go ahead and sell artwork the same way?

"For creative people, artists are not all that imaginative. In fact, I personally believe that the majority of the people that are calling themselves artists aren't artists. What's the snap course in college, that [you take] if you can't make it in math or different things? *Well, man, go for an art degree!* Or you go for Liberal Arts because you can't cut it the other way."

Shoop proved 12 years ago he is not afraid of change, not afraid to make daring decisions and bold moves. That was when his focus in life switched from making music to making sculpture. While he wanted to be a visual artist from about the age of eight, music began dominating his life when he became a teenager. He had a succession of bands from age 14, bands with such names as Dracula and the Zombies, Billy Rat and The Finks, The Rocking Blue Devils, and The Wally Shoop Show. He wrote songs and recorded "for years," he says, wanting to change the world with "deep" lyrics, songs which met an indifferent response.

"I did learn from music that people want music for entertainment," he says. "They don't want the songs that (try to) change the world—the social commentary. And I also found out that art is part of the entertainment sphere. You may get away with a subtle statement, but you won't get away with hitting people over the head with a baseball bat. You slip it in every now and then."

He played on the same bill with rock 'n' roll pioneer Jerry Lee Lewis and actually performed with rockabilly legend Carl Perkins, his idol. "He played at this club [in Sioux Falls, South Dakota] and we were the back-up band. In fact, we backed up a lot of name artists over the years because I always had a group, so an agent that was booking somebody like Buddy Knox six months from now knew that we would be around. Anyway, with Carl Perkins, he gave me the philosophy, because he was like Chuck Berry—he played the guitar and sang. And he gave me the philosophy one night in a nightclub that allowed me to pick the guitar and sing at the same time. And the philosophy is real simple: He says, 'You don't play it; you just fiddle *around* a little bit in between the lines.' And he was right. You're not *really* playing it. It's funny because you really don't become a great singer that way, and you really don't become a great guitar player, but you sure can put on a cooking show."

Weary of singing and playing guitar with bar bands five and six nights a week, Shoop wasn't sure which direction to turn. A "serious Christian" friend suggested he seek God's counsel by speaking to Him as a friend. Shoop did, and immediately propitious things happened. He had been sculpting as a sideline, and within a week he had two "really good" commissions, received publicity from a St. Paul newspaper and two magazines, and found a small farmstead near Stillwater perfect for his work needs he was able to buy at a lower price than the owner had previously turned down with money obtained by selling the house he was living in to a couple who fell in love with that house at first sight.

"So much happened in that week," Shoop says, "that is was like I got a telegram that said: 'Make sculpture, kid.' I shouldn't mess around. I gradually weaned the band down to three nights [a week], and two nights, and one night, and this [the sculpture] pretty well took off, and it's been taking care of us ever since."

Shoop tried the starving artist approach for a while, with art fairs and one-person gallery exhibits. "I had several one-man shows in nice galleries, and the cocktail opening and the whole bit," he says. "That's great for the ego, but it is not for the pocketbook at all. I knew there had to be a better way, and I just looked around for other ways. . . . I've been real selective about the galleries. I'm going back into it very carefully. When the recession came even the wealthy didn't have the extra money to buy artwork, so I went into other markets like direct mail and awards and incentives, and hooked up with a real good company [based in Minneapolis]. . . . They didn't have anything like the awards, and they thought it was a classy idea (for companies) to give fine bronzes. In fact, we custom design them for a lot of major corporations. It's their edition; no one else has it."

Shoop proudly believes he has worked harder at his craft—"12 hours a day"—than 90 percent of the people he knows. "If you're a sculptor you make sculpture," he says. "If you're a writer you write. If you look at the great writers and the great artists, those people (wrote and) painted. Van Gough, that sucker painted all the time. He had to borrow money from everybody just to buy more paints. Edgar Allan Poe. . . wrote standing up, at a bookcase. Those are artists, and those are writers. They worked hard at it. Look at Audubon. Audubon was a naturalist and an artist, but the way he made money was having these packages of prints sold. He knew if he wanted to keep on painting that he'd better figure out a way to make a living at it.

"I've taken courses in small business financial management. I read just about every new book that comes out on business and business management, because if I want to survive and I want to keep making these beautiful bronzes (I need to do it). . . . We're a corporation now. We have 20 full-time staff, a full-time office, and that's all being fed off of what I make. . . . It doesn't look like we're busy, but we have distributors, and everything is done through distributors. When an order's done it goes in our own delivery van and goes right over to the distributor and is dropped off. . . . There may be 30, 40, 50 orders going through at any one time. They're at different places throughout the system."

Shoop has created more eagle sculptures than any other image. He believes nature is life's best teacher, a philosophy he formed while growing up among Sioux Indians in Rapid City, South Dakota. While Shoop is 1/16th Chippewa Indian blood, he identifies more with the Sioux way of thinking and feeling about things. He says the values he picked up in South Dakota are his most important influence. "They may not have a lot of culture, but they have perfect values," he says of Western people.

The Shoops share their modest, old house and 10 acres of land near Stillwater with a slew of cats and dogs, two horses, and a pet Arctic wolf named Sinoauv [Sinoauv is Paiute for wolf]. Shoop, who is an activist for wolf protection, has such regard for Sinoauv that he named his company after him—Studio Sinoauv, Ltd [now American Bronze Casting]. Two of his grown sons, John and Wally Jr., work at the Hudson foundry. His third son, James, or Buddy, is involved in the design end.

Owning his own foundry allows Shoop the quality control he wants. "There are a lot of people working in bronze who send their originals to a foundry, and then the foundry does the molds, the casting and the finishing," he says. "We wanted control over that. I don't think you can work in a medium and not know the whole medium from beginning to end. I've learned so much from just doing the process that I wouldn't have known before about sculpture if I hadn't."

Total control also means he is able to price his bronzes lower than most other sculptors. His small bronzes go for anywhere from a couple of hundred dollars to well over $1,000.

Shoop's bronze sculptures are produced by the ancient "lost wax" process, which may have been used as far back as 10,000 years ago. Once an original soft-wax model is sculpted (sometimes clay is used for larger pieces), a rubber mold is made from the wax model with super-heat-resistant rubber invented for space capsule insulation. The rubber mold is used to make additional wax impressions, which are encased in ceramic shells and placed in an oven. A temperature of about 1,600 degrees quickly melts the wax, thus the phrase lost wax. Actually, Shoop designed a furnace with a trough in the bottom that collects three-fourths of the wax for re-use. The ceramic shell is then set on sand and filled with molten bronze. After the metal cools the shell is cracked away and finishing touches done by hand, with imperfections smoothed over and parts of sculptures welded together. An average production run is 100 to 300 bronzes.

The space-age technology and materials used in the production process are a far cry from having handmade foundry equipment set up in a pasture, as Shoop did in the beginning, having borrowed $2,000 from a friend for that equipment. In those days, when Shoop was ready to do a pour a friend who worked at a gas station in nearby White Bear Lake drove over to help after closing the station at 9 p.m., since pouring molten metal from a crucible is a two-person operation. "I'd try to have the metal ready at 9:15," Shoop says. "But he was on call with the wrecker, and every now and then it would happen that he was out getting somebody out of the ditch, and here I was with smoking metal."

Shoop spent many nights in a sleeping bag on the floor of the casting room—a shed that now serves as his studio—setting an alarm clock to ring every two hours so he could monitor the temperature of his kiln.

These days—perhaps it's the musician in him coming out, for musicians are notoriously nocturnal—he usually can be found in his studio from sometime in the evening until about 4 a.m. "You can concentrate then and get a lot done," he says. "There are no disruptions."

Not surprisingly, given his work ethic, Shoop has little empathy for artists who say they need to be "in the mood" or inspired to create. "Hey, if you want to be a writer or an artist you write (or create) whether you are inspired or not," he says. "You inspire yourself; you psyche yourself up. Otherwise you're going to be sitting around for 364 days out of the year and get inspired on one, and you're going to get awful hungry in the meantime."

While he gets involved in creating representations of everything from automobiles to zeppelins, he is most closely associated with birds—particularly eagles, as noted—and animals. He has done very few large-scale pieces. "I make more money off the small ones," he says. "Somebody like Merrill-Lynch will buy 200 bulls, or IT&T will buy 30 of one or 30 of another. . . . If the right person comes along and they'll spend the money, yeah, then we'll do a big one."

But wouldn't he like the prestige of having large public pieces in parks or in front of buildings? "I'm not sure," he answers. "I'd rather go into people's houses, because I think these things in the park get lost. Most people don't even stop and look at them. Besides, I'd rather make art more reasonable for average people. Up until just recently it's always belonged to the rich. In fact, you've heard of the generation gap; well, I believe there's a culture gap. I believe that a lot of people don't go to the museums and don't participate in the orchestra [concerts] and don't have anything to do with the arts because it's a culture gap. They think that only snobs go to the museums. I think average people should be able to afford it. That's why I built the foundry, because I wanted to make more pieces. . . . It's a very high-profit piece of merchandise, because the materials is just a fraction of the cost of the artwork; the rest of the cost is the creative ability and the amount of work. . . . Opportunities aren't our problem. Our problem is production and making enough work and getting people trained. . . . All the people that work here are people that may be interested but are unskilled, and then we take them in, and it may take a year to train them."

Being both down-to-earth businessman and head-in-the-clouds artist can present problems. "When you tell somebody to do something and he's seen you just walk into a wall because you're dreaming about something he doesn't pay much attention to you," Shoop says. "But when I ask somebody to do something I mean it. I've read a lot of books about it and I know exactly what I want and how I want it done."

While such famous people as Robert Redford, John Denver and President Ronald Reagan own Shoop bronzes, Shoop doesn't let celebrity sales go to his head. "I guess they're just people like everybody else," he says. "They might be famous, but that's all." He measures success and satisfaction on a different scale. For instance, when a well-liked White Bear Lake High School teacher who admired his work died from a stroke, students there contributed to a memorial fund so they could buy one of Shoop's bronzes for the school library. The teacher had been helping students put together a production of *Swan Lake* on her own time before she died, and Shoop happened to have just finished a bronze of a ballet dancer. When he met with those in charge of the memorial fund and learned there was barely enough money in the fund to cover the cost of the metal used in the piece that was of little concern to him. No other sale has given him more satisfaction.

"Bronze being a permanent medium," he says, "you think very carefully about what you're going to do when you sit down to start something. I don't want to make anything dumb, silly, ridiculous. I don't want to make any negative statements because I think art should inspire and uplift."

Shoop has learned from successful companies that "everything has to serve a purpose or it becomes extinct. . . . If you can perform a service for other people, and perform it better than anybody else, you're bound to come out ahead regardless of whether you're selling stories or insurance or sculpture or cupcakes. It's the same thing. We all have to serve, and the better servant we are to one another all the rest just falls into place. It isn't they're out there for you to take; they're out there for you to serve. And then you come out on the winning end."

☼

Metal Evolution

Jack Route ... metal artist

(And Mike Route ... metalsmith)

Of all the artists and artisans I have interviewed, Jack Route changed the most between interviews, in terms of what he created. The 22-year interval between the first and second interviews accounts for only part of the reason; the biggest factor was his thirst for artistic fulfillment. The first part of this is based on an interview from August 1, 1990.

Metalsmith artist Jon Michael Route calls himself a frustrated architect. "I've always responded to shapes and forms," says the 36-year-old Frederic, Wisconsin area resident, who is better known outside the craft community as Jack Route. His architectural leanings are evident in the geometric designs of his pewter salt and pepper shakers, desk sets, napkin rings, candle holders, and other functional items.

Route [pronounced like "dowdy," with two syllables] displays and sells his work at prestigious American Craft Expos and other top-level craft fairs, gift shops and galleries across the country, with the East and West Coasts his best markets.

"There are only a limited number of people who want or can afford this kind of thing," he says. His functional—or "production"—items range in price from $30 to $169. He also makes handcrafted one-of-a-kind vases and other decorative vessels, which are priced from $500 to $1,500.

"Hollow-ware has always been my thing in life, I guess," he says. . . . "The difficult part was trying to design them and figure out if I could make them at a reasonable price and be able to sell them. When I started I had no idea what they were going to end up costing and what people would be willing to pay for them. I wasn't that into marketing that I understood all those different parts of the business; that had to be learned step by step. I made some mistakes along the way, but I think in a large sense I was pretty lucky to kind of hit on something that people grabbed onto. In a year's time or so I had several accounts—places that were buying from me fairly regularly. It wasn't a long process of finding people to buy my work. I was able to find markets fairly fast. I don't know if that's luck or what. I hit it at a good time.

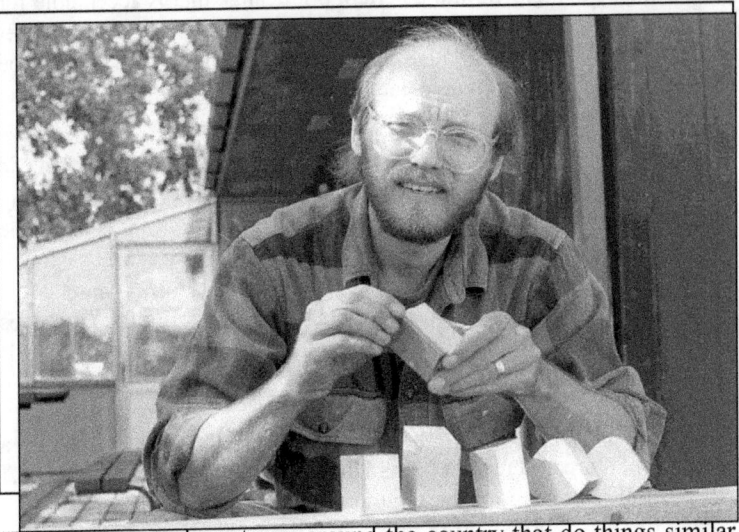

"There are several pewterers around the country that do things similar to what I do, but most of it is very traditional, Colonial, Queen Anne-type things. It's usually spun on a lathe and cast in molds and things like that.... The ways in which I work the metal, and the styles, set them apart from all of the other people. The fact that I made something a little different, I think, was in part the reason why people bought them for stores, because they're always looking for something different. If a retail store doesn't have something new and different each year, then people don't frequent it. You have to keep showing something new and interesting so that people keep coming back into your store looking for something that excites them."

Spun on a lathe, pewter items are always circular, with concentric designs. Route wanted to do something different, and the way he fabricated his items led him in that direction. He cuts, folds, stamps and solders the material. His "simplified forms" don't have a lot of decoration, except for "a little surface pattern on them. It's basically the form that slants, or tilts, or does something unusual that is hopefully what is attractive about them.... It's a nice functional metal. People are familiar with it. But the way I present it usually makes them kind of look twice and wonder if it's not aluminum or stainless steel or something like that."

While Route enjoys working with silver and gold, he usually works with those more valuable metals only on a commission basis. Pewter, a tin-antimony alloy, is "more expensive than brass and copper," he points out, "but it's a lot less expensive than silver. As far as what the price ends up being, I fit into a certain price range that is acceptable for gifts and that sort of thing. So that's part of the reason for using pewter too." Beyond that, brass and copper salt and pepper shakers would be impractical because salt would eat those metals.

Route studied his craft at the University of Wisconsin—Stout, in Menomonie, then lived in Kansas City for nearly 10 years before returning to his native Frederic two years ago. In Kansas City, he worked for an architectural metals firm and at a jewelry store.

In addition to selling his products at open arts and crafts fairs, he does "a fair amount of wholesaling" as well, renting booth space at trade shows where people come around and place orders.

"It's not real high production, like you would buy something in a department store and maybe hundreds of thousands of them are made," he says. "I just make maybe a hundred [of an item] in the course of a couple of years. It's small production. It's basically hand-done. I've got a few machines and things to help me a little bit, but there's an awful lot of handwork and hand-finishing. . . . I'm a traveling salesman, so to speak. I do between 10 and 12 shows a year. That's what I have to do. I travel to meet my market."

He has participated in American Craft Expos, held annually in Baltimore, San Francisco, West Springfield, MA, and St. Paul, for five years. The gatekeepers select only a small percentage of the artisans who apply for those major shows. "You're reaching a lot of people in real diverse parts of the country all at once," Route says. "It means I don't have to go to every city; I can just go to one market. It's sort of expensive to do, but it's a lot easier to do it that way than to go around to different cities."

Route drops certain items he feels are insufficiently successful and adds new items from time to time. "You have to," he says, "because people are always looking for something different too, so you have to keep it fresh. And in terms of my own creativity, it's nice to work on something different instead of the same thing time after time. The production work is what pays the bills, but it gets tedious. Anything gets tedious, and it becomes work. Having a chance to do larger things, and more one-of-a-kind things, is what really interests me."

He uses pretty much the same process when making larger pieces as when making small production items. "I do kind of a patchwork panel and then assemble the panels up into a form," he explains. "All of the little pieces are welded together from the back and then left so that you can kind of see the little weld marks and stuff. That adds a little bit of texture to the overall feel of the piece."

He tries to take as much as possible to shows. "I try to show a range of things," he says, "and what I'm capable of doing, in the hope that people will take a good look at it and like some of the ideas that I do." By having the opportunity to talk to people, he is able to explain how certain items and ideas could be customized to fit a certain space. "I'm making these things basically one at a time," he says. "It's not like you want a Ferrari but you want it a little bit smaller. I mean, you can't do that. But you can with what I do."

- 0000000 –

By the time I interviewed Jack Route again, in 2012, his art had evolved into something quite different and he was sharing studio space with his son Mike, who crafts items from forged metal. I interviewed both of them, individually, on May 22, 2012, then did a shorter follow-up interview with Jack about a month later, on June 15.

Like most fathers and sons, Jack and Mike Route have similarities and differences, beyond physical characteristics. While both are Frederic residents and metalsmith artists, they are following different paths in that artistic field. Jack, the father, who uses his full given name of Jon Michael Route as his professional name, constructs colorful wall pieces out of brass, bronze, copper, aluminum and pewter. Mike's art is based in blacksmithing. He forges iron and steel stock into table bases, fireplace doors, benches, sculptural pieces and other items that have a flowing, sinuous quality.

"There's something about taking a big piece of hot steel and being able to manipulate it the way you want to—to be able to make it do what you want it to do," Mike says. "I like the fluid movements of the steel, trying to make it look real fluid and organic, which is kind of a cool contrast to me; you typically think of steel as very cold and rigid, and to make it have that organic feel is pretty cool."

Both Mike and Jack display their artisan creations at some very prestigious arts and crafts fairs around the country, such as the annual American Craft Council show in St. Paul each April. For Mike, such shows are more promotional than immediately profitable. "It's been a great way to get commission works," he notes. "Typically I'll go to the shows and not sell anything, but then I'll get a few phone calls or e-mails in the following months. I've tried some other forms of advertising and they don't quite seem to work as well. It's sort of my advertising. They [potential customers] want to trust somebody who's going to build them a fireplace door or a table or something." On the other hand, shows are a good marketplace for Jack. "I usually try to have things that people can take home with them—some smaller items," he says. "It does happen that I sell big ones, but a lot of times people have to go home and think about it, or measure their wall or something like that."

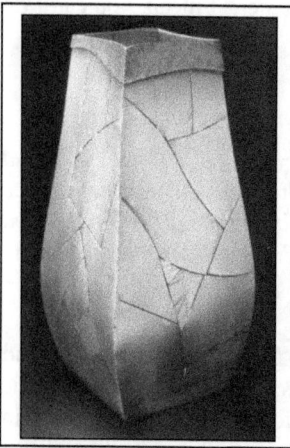 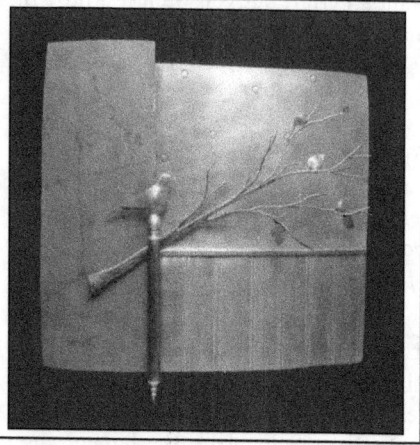

Once known primarily for grayish pewter boxes, vessels, teapots, and salt and pepper shakers, Jack's metalsmithing began taking a new direction nine or 10 years ago when he played with copper and brass and new patina solutions he found on the Internet to fill a specific kitchen wall space in his house.

"Experimentation is integral to your development as an artist, and real change requires a commitment to a new direction or purpose," he explains on his website. ". . . Looking back, it was very unnerving to try and take on a new identity that could prove to be detrimental to my income and risk what I had worked 20 years to build."

Many of Jack's wall pieces have a collage quality. They resemble small sections of patchwork quilts, or geometrically based paintings, with either a leaf or a bird on a branch highlighted out front. Serendipitously, birds symbolize peace and serenity, which makes his pieces well-suited for health care facilities. He has hooked up with "a handful" of design firms that specialize in designing and decorating such facilities. "It's been kind of more like a focus piece above an entryway or something like that, so I might just do two or three pieces, or a triptych, or something like that," he says. He estimates he has created 25 to 30 such installation pieces over the last five or six years. The idea behind such health care facility artwork is that a serene, beautiful, art-filled building should help patients recuperate more quickly than a facility with unadorned, antiseptic white walls.

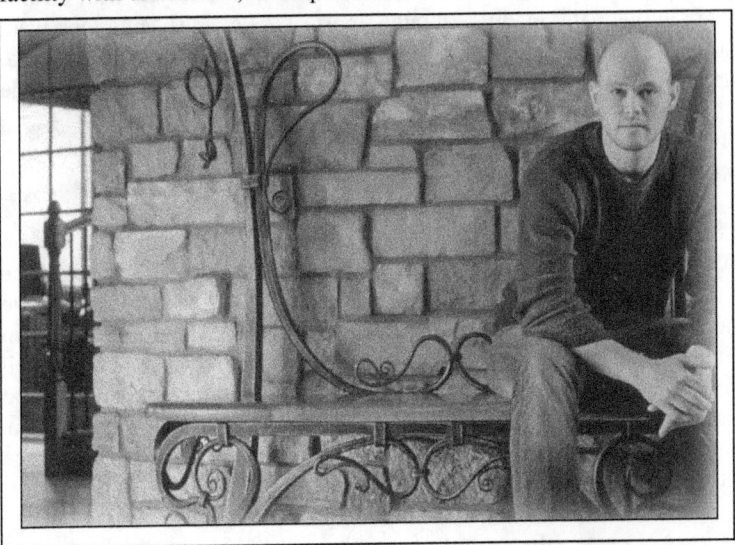

Naturally, Mike found himself drawn to his father's studio as he grew up. "I typically would work in the shop when Dad would be out of town," he relates. "Then I'd have the whole shop to myself. . . . There were things that were off-limits—some of the machinery and whatnot. . . . I would try to do some soldering and make little jewelry. I think my first art fair was at the Bayfield apple fest. I was young; I was in sixth or seventh grade, maybe. I made $700 just selling. . . sort of small jewelry kind of things. Of course, I didn't have any upfront costs; I didn't have to pay for the materials or anything because I just sort of used whatever Dad had. He had quite a scrap pile, so I would take from the scrap pile and make stuff."

Jack characterizes Mike as "a very independent kid. He was very interested in music for a while. I don't remember, until he got into maybe high school, before I could really tell that he was kind of pursuing some of the things I was doing. I brought home some iron-working equipment at one point. I had it set up at my Dad's house, and I remember one summer he went down there for a few days, and that got him pretty interested in that."

As Jack did, Mike studied metal art at the University of Wisconsin—Stout. "I wasn't really sure if he was going to take up metal, per se, or something else," Jack says. "The nice thing about Stout is they kind of made you take all these different classes, so you had to take a sculpture class, and you had to take a printmaking class, and all that stuff, so you get exposed to a lot of different things. But, no, he stayed with metal." Even in the metal medium, though, most of the classes Mike took were not geared toward ironwork. An independent study project in that area, under the supervision of professor Ron Verdon, lit a spark in him. "He basically just let me go and do whatever I wanted," Mike says. ". . . But there were a lot of limitations at the school, in terms of noise and whatnot."

Following college Mike spent two years as a graphic designer at an Atlanta advertising agency owned by an uncle. About five years ago he tired of that job and pitched the Village of Frederic a proposal that he take over two adjacent, vacant village-owned buildings in downtown Frederic, one a former automotive service garage that would work well for blacksmith tasks. The village agreed to let him use the buildings at no cost, and give him the buildings if he stayed for five years. Mike returned to Frederic and set up his Red Iron Studios in the garage building, fired by youthful energy and confidence.

"I kind of came into the business with a pretty big ego, thinking that I could make some stuff and sell it and make a living," he admits. "I learned pretty quickly that you kind of have to do some things you didn't think you would have to do to make a living and keep a business open. . . . I feel like I'm okay on the design/art end, but the business end of things is a whole different story. . . . It's always a roller coaster with finances."

Of course, the vast majority of artists are more adept at creating than they are with marketing and a business role. It is difficult for many artists to find their markets and manage the business aspects. "There's more than one way to do everything, and I just did it my way and he's got to figure out his own way," Jack says about Mike.

When Jack and his wife, Debbie, decided to sell their house four miles north of Frederic and move into town, the second building Mike acquired from the village seemed like a perfect studio space for Jack, so Jack gradually transitioned from his old home studio to his new in-town studio this past spring and summer. Pooling their resources, Jack and Mike formed a LLC [limited liability corporation] and now share ownership of the entire two-building property, which will include a small showroom in front of Jack's studio space to display the work of both.

"He really was kind of the spark to it all because he took the initiative to do it," Jack says. "I remember thinking about this building years and years ago—it's been empty for quite a while—but I just didn't have the energy to do it." For Jack, "it's been a real pleasure to now be able to work with him a little bit. He'll call me in there sometimes and say, 'I need somebody to hold this hammer.'"

Mike generally uses chalk to draw a full-scale design either on a table or his shop floor. He heats the metal in a coal forge or one of two gas forges. The coal forge produces torch-like spot heat while the gas forges give him "nice long heat." He uses a noisy power hammer and other tools to further stretch and shape the metal, and weld together pieces.

"It's noisy, and it's loud, and it's hot and sweaty," he says. "You're heating metal up to around 2,000 degrees, and then you're banging on it. . . . It's just a back and forth process: you're heating up, and you're hitting, and you're drawing out, and you're matching curves. . . . Usually you draw out your curve and you match that curve. Some sculpture can be very whimsical and just let things happen and let things be what they want to be. I try to have a little more control with what I'm doing." That said, there are times when he uses a more free-form technique, playing with a torch and some pliers to sort of let something happen.

Jack has described himself as "a frustrated architect," and his architectural leanings are evident in the geometric designs of both his old and new work. He likes mixing metals, "partly because the way the coloring process works it shows a little bit of the underneath metal, so yellow color on brass, which is already yellow, looks different than when I put yellow on copper, which is kind of a reddish color. It actually gives me more colors that way. You can also choose metal based on what you're going to do with it. If you need to do a lot of forming, or maybe real detailed work on something, sometimes you want a softer metal. I still use pewter even, occasionally, when I want to get some certain kind of look to it." Some of the metal receives "a fair amount of texturing" with hammers and other tools. He also builds up layers with metal and plywood backing to give a piece more depth and added interest.

The coloring process, which involves liquid patina solutions, produces vivid colors. The patina is applied with a sponge or a brush, or even sprayed on. Since that must be done when the metal is hot, but not too hot, Jack uses a torch to heat the metal while simultaneously applying the patina with his other hand. The chemicals in the solution react with metal when the metal reaches a certain temperature range. Whenever assembling a piece involves soldering, the piece needs to be assembled before the coloring is applied.

He generally ends up with colors very close to what he envisioned, though the coloring process is not an exact science. "The amount of patina you put on makes a difference, the metal that you put it on makes a difference, and the heat that you put it on makes a difference," he notes.

Mike gives his pieces a variety of finishes. "You have to treat metal somehow if you don't want it to rust," he explains. He either paints the metal or goes over it with a wire brush before applying a wax finish. "That makes it feel like a nice natural metal," he says. "Interior things don't look very good painted, I don't think; I like the more natural finish, which is black."

Explorative artist that he is, Jack already is doing some re-evaluating as to what direction his metal art should take in the coming years. While he "takes ownership" of the wall pieces he has done for health care facilities, and knows his identity is now tied to that work, at the same time he is searching for another potential path.

"I would like to eventually have two bodies of work—one for that kind of area and then one of my own work," he says. "Right now it's all kind of mixed up and I'm still kind of learning the color process—still searching, kind of, for kind of a direction there. It's a constant thing; it's something you've got to do all the time, is find your way where you become more comfortable."

☼

From Scrap To Sculpture

Dennis O'Donnell ... junque sculptor

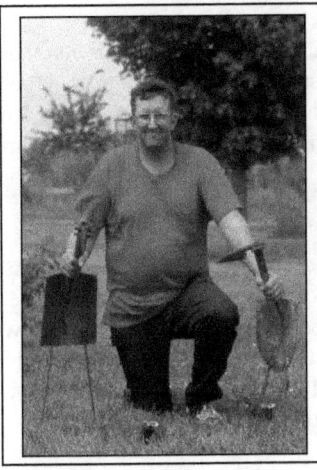
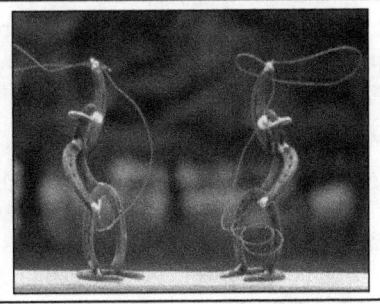

I interviewed Dennis O'Donnell on November 5, 1992, and again on August 18, 1998.

All creative craftwork has an element of alchemy. The artisan transforms raw materials into something decorative, something useful, something inspiring. When the raw materials are literally junk, as they are for Dennis O'Donnell, that alchemic transfiguration crosses a rather wide artistic bridge.

With perception, imagination and a deft touch with an arc welder, O'Donnell turns parts of old tools, farm machinery and other scrap iron into pieces of suggestively representational sculpture that sell for as much as $100. In fact, a bighorn sheep sculpture he donated to the Foundation For North American Sheep brought $325 at a fundraising auction.

In O'Donnell's hands, old rusty hand shovels become the bodies and necks of quaint birds, cattle drinking cups mottled turtle shells, milk cans stout metal pigs, horseshoes the bowed legs of lariat-twirling cowboys, and discarded gears serrated tractor tires. O'Donnell is so accomplished at this folk art genre of "junque art" that last summer he was an invited participant in both the 32nd annual Smithsonian Folklife Festival in Washington, DC, and the four-day Wisconsin Folklife Festival in Madison. In each case the event sponsor paid all travel and lodging expenses for O'Donnell and his wife, Linda. O'Donnell also had three pieces included in a traveling folk art exhibit put together by the Cedarburg Cultural Center for Wisconsin's 1998 sesquicentennial celebration.

O'Donnell is an unassuming, unpretentious man who marvels that people pay money for the pieces of rusty sculpture he puts together largely as a lark. First and foremost, he is a farmer who cares for more than 60 cows and approximately 300 acres of land about a mile from Frederic, Wisconsin.

"Dennis is just a great guy to deal with," says potter and stained glass artist Mary Dosch, co-owner of the Brickyard Pottery & Glassworks near Barronett, one of two retail outlets for O'Donnell's junk sculpture. "He's one of the most colorful, genuine people I've ever met. . . . I saw his work at a shop in Luck and I just knew that our customers would like it. He drives up with his pickup and throws it all out on the lawn. To him it's still just junk. To the people that buy it, though, it's art."

When a man came with a truck to pick up O'Donnell's items for the Cedarburg Cultural Center's traveling exhibit, O'Donnell was amused that the man carefully packed his pieces by cushioning them with blankets and tying them securely. "Don't worry about my stuff," O'Donnell said to him. "Cover up the other stuff you have in there, because if my stuff falls over on it it's going to hurt it. If my stuff falls over it won't get hurt."

Unlike other scrap metal sculptors, O'Donnell doesn't give his creations cute or fanciful names. To him they are simply birds, turtles, rabbits and owls.

Dosch reports O'Donnell's work sells "very well. . . . His birds have always sold really well, in particular the ones that are made out of the barn drinking cups. But anything he makes will sell."

O'Donnell has been a sales-oriented artisan for fewer than half of the 15 or 16 years he has played with pieces of scrap metal in the welding area of an implement storage shed.

While attending a birthday party for O'Donnell, the owner of a Luck gift shop saw some of the whimsical creations in O'Donnell's yard and asked if she could put some of his sculpture in her shop. Although skeptical anyone would buy it, O'Donnell granted her permission. To O'Donnell's amazement, the sculpture started selling, although a minority of perplexed shoppers scorned it.

Dosch doesn't find that sort of love/hate division with her customers. "People come here looking for artwork," she says, "so they think it's artwork. Dennis thinks that's hilarious because to him it's not artwork at all; it's a big joke to him."

While O'Donnell doesn't consider his junk sculpture art, he still takes obvious pride in what he produces because of the pleasure and delight people derive from it. At the Smithsonian Folklife Festival he noticed a man "grinning from ear to ear" approach from quite a distance away. "You just can't help but smile," the man said upon reaching O'Donnell's tent. "He just kept smiling, and as he walked away he was laughing," O'Donnell recounts. "And that's why I do it—to give somebody a little bit of a light spot in their life."

O'Donnell demonstrated his junk sculpture craft six hours a day at the 10-day Smithsonian Folklife Festival, held on the National Mall, which is bookended by the Capitol building and the Washington Monument. "I went through two bottles of oxygen and 10 pounds of brass while I was out there," he says. "That's a lot of oxygen and a lot of brass. We sent four boxes of junk out, and by the last day I was down to where I didn't have a whole lot of junk left. I was pretty limited on what I could make [by then]; I didn't have parts enough anymore."

He took all the pieces he made there to a marketplace area. Every piece sold. "As fast as I could make it and take it to the marketplace it was gone," he says. The festival director bought the one milk can pig he made.

The trip wasn't a financial windfall, though. "By the time we paid somebody to do [farm] chores and that kind of business," O'Donnell points out, "we didn't really make a whole lot. But we had fun."

People prefer the junk sculpture unpainted, even if parts are cancerous with rust. They also appear to prefer pure whimsy to functionality; such items as cookbook holders and bootjacks have sold poorly. "Just about everything sells, unless it's useful," O'Donnell quips.

Because of the liability factor, O'Donnell makes very few of the sort of heavy-duty lawn and deck chairs, stools and tables found on his own outdoor deck. "No matter how good it is," he says, "somebody can figure out a way to get hurt on it." He stays away from using old pitchforks in his sculpture for the same reason.

Now that O'Donnell's hobby has earned him a measure of public recognition, some people bring him their scrap iron. "It's not uncommon to come home and find a pile of iron in the yard," he says. "I'm getting known enough now that people collect stuff for me."

Most of the time he knows immediately what a piece of junk—or a part of it—reminds him of, and how he will use it. Sometimes, though, his inspirational juices simmer a long time before boiling to conception.

"I've got an iron barrel that I throw all my spare parts in—parts that I don't want," he says. "Then all of a sudden a lightbulb comes on and I think: 'Oh, I can use that part here.'"

O'Donnell suspects the popularity of junk art is a fad. Given that, he isn't likely to sell his cows and give up farming anytime soon to try to make a living as a junque sculptor. In the meantime he's "having fun with it. It's great fun for me," he says. "And as long as people enjoy looking at it I enjoy doing it."

☼

Math + Metal = Geometric Sculpture

John Ganske ... abstract sculptor

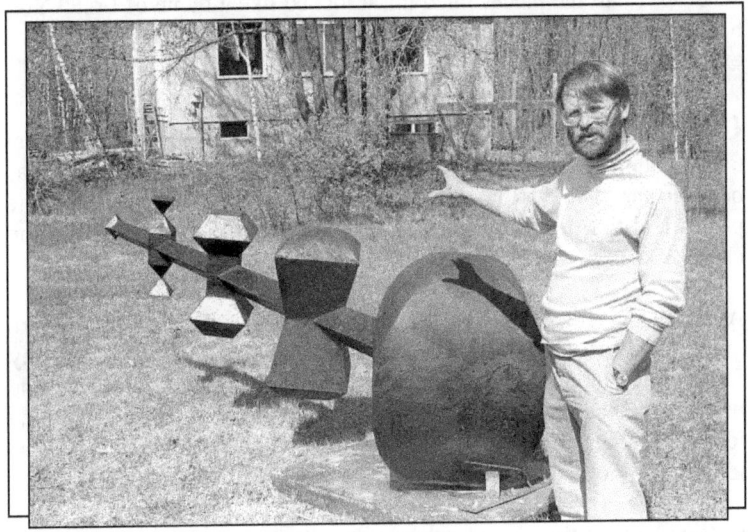

Unlike most abstract sculptors, who create their pieces capriciously, John Ganske knows exactly what his are going to look like before he begins making them. Ganske, of Spooner, Wisconsin, is a trained mathematician who likes to incorporate the laws and structures of mathematics into his sculpture.

"I plan things out, and I draw things out, and I figure things out, and reduce them to formulas," he says. "I have everything planned out. I know exactly what it's going to look like."

Many of Ganske's sculptures are multi-piece works with the pieces identical in shape but different in size, progressing in a geometrical pattern. A work called *Split Ellipsoid*, for instance, consists of five ellipsoids, the smallest of which is 18 inches long, the largest 72 inches. Based on the mathematical principle called the Golden Section, Ganske determined the size of each ellipsoid by multiplying the square root of two to determine the size of each succeeding piece. "It's geometric, because that's the nature of vision," Ganske says. "When you see something at a distance, as you double the distance the size of it halves. . . . I'm interested in perspective."

A work called *Lawn Sharks*, in its most recent reincarnation at a one-man show at the University of Wisconsin—Eau Claire last fall, is made up of 21 crescent shapes ranging from one foot long to 12 feet long planted in the ground. Viewed from the side, the row of crescent shapes resembled a line of shark fins cutting through the grass. Viewed head-on, so all the pieces lined up, it looked like a flame of fire. "You have everything line up and it becomes one point of intensity," Ganske explains.

Ganske is serious about his work, but not solemnly so. There is a certain amount of playfulness and whimsy involved. *Lawn Sharks* has been arranged in various ways over the years—sometimes with the pieces laid flat on the ground—and has undergone a number of name changes.

As a student at UW—River Falls in the mid- to late 1960s Ganske made a lot of "variable sculptures" that could be arranged in any fashion. He couldn't quite decide how to put the objects together, so he usually chained pieces to each other. "I was kind of interested in the idea of a DNA molecule and the way things linked together. That was kind of the motivation for that."

Getting back to the idea of perspective, though, and having everything come to one point of intensity. . .

"I start with a two-dimensional image," Ganske explains, "and break it all up into parts, allowing for perspective because from a distance the objects decrease at a specific rate." He sometimes makes a painting before actually constructing a sculpture, but he doesn't feel something is complete unless it is in a three-dimensional form. "I don't know what that's related to," he says. "I've been trying to figure out why. Maybe it's because we're becoming so familiar with two-dimensional formats, like newspapers, magazines, television and all that. . . . I keep thinking of the example of seeing Walter Cronkite in person. You're constantly being flamblasted with this two-dimensional image all the time, and to actually see Walter Cronkite in person makes it something special."

Some of Ganske's sculptures are made from laminated wood, others from steel. Almost all of them are painted black, with plastic roofing cement. After scratching many of the objects when moving them, he started painting them black to make such blemishes less apparent. He also likes to paint them black because he believes it makes his sculptures look important, which is what he wants.

While there is some comparison to be made between Ganske's creations and the work of well-known sculptor/installation artist Cristo, there is more difference than similarity. "Cristo uses the same size repeated and repeated," Ganske points out. "There's no end to it; it's continuous. My work is different in that I start with a particular size and then I decrease it, so eventually you reach a certain limit. The main difference between my work and his is that he would continue on forever and ever, until the money runs out. . . . I do like his work, and his energy, and his commitment. That's a big part of it. Making sculpture is quite a commitment. Just the mere fact of doing some large thing like that is a statement in itself about the nature of art."

The Golden Section is also called the Fibonacci Series, which is related to certain natural patterns. "If you look at the head of a sunflower you see the seeds spiral one way and another, and it has to do with this logarithmic spiral," he says. "Also, if you remember looking at a ram's horn: the spiral there. Or the shape of a nautilus shell; it's got a certain spiral to it. And it's related to this series, the Fibonacci Sequence."

Ganske was so interested in depth perception he took a college course in "optomology." "The neuron sort of suppresses information," he notes. ". . . The brain does not accept all information; it's selective."

Not by choice, Ganske doesn't sell many of his sculptures. "When you're making large pieces of sculpture, it's pretty hard to get people to buy things like that," he says. While awaiting his big break in the art world, he makes a living as grounds superintendent of the Spooner Golf Club. Not surprisingly, perhaps, he perceives a connection between his sculpture and the game of golf, which he has played for years. Just as he tries to line up everything in his sculptures, to have one point of intensity, golfers look for a straight line to a hole. "I'm interested in that image of a straight line in a natural environment," he says. "That's kind of opposed to the natural environment, which is sort of a curvilinear thing. There are always curves. But I try to impose this straight line in the natural environment." - *May 20, 1981* ☼

Riding High

Mike Polodna ... high-wheel bicycle builder

Many bicyclists like to say biking produces a natural high. For Mike Polodna, that is true both figuratively and literally. While biking of any sort brings him aerobic euphoria, he has a particularly high time when riding one of the several high-wheel bikes he has built and restored.

With front wheels ranging from 46 to 64 inches in diameter, someone perched on the lofty saddle of an old-fashioned high-wheeler, with its peculiarly discrepant wheels, presents a striking picture of high-spirited, high-keyed sportiveness.

"You ride right on the streets," says Polodna, an Onalaska, Wisconsin, machinist who currently owns four high-wheel bikes—two he built from scratch and two he restored. "You ride them like a regular bike. You've gotta look out for traffic because you don't stop on a dime with these at all. You're looking out for yourself."

Other people, of course, take long looks *at* him. "You're always getting people looking. They can't help it. It's an odd thing. A lot of people have never seen them before. You hear remarks like 'How's the weather up there?' and 'Do you ever get nosebleeds?'—things like that. They've been a lot of fun. Little kids really get a charge out of them. 'Where'd you get that bike?' Stuff like that. It's really strange."

Polodna and other Wisconsin members of The Wheelmen, a national club for antique bike owners, ride in La Crosse's Oktoberfest parade and several other parades each year, wowing spectators with synchronized circular riding patterns and gymnastic-style tricks.

With the front wheel 46 to 64 inches in diameter and the back wheel only 18 to 20 inches in diameter, balance is a big concern. So why did manufacturers build such ungainly creations? "I think what they were doing was, they put the rider very close to the center of the top of the front wheel so the front wheel did support the majority of the weight, and then the back wheel was just there for balance or stability," Polodna says. "They also figured that since that big wheel weighed so much that if they added to those big wheels they would have an awful heavy bike that would be kind of hard to handle, so therefore they figured they would keep the small wheel just as little as they dared and keep the weight down. The only reason I can come up with, really, why that big wheel is the size it is is because of their thinking that the bigger the wheel the faster they could go." And was that the case? "I think so," Polodna responds. "Yup. The larger the front wheel, the faster they would go."

With a 54-inch bike, for example (wheel size increased in two-inch increments), one turn of the foot pedals moves the bike about 15 feet.

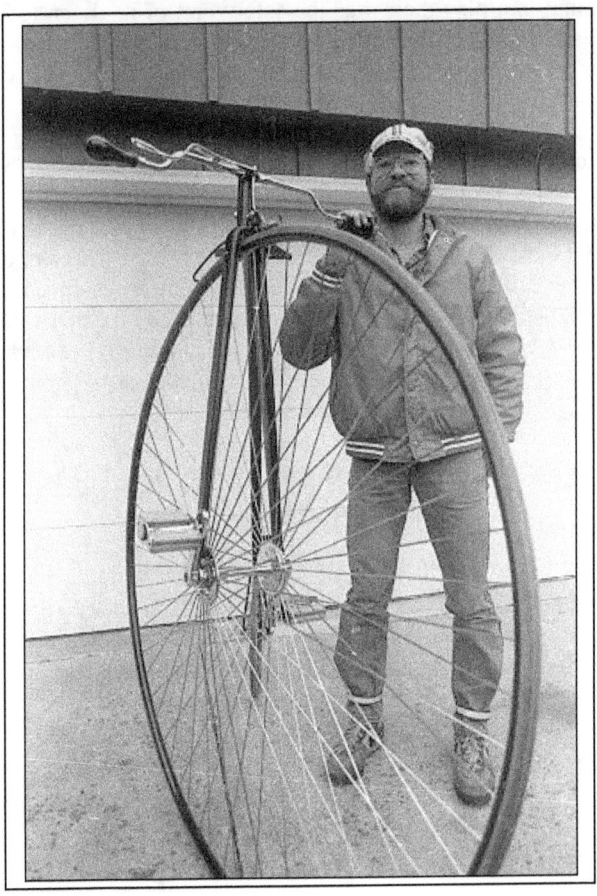

"If you did some calculating you could do a nice comparison between that and a modern bike," Polodna says. "I'm sure you would be kind of surprised."

Polodna is a thirtysomething man whose handlebar mustache (he also sports a beard) gives his face a 19th Century appearance.

While high-wheel bikes generally are associated with the Gay Nineties in most people's minds, the bikes actually were manufactured before that time, from the mid-1870s through the 1880s, in the United States.

"I think you could still buy a high-wheeler in 1892 or 1893," Polodna sayd. "I think that was about the tail end. I think the big aspect that was coming into play there was the safety part of it. Even today you can hit a chuckhole on one of our nice blacktopped roads and do a nice little header. In the 1880s, what were the roads like? Pretty sad, I think."

It is much easier to go headfirst over the handlebars on a high-wheel bike than on a bike with two equal-sized wheels. When bikes with equal-sized wheels began appearing in the 1890s they were referred to as safety bikes. The size of the large wheel on high-wheelers differed to suit the different statures of people. "On a ten-speed today," Polodna explains, "if you're a tall person you get a bike that's got a big frame; the wheels always stay the same (size). But on (a high-wheel bike) a short person has to ride a bike with a smaller [front] wheel. That's why they had different wheel sizes."

Polodna owns one 50-inch bike, two 54-inch bikes and one 56-inch model.

"I guess I've always liked bikes," he says. "I wanted to get ahold of a high-wheel bike. I couldn't find one, so I just figured: 'Well, I'll build one.'" By coincidence, Polodna, who was then still living in Prairie du Chien, Wisconsin, where he grew up, happened upon a story in a Dubuque, Iowa, newspaper about an Illinois man who builds high-wheelers. Polodna contacted the man, visited him, and spent four hours making sketches of the parts of one of his antique bikes. "I caught most all the dimensions," he says. "There were a few that I kind of glossed over or skipped over or fudged. But I had enough to make a nice-looking bike."

Since then he has built two others and restored five high-wheelers, four of those on commission. He also has made and sold many parts. This winter he will work on another restoration and three more reconstructions.

He estimates it takes about 800 hours to build a high-wheeler from scratch.

"It's one of those deals where if you were to make a business out of it you'd quit your job and you would go at it full time," he says. "But since it's not [a full time job], since it's an enjoyment, I guess, I'm not geared fully into that direction; that's why the hours are what they can be. There are just a lot of things that I'm not set up for yet. Possibly if I keep going the way I'm going, in another two years I could knock a couple of hundred hours off it real easy."

Meanwhile, he plans to keep his job as a machinist at a tool-and-die company.

Polodna's basement workshop is filled with 10 metalwork machines—the sort of machines found in any typical metalwork machine shop. He works mainly with salvaged stainless steel for handlebars, foot pedals and spokes, some of which are $1/8^{th}$ inch in diameter. "I like to get the scrap stainless because then the price is lower," he says. "As long as I can get parts out of them, what the heck. As long as I can be quite sure as to what [grade] the material is, then I'm okay. I've had to buy some new steel tubing for rims and backbones—things like that."

Most of the antiques Polodna restores are in poor condition when he acquires them. A 52-inch Columbia model he is currently restoring, for example, came without spokes. "It's kind of strange that they rotted out that much," he says. "I don't know if the thing was lying in the weeds or what, but there were really no spokes to it. There were stubs hanging out of the rim and stubs hanging out of the hubs, and that was it. It was minus spokes, minus tires, and there was no seat leather." Also, the large rim was so badly pitted Polodna was unsure whether or not he would use it for fear it might collapse while someone—maybe him—was riding it.

Polodna takes a bit of liberty by using stainless steel for replacement parts, for most high-wheelers originally had plated steel parts. There is a solid reason behind that deviation from historical authenticity. "If you plate regular steel," he explains, "eventually you could chip your plating and your plating could rust through. It should originally have been nickel plating, and nickel doesn't stand up to weather very good. After a while nickel plating will start to dull, even—almost tarnish, or get to the point where it looks like aluminum. . . . And another thing, too, is in order to get something plated you have to buff it out real nice and smooth. Well, if you're going to buff it out, why not just buff out a piece of stainless steel and be done with it? Stainless steel is a little tougher to work with, but I think it's a pretty decent trade-off. . . . If you crash a bike and scuff the handlebars or something like that all you have to do is take it off and hit it on the buffer and that's it; it's done. If it had been a plated part you would eventually have some streaked rust there, or something like that, and you'd have to end up stripping the whole part and getting the whole part plated."

Polodna buys rubber for tires from an Indiana man who buys large amounts of the material from a manufacturing source. At $2.50 per foot, that works out to about $37.50 for a 54-inch tire. "The rubber has a small hole in the center," he explains. "You cut your rubber long. You don't want to cut your rubber the exact circumference of the wheel; you want to have extra. On a front wheel you probably want a good six inches of extra rubber. If you just cut the tire the exact circumference and mount the tire on the wheel it would be apt to creep and gap as you rode it. By having extra in there to begin with the tire will always be holding that joint. It will actually always be butting itself up good and tight. You string wire through, and with a tire machine of some sort you have to pull that wire good and tight and at the same time keep the rubber apart so you can get in there and work. You pull the tire wire good and tight, and that will draw that tire right down on the rim. You lock it, clamp it, cut your ends, and then you have to position your two ends side by side and just silver-braze them. Then once it's cooled down, undo your fixture, pull it out, and then your tire will actually kind of make an attempt to close up right away, but you usually have to work it together by hand. That's it. It's like a wire bead in the tire."

The hard rubber has little give to it. "It's almost like riding on a bike with hundred-pound tires. But you don't have to worry about hitting too much. You can about run over anything and you won't lose your air; there's nothing to lose."

A hundred years ago, buyers of high-wheel bikes had the same color option as Model T Ford buyers did later: They could have any color they wanted, as long as they wanted black. In keeping with that authentic look, Polodna paints all of his bikes a high-gloss black.

Buyers did, however, have a choice of different styles of handlebars and grips. Some bikes had spade/shovel-type grips, others a bulb-type grip. Some handlebars were straight, others bowed so that the grips were lower, relieving arm strain because a rider did not have to hold his arms in a bent position, as he did with the straight handlebars used on early high-wheelers.

Polodna says he had no trouble mounting a high-wheel bike the first time he rode one. Dismounting was a problem, however. He likens getting off a high-wheel bike to climbing off of a roof onto a ladder that is too short. A rider has to step down, backwards, onto a small step above the rear wheel. "It's kind of hard to find [the step] until you get the hang of it," he says.

To mount a high-wheeler, he explains, "You grab the handlebars, get your left foot—just your toe—up on that little step, then with your right foot you scoot along so you get enough momentum to where the bike will carry you along pretty good. Then when you have your momentum you want to just straighten out your left leg and get yourself situated on the seat and catch the pedals. It's pretty simple." As the saying goes: that's easy for him to say.

Polodna says riding a high-wheel bike is "about like having a ten-speed and starting out in tenth gear. It takes a little bit of effort to get it going, but once it's rolling it rolls pretty good. Since you have more of an upright position on these, if you have a headwind you end up fighting it more because you can't get down out of it as easily. You can tuck in pretty good on it, but you're hanging over the front wheel quite a bit then." All high-wheelers had a front brake.

"There are a lot of people interested in these bikes, but it's a matter of finding them," says Polodna. "And they're expensive once you do find them. They're like anything antique; they're worth as much as the traffic will bear, price-wise." The average value of antique high-wheelers is $1,500 to $2,000.

National Wheelmen meets, held twice each year, consist of competitive judging, marketplace buying and selling of parts, races, and generally a 100-mile Century Ride on antique bikes. Polodna has four Century Rides to his credit, on high-wheel bikes. To keep their spirits high during this grueling endurance test, can't you just hear a group of Wheelmen singing "High-ho, high-ho, it's down the road we go. . ."?

- October 17, 1987   ☼

Fancy Framework

Tim Paterek ... bicycle frame builder

"Fifteen years ago," Tim Paterek says, "custom bicycle framebuilding in this country was almost unheard of. The only custom builders at that time were in France and England and Italy." Now there are scores of fine frame builders all over the United States.

Paterek, a lifelong bicycle enthusiast who lives near River Falls, Wisconsin, spent more than two years putting together a bicycle framebuilding manual for the expanding framebuilding community, which he says is much more comprehensive than two other manuals written in recent years. The first printing of 500 copies of the $35 manual, which Paterek self-published, has already sold out. Another 500 copies will be printed soon.

Paterek opened his own bike shop in the basement of his family home in 1966 or 1967, while in high school, and later started a downtown bike shop in River Falls. He learned the basics of framebuilding from a Minneapolis friend in 1978 and picked up other pointers by touring bicycle factories in France, Great Britain and the United States. "Plus," he says, "I hobnob with different frame builders. We're a pretty close-knit group. If we need a certain paint color and it has to be custom-mixed, you call someone and say, 'Hey, do you need some of this?' And the other guy might say, 'Yeah, I want to do some bikes in that color.' So you go together on some paint, because custom-mixing of paint is pretty expensive." Custom frame builders also exchange advise, opinions and news.

Paterek has built nearly 100 frames, including a half-dozen tandems. Touring and racing frames take 25 to 30 hours of work, tandem models close to 60 hours. Some of his bikes have been sold to serious bikers in such distant states as Florida, California and Texas, with an average racing bike going for about $1,600.

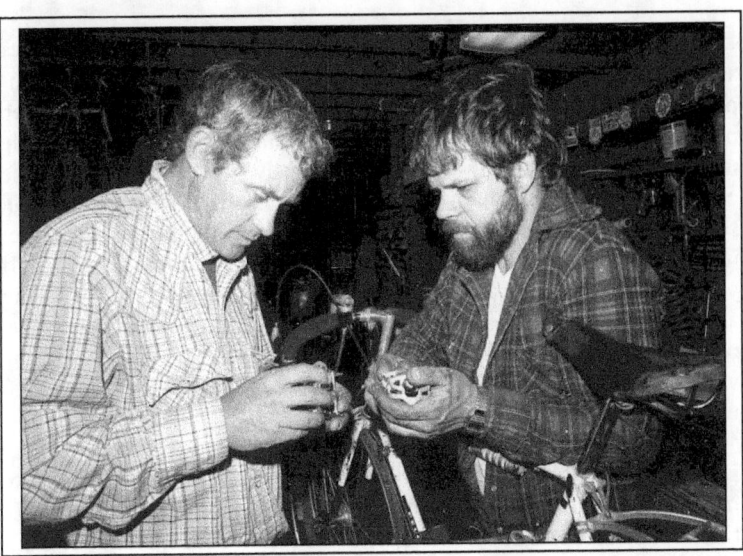

Essentially, custom framebuilding involves three things: custom sizing, custom materials and custom finishing. "There are limitless ways that you can change a bike to fit someone's own individual needs," Paterek [on right, in photo] says. "That's basically what I do here." Each bike is designed to be as efficient as possible for a buyer's physical proportions. "Right here in the shop right now," he says, "I've got probably enough different combinations to build 20 completely different bikes. No two would be the same."

By using lightweight tubing—he uses tube sets of either chrome molybdenum or magnenese molybdenum—Paterek keeps his bikes to about 20 pounds, which is slightly more than half of what a chain-store bike weighs.

"Most of the people who come in are at the end of a succession of a whole bunch of bikes or a whole bunch of frames," Paterek says. "And then they finally decide they want a custom frame. So they come in, and they've got all these components that they've put on their bike from before, and they don't want to spend all the extra money on components, so oftentimes I build them a frame that will match up with their components. They'll pull the components off their old frame and put them on the new one. Sometimes they'll buy a whole new bike. Then I'll build up a whole bike for them."

Paterek's framebuilding manual covers the geometry of bicycle frames and how that affects riding and handling performance, lists and compares thousands of parts and materials, and presents step-by-step building instructions. He says anyone with experience in bicycle mechanics, metalworking or welding already possesses some of the necessary craft. While he uses expensive, specialized tools (he has tool sets worth $1,200 to $1,300 each), he says someone does not necessarily have to own all the same tools in order to build a frame. "If you can find another frame builder that will do your milling and facing and cutting and reaming and so forth, you don't have to lay out twelve or thirteen hundred dollars for a tool case," he says. "You can get by without a lot of that equipment. It depends on whose wing you can go under and who you can get help from."

For fees ranging from $625 to $1,225 (for level two tandem bike instruction), Paterek takes people under his wing for individual instruction in his basement shop. "I teach about half a dozen people a year," he says. "Last fall I had a guy come all the way from Hawaii to learn how to build bike frames."

Paterek builds all his frames on a stone-surface table. "In doing that, I know for sure that they're completely in one plane," he explains. "A bicycle has one plane running right through the center of it, and things on each side of that plane are symmetrical." If the plane isn't precise there will be handling and shifting problems.

He uses silver solder on his frames, which means he can build them at a lower temperature than the temperature at which factory bikes are built. Silver solder goes together at about 1,400 degrees, whereas brass solder goes together at about 1,800 degrees. "That higher temperature is right about at the critical temperature of steel," he says. "The critical temperature of steel is where the steel re-crystallizes and loses a lot of its strength characteristics. So if you use silver you stay way under that critical temperature of steel, and end up building a much finer product as a result."

Ironically, Paterek spends so much time building bikes he no longer spends much time riding them. "There are a lot of people around who buy real fancy bikes, and they don't deserve having fancy bikes because they hang up all the time and nothing ever comes of them," he says. "And I would probably be one of those people who doesn't deserve to own a fancy bike because my bikes hang most of the time."

- May 20, 1985 ☼

Feats Of Clay

Marty Pearson ... potter

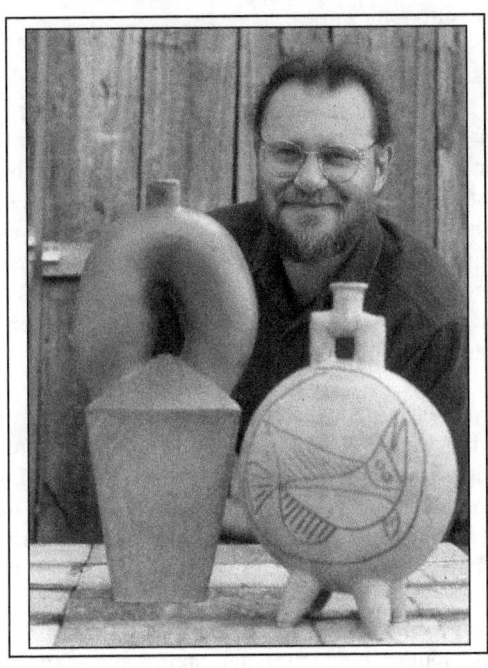

I first interviewed Marty Pearson March 26, 1993, then a second time May 5, 1997.

The popular slogan Think Global, Act Local could easily be applied to Marty Pearson, a potter who lives near Cozy Corner, a hamlet in the wilds of northwest Wisconsin. While Pearson's pottery has been influenced by a Japanese firing technique and pre-Columbian South American designs, he makes use of local clay and other local products in the production process.

"It's important for me to make art from local materials," he says. Although he "would probably be money ahead" if he bought all his clay rather than dug some himself from a vein the Webster area where

Native Americans dug clay for their pots hundreds of years ago, digging his own clay is "part of the fun of it," says Pearson, who lives in a self-built log home that is as close to the middle of nowhere as pink is to red.

Partly because of the use of local clay, partly because of his firing technique, and partly because of his symbolic decorations, which resemble ancient petroglyphs and pictographs of Native Americans, pre-Christian Scandinavians and Australian aborigines, Pearson's pots are, he says, "totally different."

While "there is clay that goes from Webster all the way to Lake Superior," he notes, a three-foot-thick vein of clay between Clam Lake (two miles north of Siren) to north of Webster is sort of special because it contains fewer impurities than the clay found further north. The lime content of that clay makes it unusable for pots. The clay Pearson gathers from the Webster area is "not a very strong clay" either, so he mixes it with sand and fire clay to make it work for him. Pearson's mix calls for 60 percent local clay, 20 percent local sand and 20 percent fire clay—the sort of clay used for firebricks. He experimented for six years before perfecting the recipe.

That experimentation began when he was an art teacher in the Webster school system between 1976 and 1984. "Ed Oerichbauer from the Burnett County Historical Society came to my class and asked my class to re-create the large storage pots that the Woodland Sioux made, using local clay and the firing techniques that they used," Pearson relates. "So we started messing around with that as a class, and it was a disaster. The pots all blew up. Nothing worked. I kind of was intrigued by the local clay, so I started messin' around with it, and six years later—after adding and adding things to it, and taking things away—I figured out how to use it, how to get it to stoneware temperature. . . . The more fire clay I added, the clay became too porous. I could fire it at a high temperature, but yet it would still chip easy. And then if I didn't add enough the clay would bubble and sag."

After a relatively lengthy processing and aging process prepares the clay for shaping, Pearson "throws" bowls and mugs on a potter's wheel and makes platters and other pots by coil and slab methods.

He draws symbolic designs in the clay while the pieces are still wet. "My drawings on the pots are like a diary—sounds and things that I hear that week, or sometimes dreams," he says. Wavy lines going out from a coyote, for instance, represent a coyote's call. "The Ojibwa would draw song pictures; they would draw pictures of their songs. And they would show wavy lines. It could be animals singing, people singing, trees singing, water singing. I liked that idea of drawing pictures of sound, because the coyote howling out here influences me. I've made my own symbols, but I'm influenced by Scandinavian petroglyphs, where they've carved into the rocks in Iceland and Norway. And then I'm also influenced by the pictographs in the Boundary Waters [Canoe Area], and Picasso."

Pearson draws his designs with a pencil, paints a porcelain slip over the lines, lets the piece dry to a leather-like texture, then scrapes off the porcelain, which leaves porcelain in the etched lines. After being bisque-fired and glazed, the pots are kiln-dried in a small wood-fired downdraft kiln, which reaches a peak temperature of about 2,200 degrees. This firing takes six to eight hours, sometimes longer. "I can do three firings on a pickup load of slabs [slab wood], so it's a pretty efficient kiln," he says. ". . . I start off real slow and relaxed, and at the end I'm running around throwing it in because once it gets really hot it kind of becomes alive. It roars, and flames shoot out about eight to ten feet out of the chimney, just like a blowtorch. . . . If I was more of a production potter, where I just did casseroles and a gazillion mugs, this [a small kiln] wouldn't work. But since I do a few bowls, and mostly sculptural, one-of-a-kind pieces, I can make a living with a small kiln like this."

Humankind's relationship to nature is a dominant theme in Pearson's drawings, just as it was in the primitive artwork of many cultures. His drawings are so similar to Native American pictographs that some people assume he is a Native American potter. He is not. He has Swedish and French ancestry.

"You would think that you would come up with something original," he says. "You think you do come up with something original. You don't see people decorating their pots this way. Okay, I go to a museum in Minneapolis and there's a whole dang shelf of them. They did it a thousand years ago. So it's pretty hard to be original."

Pearson's South American influence traces to the time he and his wife, Jeri, traveled to Columbia to bring home an adopted boy named Roberto. "When we were in Columbia we went to a number of museums," he says. "And when I saw the pots it was as though something hit me with a sledge hammer. Those were the kinds of pots that I wanted to make. I really fell in love with their shapes. . . . A lot of the pots in South America have two spouts. There will be a double-spouted pot with a handle between the two spouts. I experimented with the handle by stretching it or squeezing it and not making it a handle anymore."

Besides wood-fired pottery, Pearson also makes distinctive raku pottery, which has a Japanese derivation and more abstract, geometric designs (Pablo Picasso's influence is also noticeable here).

"Raku," he explains, "is a Japanese type of firing where you fire one pot at a time." He uses thin strips of masking tape to create designs, then brushes a thick glaze on areas that will be colored. Unglazed areas, including the lines left when the tape is removed, before firing, turn matte black in the firing process while glazed areas become metallically shiny.

"When the glaze is a liquid I take it out of the [gas-fueled] kiln," Pearson explains. "The hot glaze hitting the cold air will make it crackle. Then while it's still really hot I put it in a bucket of wild rice hulls. The rice hulls start on fire, I put a lid on the bucket"—which is buried in the ground—"and the clay absorbs the carbon from the flame and turns the exposed clay—the unglazed clay—black. . . . Because you get a shiny, metallic glaze, and you have the matte black, that's a good contrast. You can do some really nice decorative design work on the pot, and that's why it's really popular, because if you know your glazes you can get 'em to do some really neat things." Pearson believes many people like raku pots because the crackling makes them appear old.

By beginning with a basic white glaze, then adding and overlapping cobalt and copper glazes to various sections of a pot, Pearson creates one-of-a-kind color combinations he cannot totally control. "I never really know what it's going to look like. I know the design, but I don't know what the color is going to be. . . . I'm becoming better at knowing when to yank things out to get certain effects, but I can't guarantee it. Some of my friends who have a masters degree in pottery know the molecular structure of the glaze, and what it's going to do, and they approach it in a more scientific manner. I don't have that type of training. . . . My raku is a little bit different than a lot of the raku that's out there. Mine is a little more subdued. Raku can be really flashy, with bright, vibrant colors. I tone it down some." Pearson's raku pots are characterized by restrained reds, soft greens, tarnished coppers, neutral grays, and other muted hues. "Pretty much every [art] fair that I go to there are a lot of raku potters. What is interesting is that we all have a different twist to the technique." Most raku potters put their kiln-fresh pieces in sawdust, for instance.

Pearson happened upon his idea for using wild rice hulls when visiting a local Ojibway elder to learn how to make black ash baskets so he could incorporate that Native American craft into his art classes at Webster. The Indian elder was burning a large pile of wild rice hulls that day, and the thick, sooty smoke produced inspired Pearson to think the hulls might work well for his raku pots. A combination of dried grass and pine needles he was using didn't give him the nice carbon-black and the consistency wild rice hulls have proven to provide.

"With raku," Pearson says, "it's strictly a decorative pot because in order for the clay to go from a hot kiln to the cold air without breaking it's gotta be porous; the clay has to be able to give. So if it's able to do that, it means water passes through it, so you can't put a bunch of cut flowers and water in it." Since the local clay used in the wood-fired pottery cannot withstand a drastic temperature change, Pearson uses a different mix of clays, heavy on fire clay, for raku pots.

Each winter Pearson moves his pottery operation from a small shed-like studio to the basement of his house, where he devotes the months of January, February and March to making large pots and other more sculptural creations that are more for the satisfaction of his artistic soul than for commercial consideration.

"It's a good balance for me to take three months of the year to make those kinds of pots," he says. "The other nine months I then make pots that are in more demand and aren't as time-consuming as the larger pieces. I can work two weeks on one big piece, then it can sit around for several years. Which is okay. . . . I'm finding that it's more fun and satisfying for me if I just take these three months and make whatever I want. I don't care if they sell or not. It's just the enjoyment of making the pot. That's been the goal now. I get these ideas during the year and then I save 'em for those three months."

☼

Accent Artists

Wendy Penta, Laura McCaul & Mark Tomlinson ... tile makers

I interviewed Wendy Penta on May 10, 2002 and Sept. 8, 2003, Laura McCaul on Sept. 9, 2003, and Mark Tomlinson, by phone, on Sept. 17, 2003.

Picture yourself in a boat on a river, with purple cattails, pink reeds and iridescent dragonflies. Tile maker Wendy Penta created this Wonderland/*Lucy In The Sky With Diamonds* imagery—minus the boat and the river—for clients who wanted tiles that coordinated with a particular carpet. Penta, who makes custom ceramic [clay] tiles in her Stone Hollow Tile studio north of St. Croix Falls, Wisconsin, uses this commission as an example of her keep-the-customers-satisfied approach to her craft. That bold, dreamlike color combination veered from her more well-trod artistic path. She is best known for soft, subtle, and more naturalistic coloring.

Handmade tile crafting "was kind of a lost art here [in the Midwest] for a while," says Penta, one of several western Wisconsin artists involved in the craft's recent resurgence. One popular line of thought is that people crave the handmade and the homegrown as humanistic touchstones in an increasingly technological world.

Except in homes of the wealthiest people, handmade design tiles are too expensive to use over entire walls, or half a wall. Each tile can cost anywhere from $20 to $300. Most handmade tiles are used as accent pieces in fields of mass-produced production tiles. They add spice to a space, whether they make up only a few spots in an otherwise uniform field or form a complete kitchen counter backsplash.

"People wonder why they're so expensive," Penta says. "It's because they are just very putzy. You handle these things umpteen times, even a little two-inch one."

With a growing number of tile artisans competing for sales and commissions (a 2003 directory of Upper Midwest tile makers who belong to the Minneapolis-based Handmade Tile Association lists 30 tile makers, up from 12 in 1999), most tile makers seek a niche where they can thrive. Penta, for instance specializes in designs and colors that reflect the Arts & Crafts decorating era popular from the late 19th Century to the 1930s [examples below].

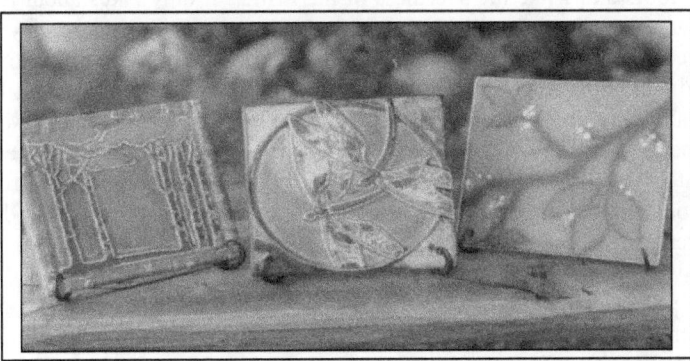

River Falls tile maker and relief sculptor Mark Tomlinson has built his reputation with large-scale works for residential, commercial and public buildings. Laura McCaul [pictured below] produces tiles with a distinctive earthy appearance through a variation of the blackware firing process used for centuries by Native Americans in the Southwest.

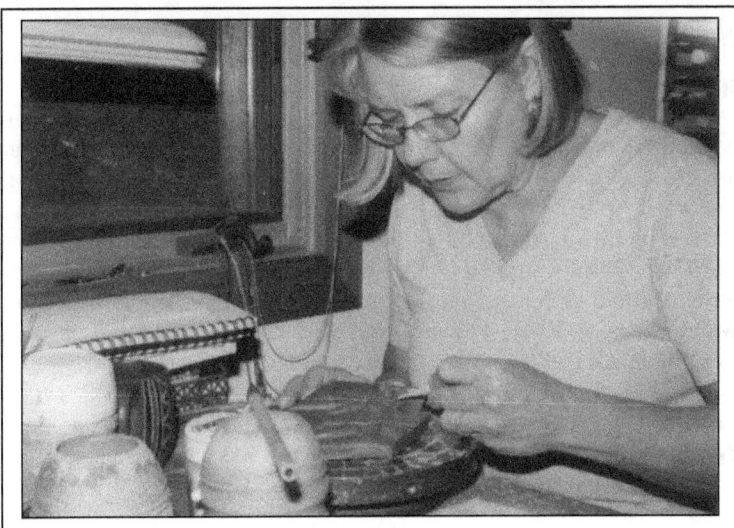

"I've been doing it about 16 years," says McCaul, who lives on a lake southeast of Danbury and produces tiles under her Earth Wood & Fire studio name. "It takes a long time to just learn the techniques. And there are so many types of firing in the clay world that you have to kind of experiment and find your niche, and narrow-focus more, because it can be overwhelming. I was overwhelmed for a long time. But when I found this method it just seemed to be really fitting 'cause I love firing outdoors and I like the shortness of the firing. It only takes about two hours, from beginning to end, where most wood firings take a day or three days—(with) those huge kilns. I'm considered low-fire primitive, and that's just where I want to be. . . . By the time I started making tiles I had pretty much determined that I was going to go with the blackware process, but early on I tried everything, when I was taking classes and that in the Cities [Minneapolis-St. Paul]. I tried every method of firing I could. I took probably 50 classes or workshops, just to work with different artists and teachers and try to figure out what I really wanted to do with it."

Tomlinson has been involved in ceramics and relief sculpture for more than 30 years. He taught at Ohio State University before establishing his own studio in River Falls in 1978. His tile work "sort of covers the waterfront," with about half of it being representational design and half being abstract design. "It goes in spurts," he says. "Sometimes I'm doing nothing but representational work for six months, and then for a couple months I'm doing nothing but abstract, patterned kinds of things."

He has been involved in the craft long enough to have a long-view perspective. "When I started doing wall pieces in the '70s," he says, "I wasn't aware of anyone doing that—making a relief object and then hanging it on the wall. And I was a professor then, so I would show in art galleries, and I really didn't have much of an expectation of selling my work. But I liked doing it. And then when I quit teaching and started my own business I modified the work more toward being more saleable, not showing in art galleries, but dealing directly with interior designers and architects and liturgical consultants—people that work with buildings—and just kind of bent the material around to be applied to a building rather than installed on a building as a work of art."

Tomlinson and an assistant create special tiles for kitchens, bathrooms, swimming pools, fireplace surrounds, bar fronts, and other spots in houses, hotels, restaurants, banks, churches, and other buildings.

He also is in demand for his replication ability. "Architects and interior designers know that I can match a tile made in 1913, for example," he says. ". . . I think if you've been in the business for 35 years you start to learn the nature of the different materials, their properties, and how to use them to create a certain impression. So even though a tile made in 1913 was made by fuel oil or coal fired in a kiln, and (that) creates a certain impact on the glaze—say, for instance, a black, speckly blotch, which is carbon falling from combustion onto the tile—I can do that by using colorants and create the same visual effect, and fire it in my kiln, which is controlled by computers."

Essentially, the tile-making process involves these steps: An artist carves a design onto a tile-sized slab of clay and creates a plaster or Ceramical mold of that design. To create duplicates of that impression, the artist rolls clay into a slab on a slab roller, cuts the slab into tile-sized squares or rectangles, presses a clay square into a mold, removes the tile from the mold, lets the tile dry in the open air for several days, until it is at a leather-like stage, smoothes and perfects the tile with various tools, gives the tiles a bisque firing in a kiln to further dry and harden them, brushes on glaze, and finally puts the tiles through an intense glaze firing, which further hardens the tiles and transforms the glaze into a glassy coating.

The liquid glaze color generally is not the finished color. A white glaze might come out green, a green glaze as brown, and a gray glaze a different shade of brown. Tile makers discover what works and what doesn't work through years of trial and error. Unlike most tile makers, Tomlinson makes his own glazes rather than buy prepared glazes. "In the pottery field it's the norm to develop your own glazes," he says. Of all the things he learned in his first years of training, he says, the most valuable knowledge he acquired was "understanding the nature of the materials and being able to use them to fit my intentions."

McCaul uses what could be called a refined slip, or a clay paint, for it is clay and water, rather than glazes. "It's really old," she says. "They used it on really old Greek pots and (objects such as) that. I just brush it on like paint. It usually takes many, many coats; I would say, on average, seven coats. But it can be done pretty quickly, and is absorbed pretty quickly into the clay. Then when it oozes that wet look I just take a cloth and buff it, and it comes to a really nice sheen. . . . My palette is basically three or four colors." Different firing produces different tints of those four colors: subdued browns, greens and black.

Once tiles are placed in a kiln for a final firing a tile maker loses control, to a degree.

"Even though I'm making them from the same mold, no two pieces fire alike," McCaul says. "I don't think I could get two pieces to fire alike if I wanted to. So that makes it more interesting, at least for me. And then nobody's getting the same tile, really."

Clay shrinks during the firing. McCaul's tiles shrink six percent, Penta's 14 percent, given she fires at a higher temperature and uses a different "clay body." McCaul uses a "low fire" red earthenware clay. She does a bisque firing in an electric kiln and the finish firing in two three-barrel outside kilns, which consist of a small barrel with a lot of holes in it inside a medium barrel inside a larger barrel. When the wood-heated barrels reach 600 degrees she pours wood shavings and sawdust between the inner and middle barrels. "That starts smoldering, and the carbon that is released from that sawdust is trapped in the pieces," she explains.

"I don't know that anybody else is doing the blackware process [in this area]," McCaul says. "I've taught a couple of workshops, but I haven't seen any work displayed in galleries that uses this same technique."

Many of McCaul's pieces are incorporated into tables, mirrors and other pieces of furniture her husband, Jim, builds. He turned his woodworking hobby into a furniture making career a couple of years ago. "I always thought her tiles deserved to be framed, at least, and maybe put to furniture," Jim says. "It works pretty well." While collaborating with Jim is fun for McCaul, it also presents challenges. "Part of it is because woodworking is: you've gotta be so specific," she says. "It doesn't allow for a percentage slop factor, really. . . . Part of making handmade tiles is that you want it to look handmade. I don't want mine to look like they're made by a machine, so an uneven line doesn't bother me. But if you're trying to put it in a straight wooden frame. . . you can vary a little bit, but you've got to watch what you're doing."

Dimensional precision generally is not McCaul's most pressing concern. "What I usually do," she says, "is carve the design and then trim it to what seems appropriate for the design. So I don't have the standard six-by-six, four-by-four tiles; I'm just not traditional in that way. I can do it, but I haven't really found a need. Most people don't do entire walls of my tiles; they use them more for accents, or just for hanging on the wall. It seems the possibilities are endless, what you can do with them."

Both McCaul and Penta are primarily nature-oriented in their choice of subject matter, with trees, leaves, birds, butterflies, frogs and flowers dominating their designs. "I just have to look out my window and I'm pretty inspired," McCaul says. "Or go out on the lake. We've always been campers, canoers and all that too. I do abstract designs too, but not as much lately. There are a lot of bird nuts and nature nuts, I call 'em. We get along just fine."

Owners of bungalow and prairie-style houses built during the Arts & Crafts era like Penta's "tonalist" tiles. "They look like tonalist paintings, that were plein air paintings that were very popular from that particular period too. . . . Everything was very earthy and very subtle." Last year the Twin Cities Bungalow Club commissioned Penta [pictured below] to produce 250 tiles of a bungalow house design.

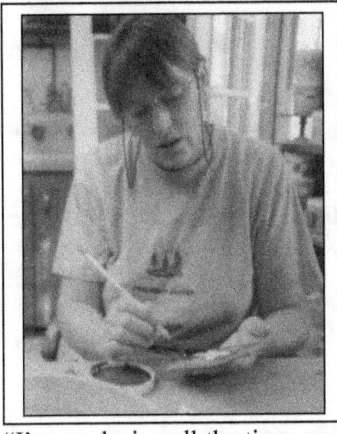

Not all of her customers live in bungalow houses, though. Given that her tiles "go very well with nature," she has created tiles for people with log cabins and log homes. "Of course, they're very nice cabins," she notes. "You know what I mean?"

Commission work is not her bread and butter, though. Most of her sales are at art shows—two or three each year—and through retail stores, sometimes on consignment. "I'm producing all the time, even if I don't have a [commission] job," she says. "I'm still making finished product, in preparation for something that might come up."

Tomlinson has had commissions from such companies as Honeywell, Land O' Lakes and AT&T, the States of Montana, Minnesota and Wisconsin, and such celebrities as actor/playwright Sam Shephard and Rolling Stones guitarist/songwriter Keith Richards. "That was a referral from an architect," he says of the Keith Richards commission. "That architect works for probably the largest firm in the world that does large public buildings. And they also do work for distinguished individuals—that sort of thing. . . .They were designing a house for Keith Richards and Patti Hanson. And the interesting thing in that commission was they had selected a tile that they wanted to have and it wasn't available any longer, so I was called in to come up with something 'in the feeling of,' 'something that is like this,' or 'has that feeling,' and I ended up making the tile for two kitchens 'cause both Keith and Patti have their own kitchen. And that was kind of fun. . . . And then I made a birdbath for them the following spring. That was in a kind of Islamic pattern—very geometric. . . . That was a fun project to do too."

Tomlinson, who studies, practices and teaches tai chi, especially relishes every opportunity "to make spiritual artwork that makes values tangible, . . . to make things that transcend the sort of concrete here and now." One such commission was for large, painted stained glass windows for the cathedral in Kansas City, including a 12-foot-diameter round window. "That's all painted," he says. "Basically it's the same kind of paints that you put on ceramic tile; it's a low temperature glaze."

Tile work is "part of the mix of the work" that comes his way.

While Tomlinson, McCaul and Penta are part of a blooming handmade tile movement, they also are part of a larger strong clay art contingent in Wisconsin and Minnesota. "This area—Wisconsin and Minnesota—is just incredibly rich in potters and the clay world," McCaul notes. "It's unbelievable how many nationally and internationally known clay people there are." Maybe more Midwestern kids simply never lose their love of playing with mud.

☼

Diane Keeler's Small World

Diane Keeler ... collectible doll maker

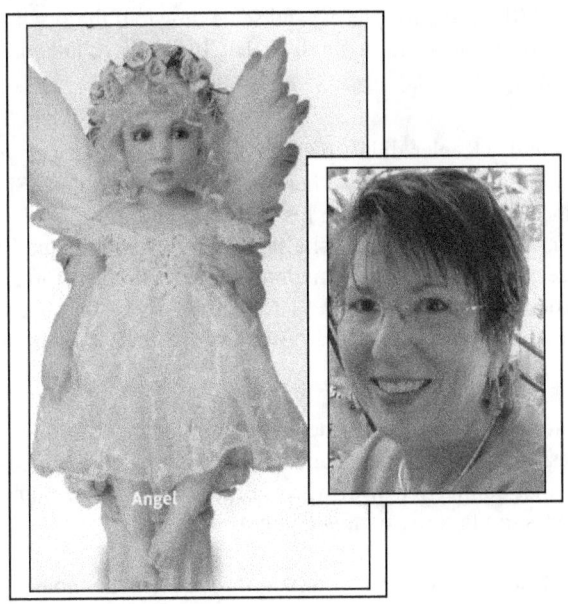

Angel

It's interesting how Diane Keeler generally refers to her handcrafted, one-of-a-kind collectible ceramic dolls as pieces. While many artists, writers, composers, and other creators refer to their artistic works as pieces, there is a little twist to it when the word comes from a doll maker because her creations consist of so many actual pieces, which is to say parts.

When Keeler was young she carved hands, feet and other body parts from "awful" soap her mother made one year, which she and her sisters refused to use. Even her early sketchbooks contained drawings of body parts. "I never did anything whole, which I think is kind of bizarre," she says. "I did eyes and lips and noses, and never put anything together until I started with this."

The way Keeler, who lives in the Frederic, Wisconsin, area, puts everything together puts her in a rather rarefied world of high-toned galleries, wealthy collectors and inventive artisanship. She finds satisfaction in the way doll art allows her to combine a lot of artistic activities she dabbled in over the years.

"I like experimenting with anything," she says. "I've done weaving, and spinning, and basket making, and quilting. I made my own clothes since I was eight years old. Just give me a medium and I'll try and work with it. . . . Now I can make little, tiny baskets from basket weaving, and little quilts for pieces, and scale down all the sewing I've done for myself and now do in small scale. It's really challenging. I'll be doing this until the day my eyes and hands give out."

Interestingly, Keeler didn't play with dolls when she was young. She was something of a tomboy—her father's son, she quips. She followed her father around, played with his tools and built things. "I played with *stuff*; that's what I enjoyed," she says. "So it surprises me I've gone in this direction. But there's something about the human form, being able to reproduce the human form. There's something that happens during that. You get really connected. And I've figured out who I am by what I'm doing."

She notes that when she teaches classes in full-body sculpting a sort of calmness comes over her students when they sculpt torsos "because there's that connection with who we are—that core of doing the torso. And that's my favorite part, is doing the torso."

Keeler teaches short-term classes throughout the country to small groups consisting mainly of women. "It's really interesting," she says, "when you have a student in a class that hasn't done a lot of it, but seems to have that natural talent. It really gets exciting. I really try to develop that." Other students are there more for the social aspect—"because they just love the socializing." A class in full-body sculpting can last as long as four days; other classes may be two-day affairs.

With 17 years of hairdressing experience—she worked at a shop in Frederic much of that time—Keeler developed a technique for making doll wigs that set her up as a wigging expert. "I understood hair, and I understood how it worked, and I understood wigs enough, so I developed this technique," she says. She works with mohair, which "isn't that much different than human hair." She used to buy "the most wonderful hair" from a supplier that went out of business, so now she buys "raw" mohair that "still has all the grease in it, like sheep [wool] that has that lanolin." She soaks the raw mohair in the hottest soapy water it will take to get it to the right condition.

For Keeler, who sold her first doll in 1990 and now turns out 15 to 20 figures a year, the most difficult aspect of doll art is scaling. Fabrics, hair and body proportions all must be the proper scale. "I can spend more time on the costuming than anything else I do," she says.

She makes women, children and pixie dolls. A good majority of them are approximately 18 inches tall, with the average price in the $2,500 range. Some doll makers create much larger pieces that sell for $10,000 or more. "I just don't want to work that big," Keeler says. "It's hard on the body moving that amount of clay. So that's why I like working smaller. Eighteen inches is really a nice size for fabric to drape, and to get the scale."

Contemporary doll-making involves design, engineering, sculpting, costuming, and more. "It's amazing what it encompasses," Keeler says. "I've known traditional artists (who) are maybe painters or plain sculptors and they've tried this and said, 'This is too much work,' because it is a lot of work." Membership in the National Institute of American Doll Artists organization, which actually has a worldwide membership, requires that a doll maker "do it all."

Over the years, through experimentation, Keller developed her own particular two-clay formula for the polymer clay she uses to sculpt doll parts.

Her faces generally are an amalgamation of photographs she cuts from magazines and posts at her workbench to guide her as she sculpts a clay skull over molded tinfoil. She doesn't use solid clay because there would be contraction and expansion with that, which would produce cracking around the eyes, mouth and other areas. She sculpts arms and legs around wire armatures.

While she could do all of the sculpting with only three tools, her workbench includes an array of tools—snubby paint brushes, knives, pick-like instruments, double-pointed knitting needles, toothpicks, and other items that sometimes prove useful. She says most doll makers get every tool they can in the beginning, thinking there will be some magic tool in the bunch. "Then," she says, "you just hone it down to a few, and that's pretty much all you need."

Keeler sculpts in stages, baking the parts to harden the clay.

With a head, she will sculpt the front, then bake that—usually in a toaster over—for about 10 minutes to "set" the clay. She then puts on the back of the skull, and the ears, and places it back in the oven for another short baking. Eventually the head is attached to a breastplate and there is a final baking at a constant 265 degrees for 45 to 60 minutes. After the baking comes a little sanding and cleaning. She does "a quick wash with acetone," being careful to not allow the acetone to eat away at the surface. That washing pits the surface of the clay enough to allow it to "take the pastels and acrylics" well. She does "very little painting. It's mainly just pastels. Then I'll do a quick little shading around the eyes, and the blushing. And then for the eyes and eyebrows and lashes I'll use acrylic. . . . I used to use the glass eyes, but trying to get them tracking as you're sculpting will drive you crazy. So I do the painting." Her wigging technique allows her to remove the wig from the doll's head while she finishes the piece, then slips on the wig and styles it as the final step.

Several cupboards in her studio are filled with fabric. Fabric selection is part and parcel of the doll-making process. She may be thinking about what fabric might work well as she sculpts a face. "A lot of times they tell me what they want to be," she says. ". . . I love really lush fabrics because I don't have to use a lot." She has gathered antique fabric for years.

Keeler sells mainly through galleries, dealers and art shows, but also will sell directly off of her website. She likes having the freedom to work without having to concern herself much with marketing. "Sometimes customers can be a little demanding and have certain expectations, and it's really nice to have these dealers," she says. "They do the advertising, they do the promoting of me, they do the legwork. So as far as I'm concerned they earn their percentage."

She gets bored "pretty easily," so she keeps things exciting and interesting for herself by doing different categories of dolls and continuing to challenge herself and her set of skills. She has sculpted mermaids, fairies, angels, 1920s flappers, women and children.

"I want to try and do ball-jointed dolls," she says. "They are the big thing now. So I want to figure out how to do some jointing—if nothing else, just do the legs so I can have a piece that either stands or sits, or maybe do the arms so the arms can move. That's going to be my next challenge. You get a little tired of doing the same thing over and over again."

Her dolls are in galleries in Massachusetts, Florida, Alabama, New Jersey and California. The galleries tend to be on the East Coast in part "because they deal with a lot of European collectors." It may surprise most people that Russia is a big market for collectible dolls these days. "I've got probably four or five pieces in a palace in Russia, which is really cool," Keeler says. "They have a room called the Doll Room, and (the dolls are) in these cabinets in this palace. I guess it's just magnificent. . . . I've got a lot of pieces in Russia, and just all over Europe. You just never know."

With the Internet such a force in the world of doll art, Keeler now attends fewer doll art shows than in the past because there simply are fewer shows for artists and buyers. Whereas she formerly participated in four or five shows a year, she now attends three. Her big "wholesale show" is in Orlando, Florida, in January. That used to be part of an annual Toy Fair held in New York City and—later—San Francisco. That Orlando show includes all sorts of dolls, not only art dolls, which Keeler finds fun.

Doll art has a long history. As Keeler puts it, dolls have been around since humans learned to carve and mold, and used those skills to create doll deities. People have made dolls out of corn husks, rags and other inexpensive items down through the years. Doll art is revered in some cultures, such as the Japanese culture.

It often occurs to Keeler that the dolls she makes will be among the antique artifacts of the future.

"Some day my work will really be valuable," she envisions, joking she probably won't be around to see that day because the value of most dolls remains fairly steady while the doll maker is alive.

Keeler cannot imagine not continuing to make dolls. When she finds herself "getting a little stagnant" she forces herself to stay away from her studio for a while and finds herself drawn back when her mind starts working on something while she does household chores. "I sit down and just start picking up something and playing a little bit," she says. "And then the vacuum cleaner gets left for a week or so."

- *October 16, 2009* ☼

Shades Of Grace

Mike Bloyer ... stained glass artisan

Tiffany. Like Rolls-Royce, Chippendale and Steinway, it is a name synonymous with elegance, excellence and grace, both in the field of jewelry and the realm of lamps. Original Tiffany stained glass lampshades, last made in 1933, command tens of thousands of dollars. They are masterpieces as treasured as turquoise, as valued as the rarest of rare coins. While it is possible to produce print reproductions of great paintings and plaster-cast reproductions of sublime sculptures, Mike Bloyer points out "there's only one medium to use to reproduce a Tiffany lampshade, and that's glass." Bloyer, a Hudson, Wisconsin, resident, does just that in his spare time. He has handcrafted more than 25 Tiffany lampshade reproductions, to exacting standards.

"Because of the detail, and partly because of the way I approach it—I'm fairly demanding and particular about my coloration in the glass and that type of stuff—it takes a long time to do it," he says. He estimates he has devoted as much time as 200 hours to a single shade.

He charges between $4 and $7 per piece for his reproductions. The price depends on the pattern difficulty, the cost of the glass, and other variables. Each shade consists of several hundred, or even more than a thousand, hand-cut pieces. At $5 per piece, a 700-piece shade would be priced at $3,500.

In Bloyer's view, most stores that sell "Tiffany" lamps sell lamps that are "kinda sorta" reproductions, in a broad sense. "If you took a lamp I reproduced and put it up against one of those in the store you would find differences—maybe subtle, but differences—in the pattern." The one in the store wouldn't have the same number of pieces, for one thing. "Those are artist renditions of Tiffanys" Bloyer says. "Somebody's looked at it, and kind of drawn it, and they've kind of figured out some of the sizing issues and that type of stuff. So they're stained glass lamps." His own, he says, are true reproductions.

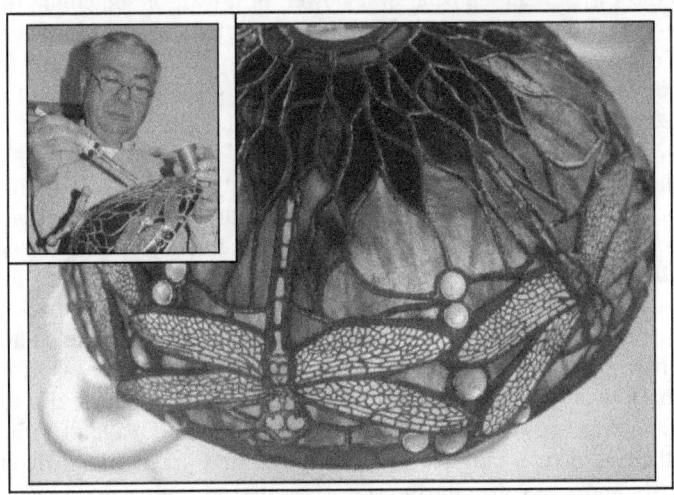

Bloyer works off of fiberglass forms that have actual etched tracings of Tiffany patterns. He has a stock of about 20 forms—"And there are many more to be had."—he bought from the only company in the world licensed to make actual Tiffany patterns. With a few exceptions, each pattern repeats itself several times in a shade, just as a wallpaper pattern repeats. Bloyer traces every piece of a pattern on Mylar plastic, numbers each piece, cuts each piece from sheets of glass, and lays out the pieces on a glass-top light table.

"You use the form to solder, because that's what you need to maintain the shape," he says. "It's kind of like putting a puzzle together." The pieces are held together with a bonding agent—copper foil. A "tacky wax" is melted and lightly coated over the entire form so each piece of glass will stay in its proper position during the soldering process. A characteristic of Bloyer's work is that he tries to keep solder lines as thin as possible. "The bigger the solder line, the less glass you can see, so I try to keep it as small as I can." Other than having the advantage of an electric soldering iron and an electric, diamond grinding wheel, the rest of the shade-making process is the same as that used in Tiffany studios a hundred years ago.

So how are the contours of a shade achieved with pieces of flat glass? Part of the magic, Bloyer says, is the way Tiffany company designers oriented the pieces. They understood the contour of each form and used smaller pieces of glass where there are contours so pieces would not repeat. "If I want to dimensionalize a piece a little bit," Bloyer says, "I roll that wax up in little balls, stick it underneath, and tilt the glass the way I want—a petal of a flower, or a leaf, or something like that—to get a little different deflection of the light." In some instances, the Tiffany artisans heated flat pieces of glass in a kiln, placed the heated glass over a plaster of Paris form so the glass would slump to a desired contour, and incorporated those pieces into the shade.

Another big difference between most Tiffany-style lampshades sold in stores and the reproductions Bloyer crafts is the quality of the glass. "This glass," he explains, "is an art glass—handmade, typically; hand-rolled, anyway. There are only maybe 10 studios in the country that produce it. There are only one or two still in existence from back in Tiffany's time. That was one of the issues that kind of catapulted him into making the lamps. He wasn't satisfied with glass that was available back when he first had the idea of coming up with lamps. He felt the glass was too monochromatic—too one-colored. It didn't reflect well the true nature, multiple colors. And so he worked with different chemists and glass manufacturers. They played with it for years to come up with what they termed polychromatic glass—multiple-colored; stuff that gives you the depth. He has mottling in there—multiple colors; it's not just a green green or a blue blue. . . . If you look at water, if you study it hard enough, it's not just one color; there's multiple colors, from foliage, from the sedimentation. Look at the sky; it's not just blue. Grass is not just green; there are different colorations in it. It's more or less like painting. Most artists won't just paint a blue; they use some other colors to highlight, to get more depth." Not surprisingly, this art glass is "significantly more expensive." It is used primarily for lampshades, not stained glass windows.

Hand-rolling produces remarkably different areas on a single sheet of glass, and differences from sheet to sheet, both in coloration and degree of thickness. Bloyer likes to lay out all of the pieces of a shade before beginning the assembly process so the colors have a certain flow he finds appealing.

There also is glass texture to be considered. Some glass is smooth, some fairly grainy, and some deliberately rippled.

Bloyer found stained glass fascinating from an early age. "My mother always got mad at me," he says, "because I told her the only reason I went to church was to look at the [stained glass] windows. She didn't appreciate that too much. . . . I liked the colors, and liked to watch the different light that came through the glass at different times. Not that I studied it intensely, but I liked it a lot.

"Then when I was in high school, my sister, who was a sculptress, asked me to help her save a coffee table that (she) and her husband had purchased and one of their dogs had put a deep scratch in the top of it." His sister was interested in trying to resurface the table with a colored glass mosaic top, as described in a book she owned. "So I went over and helped her do that," Bloyer says. "It was painful; it was absolutely painful trying to cut that glass. . . . That was back in the '60s. We got the project done, and it turned out fine and that, but I always thought there must be an easier way than that."

He didn't tackle any more art projects until 1979, when he and his wife purchased a stained glass lamp for the kitchenette of a new house. "It was just a panel lamp," Bloyer says. "It was in no manner, shape or form a Tiffany. It was just a panel lamp with a stylized version of a maple leaf in it—two-color, kind of a caramel-y background and dark brown leaves. . . . I thought: *You know, I should be able to do that.*" Soon after he noticed a community education course for beginning stained glass advertised and signed up. "What I got out of that," he says, "was the fundamentals of glass cutting, which was a big issue—getting past that, and all the anxieties associated with doing that. And from that point I just pursued little projects, mainly doing flatwork—being windows, or things that hang in windows—for friends, and that type of stuff. . . .

"I was always kind of interested in the Tiffany lamp forms themselves; I just kind of had it in the back of my mind. And then one of the art glass places where I purchased my supplies from got in a new product. They came out with a fiberglass form with pre-etched Tiffany patterns. All these lampshades were in the public sector somewhere, and they have permission to take a shade and trace all of the pieces in that. . . . I decided that I wanted to try that, and found that it worked pretty well, and I liked it. The thing that I really liked about it is that if I spent all the time making a shade I didn't necessarily have to have someplace it was going to go; I could just keep it. I could always use a lamp someplace. And so that's kind of the way it went, and has gone through the years. I've sold a number of them, and have a number of orders for them. . . . I've sold them to family members. I've sold them to people I've worked with. I don't advertise or anything because it's just a hobby and avocation. When I retire, part of my plan was to do it more on a fulltime basis. . . . I don't know that it would be so fun to do it fulltime. . . . Sometimes if you're not in the mood for it you just have to kind of walk away from it."

Bloyer's largest Tiffany reproduction is 22 inches in diameter, as measured across the bottom of the shade. He has made two Tiffany patterns twice, with color variations, just as shades produced by the Tiffany studios had color differences for the same patterns. "When you do something like a Black-eyed Susan, and you want to do it fairly close to nature, you don't have a lot of options," he says. "Where you have more discretion is in the background. But as far as if you want to stay close to nature, you're going to get a gold yellow and that's what you're going to have. . . . I don't travel too far from nature. Nature, I think, has done a good job on all this stuff. . . . This is the Art Nouveau, the Tiffany stuff. They captured a lot of natural things. It was flowers; there was some fish; there's even some scenes—nature scenes—in them."

According to Bloyer, a worldwide organization called the Tiffany Lamp Club has approximately 1,000 members, and most make lamps.

"I wish I were more of an artist, per se," he says. "I consider myself more of a crafts person. I can take this and transform glass using these patterns, and that type of stuff. . . . There are many Tiffanys that I would like to continue to reproduce, but what I'd really like to do is make my own. It wouldn't be a Tiffany; it'd be a Bloyer, I guess, now that I've got the techniques down really well. A lot of the people in this worldwide Tiffany organization design their own also. Eventually that would be where I'd like to go with it."

- *March 11, 2006*

☼

Dancing With Heat

Jim Engebretson ... glassblower

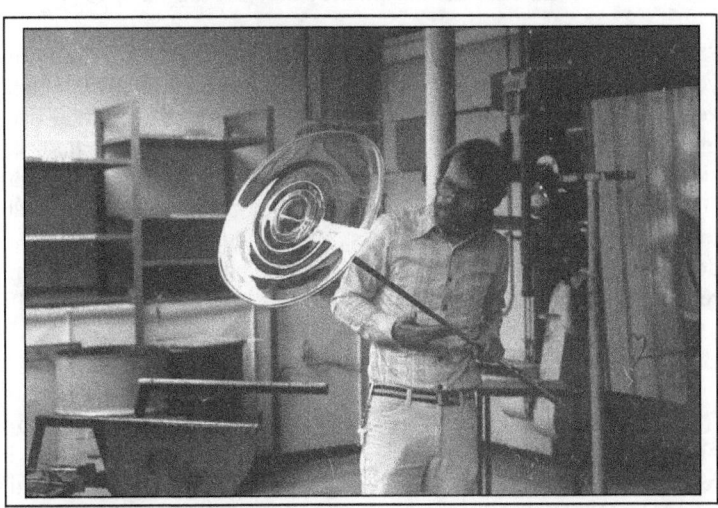

If ever there was an art form characterized by the old Army maxim "hurry up and wait," Jim Engebretson says, it is glassblowing. Engebretson, a Hudson, Wisconsin, resident, is a professional glassblower whose work is displayed in 45 or 50 art galleries throughout the country. He also teaches glassblowing at the University of Wisconsin—River Falls.

Working out of his home studio, which he calls UpCountry Glassworks, Engebretson produces pendants, goblets, bowls, tumblers, hanging roundels [discs], sculptures, birds, paperweights, pitchers, candle holders, and a variety of other objects.

"My designs for glass are clean and simple," he writes in his brochure. "Functional as well as decorative."

He used to concentrate on making pieces that retailed for between $30 and $75. Now he works mainly at the lower end of the price scale, making birds that sell for $7.50 to $10, and at the high end of the scale, making one-of-a-kind objects, such as hanging roundels, that sell for $300 to $400. With much of his time devoted to teaching, though, his output has declined recently.

Engebretson, a native of Hudson, attended UW—River Falls, then proceeded to graduate study at the Rhode Island School of Design, where he received a Master of Fine Arts degree in 1973, before establishing UpCountry Glassworks at the Windsor Mill in North Adams, Massachusetts. He moved the studio to Hudson in 1977.

"Basically," he says, "you need a furnace for melting the glass (and) you need an oven in which to place the pieces you've blown, which is kept at one thousand degrees, which is more or less the point at which glass freezes. Then that oven is also used for cooling the glass very slowly to room temperature, to remove any stress or strain on the glass. Beyond that, you simply need a bench to work at, perhaps a steel table to also aid in the forming of glass, and various hand tools. It really doesn't require a lot of equipment. It's simply that the equipment is relatively exotic. It's difficult to buy, so you have to build it yourself."

Engebretson buys broken glass from a West Virginia factory for his own studio. The broken glass used at the UW—River Falls studio is from a Minnesota bottle factory. "Glass that was formulated to be blown by a machine sets up very quickly and has a very short working range," he says of that bottle factory glass. "Glass that is formulated to be worked and manipulated by hand stays soft for a longer period of time. You can do different kinds of things with different kinds of glass. Basically the glass comes in broken-up form, that we melt. . . .

"If I tell someone that I'm a glassblower they automatically assume that I do supermarket openings and things like that, that I have a little torch and Pyrex tubing and I make sailing ships and things like that. I don't do any of that. That's a different type of glassblowing; it's more related to the scientific glassblowing. I'm a glassblower (who) works with a furnace where I melt two hundred pounds of glass, use steel blowpipes, and actually gather the glass, or get the glass out of the furnace, and then blow it from that point."

The gas furnace melts glass with 2,300-degree intensity.

"Metallic oxides are used and mixed in with the clear glass while it's being melted; you can get colors that way. A lot of glassblowers use that method. There's another technique that we use: We buy colored glass rods that can be broken up, and a small portion of this color (is) put on the blowpipe as just a solid bit of color, and then if we put clear glass over that and blow it out the color is strong enough so that it remains blue or yellow or whatever color it was."

The blowpipe is a five-foot-long, hollow steel rod that is to a glassblower what brushes are to a painter. The end of the blowpipe is dipped into the molten glass, which is the consistency of honey. With the aid of a wooden cup, a ball of molten glass is formed at the end of the blowpipe. The ball of glass is then removed from the furnace to cool as the glassblower rolls it across a sheet of steel to maintain a desired shape. It is then placed back into the furnace so more molten glass can be added to the ball, then cooled again. This process is repeated several times. Occasionally the glassblower blows through the blowpipe to expand the hollow center of the glass ball. This process of repeated heating and cooling, of working and waiting, is sometimes called The Glassblower's Dance. A glassblower needs to work the glass quickly when it is hot, before it cools. It takes experience to know when the glass is hot enough to blow. The most common mistake students make is to try to blow glass when it is not hot enough.

After being blown to a desired shape and size, the ball of molten glass is fused to a solid rod called a pontil and severed from the blowpipe. Attached to the pontil, the glass is reheated and formed into its final shape. When satisfied, the glassblower breaks the piece off of the pontil and places it in an oven, or kiln, where it takes it about 12 hours to cool to room temperature. After cooling some of the pieces are polished, ground, sandblasted, or even painted to produce decorative designs.

"If it [the glass] didn't do exactly what you wanted it to do it doesn't necessarily mean that it's a bad piece," Engebretson says. "Perhaps it's a better piece for it. But more often than not glass artists start with something definite in mind—I do, and I try to force the glass to my way, to do what I want it to do. I will accept some variations the glass forces upon me, or my lack of technique or technical ability doesn't allow me to do. I'm open."

In general, glass is glass. Certain types of glass are more suited for different objects, though. "There are probably a thousand different formulas for glass, depending on its end use," Engebretson says. "But it's all glass. It just has different grains, or textures, or degrees of hardness or softness."

Glassblowing was introduced into college curriculum at the University of Wisconsin [Madison] in 1962. UW—River Falls launched its glass program only five years later, in 1967.

Engebretson, who teaches two courses, plus a course in stained glass for the University of Wisconsin—Extension program, says students "have a lot of trouble with burns and cuts. We minimize that as much as possible—or we simply make every attempt to. But it still happens, people still get burned or cut. We haven't had any serious burns or cuts ever, to my knowledge, in this program. I've been burned to the point where I couldn't work for a couple of weeks. Burns are usually the result of carelessness. But the glass is so incredibly hot that, in general, people are very cautious. They know that there's no way they can let go of that hot stuff quick enough to prevent getting burned, so they tend to respect the glass, especially after they've been singed a little one time." Engebretson's bad burn was between a thumb and a forefinger. "No scars," he reports, "but there was sure one big blister there that prevented me from opening and closing my hand."

"Feel the burn" means something completely different in glassblowing than it does in aerobic exercise.

- *November 12, 1981*

Splendor In The Glass

Nancy Potek ... beadmaker

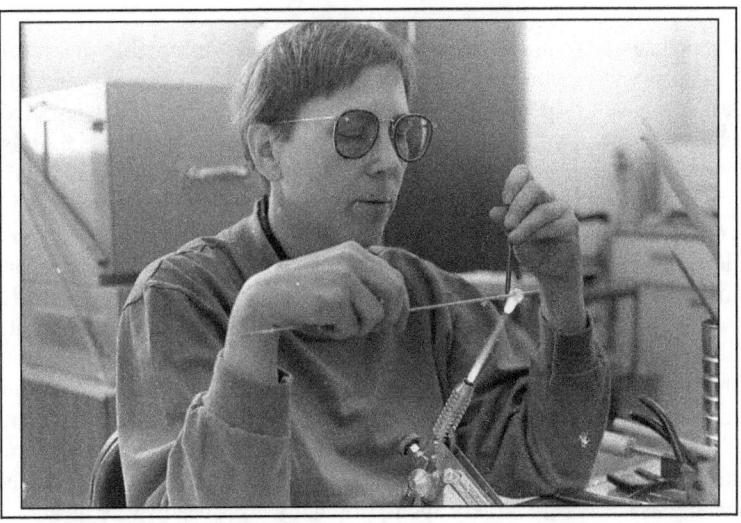

I interviewed Nancy Potek March 16, 1993, and again May 12, 1993.

A small torch-flame licks a rod of colored glass. Artist Nancy Potek collects the melting glass on a stainless steel mandrill the diameter of a bicycle spoke. She spins the mandrill slowly, with her right hand, with practiced, deft wrist action, to form a small sphere of glass on the mandrill. The sphere grows gradually larger as more honey-like glass melts onto it. Another handcrafted glass bead has begun taking shape in Potek's rural Dresser, Wisconsin, studio. The bead Potek is creating at the moment is called a lampwork bead because the creation occurs in a flame of fire. It may also be called a flamework bead or a torchwork bead.

The lampwork method is one of Potek's two main beadmaking methods. The full-time bead artist also fuses together layers of glass in electric kilns, using molds, to make larger pendant beads—beads the size of hotel soap bars.

An average lampwork bead is approximately marble size, although Potek makes the beads in an array of shapes and sizes. Using various instruments—tweezers, dental tools, etc.—she forms beads into the shape of everything from human heads to alligators to vegetables.

"I think beads were real, real popular in the '70s, and then all of a sudden everything went kaput and you didn't hear about beads," Potek says. "Now the whole bead movement's coming back, and I think it's here to stay because you have people doing unique things in beads."

Potek likes to think of beads as tiny sculptures—affordable pieces of sculpture. "Somebody can buy one, and they've purchased a piece of art and haven't spent a tremendous amount of money. It's not like having to spend a thousand dollars on a painting or something." At as much as $50 per bead, though, she admits that some of her beads may seem fairly expensive to many people. Her most expensive beads contain a layer or two of dichroic glass, a glittery sort of glass developed through space technology. It is even more expensive than the gold leaf Potek also uses occasionally. "Some of the dichroic is backed with black," she says. "That makes it opaque, so you can see it. Some of it isn't, and it becomes more translucent, so you can see through it." People are more attracted to beads that contain dichroic glass. As Potek puts it: "Everybody likes the dichroic. It sells better. The sparkle gets people's eyes." Most dichroic beads are shades of blue, violet and green. They look a lot like precious stones, which is what glass beads are largely about; originally glass beads were meant to imitate stones. "It still sort of has that use, I think, in jewelry today," Potek says. Potek combines a layer or two of dichroic glass with five or six layers of other glass in various ways to create variegated effects. "People tend to like the blues and the purples," she says. "I do have a lot of the warmer gold colors, but people like the cooler colors more."

Beadmaking involves many steps, including two kiln cycles for fused beads. "Each firing takes 24 hours," Potek says. "The first firing goes up to about 1,450 to 1,500 degrees Fahrenheit. The second firing goes up to about 1,350. And then they're annealed at between 950 and 1,000 degrees Fahrenheit. . . . When you work with glass, either lampworking or this kind of glass, you're putting strain on the glass; you're poking it and prodding it and everything else. You want to even out the strain in the glass. The way you do it is, you bring it up to a temperature—say, for example, a thousand degrees, which is the temperature that you anneal borate silicate glass at—and the glass is at a point where there's no strain in the glass, but it's lower than the point where the glass would start to melt and flow. At that point—the annealing point—all the strain is evened out. And then you slowly take the glass down from the annealing point to the strain point, where it's at a point in the cooling cycle where some stress could reoccur in the glass, and you leave it there at the strain point for a while, and then you slowly bring it back down to room temperature. It makes the glass strong."

The labor-intensive nature of the beadmaking process is another reason why handcrafted beads are relatively expensive.

Besides her home studio, Potek has a second studio in Minneapolis in a building she shares with several other glass artists and potters. She grew up in North Minneapolis and studied glass art at the University of Wisconsin—River Falls, from where she graduated in 1980. UW—River Falls is one of the few universities in the country that still has a glass art program.

"I did a lot of flat glass fusing work and sold it through galleries," she says. "Then I went back to get my teacher's certificate, and did some more art. Then when I finished that I was trying to decide how I could re-use my glass skills in new ways, and beads were becoming popular again. . . . I go around to some of the bead shows, like the Chicago Bead Bazaar, and sell my work. And jewelers buy it."

She believes interest in beadmaking will grow as she and others teach the craft to others.

"Beadmaking, historically, in Europe, has been a cottage industry kind of thing where a lot of women have made beads and never really gotten the recognition," she says, adding that jewelry designers received the recognition the beadmakers deserved.

Women still dominate the beadmaking craft, as evidenced by classes Potek teaches and attends. "I think it's a matter of women tending to have more time to take the classes rather than men not having an interest," Potek offers. "A lot of them are homemakers and take the time to take the class, or they have jobs that allow them to take time off more than men. You might be seeing, in the future, more men taking classes as they have early retirement. . . . They'll have more time to do some of the arts things that you traditionally see more women involved in."

☼

Extra Texture

Julie Crabtree ... embroidery artist

Ah, yes, the double take. It's a classic comic gesture. Someone casually glances at something, then starts turning his attention elsewhere when something in his brain clicks and he realizes what he glanced at was odd or remarkable, so he quickly swivels his head back for a longer, often bug-eyed look. A version of the double take is often displayed at art fairs when people notice out-of-the-ordinary artworks. Julie Crabtree's dimensional embroidery art creations draw a large number of double takes anywhere they are displayed—at art fairs, in galleries, or wherever. Frequently, as people walk by her booth at an art fair, their eyes scanning what they think are paintings, a sixth sense kicks in and they realize that these pictures have deeper dimensions than paintings do, that they, in fact, are not paintings. So they inspect one of the landscapes more closely and see there is thread there, that stitchery is at play. Almost invariably upon this discovery, someone's first question to Crabtree is: "How do you do it?" "So then I explain how I do it," Crabtree says. Most often, the next question is: "Well, where did you go to learn this? Who taught you how to do this?" Crabtree's response: "My background, but. . . I've evolved this over the years of doing it."

The art fair double take never ceases to amaze Crabtree. "It's quite amusing, really," she says. "But I enjoy it, and people are getting very interested in wanting to do it. . . . It's something that's just starting to catch on a little bit here, with the quilters and with the art groups, especially the machine embroidery, what that can do. It's very diverse. You can do lots of textures and things."

So where *did* this Grantsburg, Wisconsin, area artist learn to fashion landscapes with embroidery art? She learned in her native England, at the Mansfield College of the Arts in Nottinghamshire, where she later taught. She also earned degrees in embroidery and fashion from the City and Guilds of London.

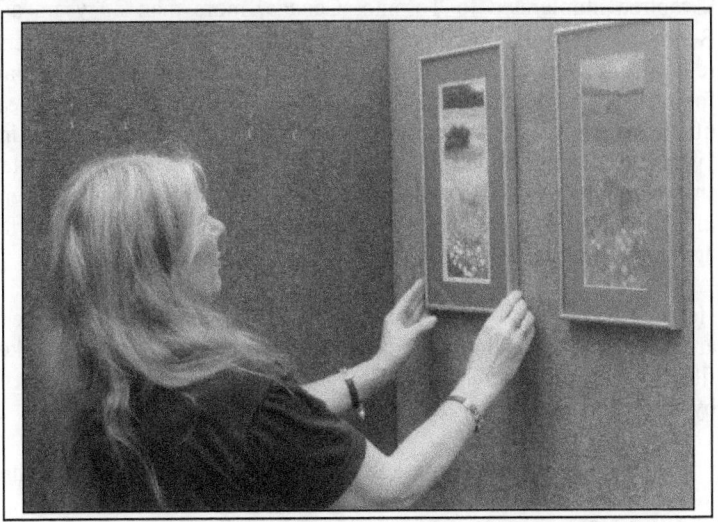

In Great Britain embroidery art "is really on a par with fine art," she says. "They have huge exhibitions over there. It's taken, I think, a little more seriously than it is here."

Crabtree aspired to art college since she was very young. After being accepted into Mansfield College she found that graphics and fine arts really didn't interest her all that much, so she drifted toward fashion. After a year of study, she decided fashion was too structured. "I needed to do something more creative," she says. "And just by chance there was a new tutor started at the college for embroidery, so I switched to embroidery. I was one of the first group of students to do this, back in the early '70s."

She loves embroidery art because it has a structural base but also allows an artist experimental liberty. "You can be as free and textural as you want to be, combining different techniques," she says. "This was perfect; this was for me, because I could combine all these things. After doing all the traditional techniques you experiment—you combine techniques, and combine other areas. I combined textile printing. I used to enjoy textile printing. So I combined those. And then my art background—painting and stitching. And that's where I expanded. The one particular technique I like is machine embroidery, because you can do so much with it, and experiment. It's just a regular sewing machine; I just use a straight stitch, and a zig-zag stitch."

Crabtree immigrated to Toronto, Canada, more than 20 years ago. Before moving to her log home in the lightly populated "sand barrens" region southwest of Grantsburg last year, she also lived in River Falls for 11 years, as well as in Massachusetts, southern Wisconsin, and east of Luck. She started getting back into embroidery art while living in a "very artsy area" of Massachusetts. "I started doing some gallery shows, and I was teaching again. It was just the right time. Then I moved back to Wisconsin. It was a perfect move for starting this again." She has been a fulltime artist the last two years.

Her basement Bratch Sith Studio [pronounced *bra-ta-shay*], centered around a sewing machine, is a warren with small cabinets and baskets filled with hundreds of spools of thread, bits and pieces of fabric, sorted by color, and other materials used in the textured artworks.

She specializes in landscapes, from "miniatures" about two by three inches to pieces as large as computer keyboards, in both vertical and horizontal formats. She does embroidered clothing and accessories, and textural pieces, as well.

"It's like painting," she says of the landscapes. "You start in the background and work forward, then get a lot more textural as you get further forward."

The first step involves painting a "rough idea of background" on cotton cloth with watered-down acrylic paint. Then she rips up fabric and stitches with that fabric. "Basically," she says, "it's just a matter of layers of fabric, layers of stitching, going between hand-stitching and machine stitching. I add little bits of dried cheesecloth, and that gives it extra depth. It also stiffens fabric." Other materials are stitched in too—sparkly "angeline" fiber, beads, hand-dyed ribbons and handspun thread. While more expensive than manufactured thread, that handspun thread adds a textural element more common thread cannot. Hand-dyed ribbons, which Crabtree also stiffens with fabric spray, have more gradation of color than mass-produced ribbon does.

"I'm constantly changing threads," she says. "It's like a painter's palette. It's just like paint, but in thread. . . . There's a lot of machining, a lot of stitching."

String wrapped with fabric or stitched with thread creates tree trunks and branches. Woodsy, north woods scenes are popular with people.

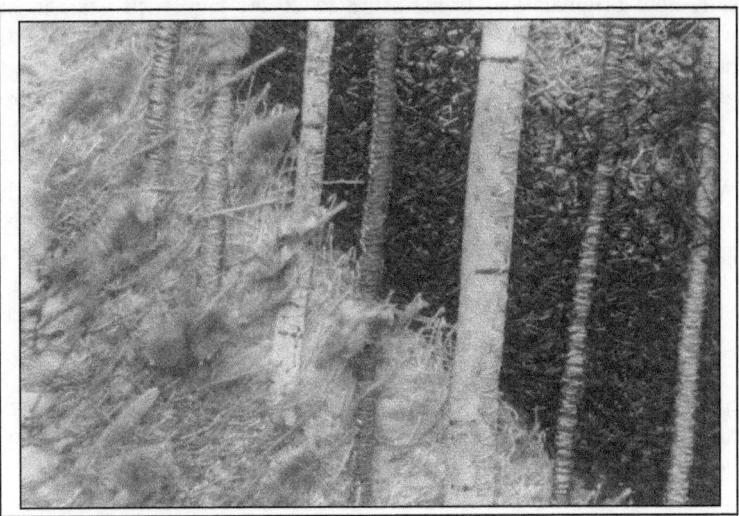

Crabtree constantly experiments. "You learn the basics in college," she says, "and then over the years I've developed combining stitching, experimenting."

Other than "How do you do it?," the question people ask Crabtree most frequently is: "How long does it take you to do one of these?"

"It takes me a long time," Crabtree says. "And it depends on each piece. Some come together easier than others. There's the time painting with fabric, dying the bits of cheesecloth and things that I use. If I'm putting trees in, it's making the trunks, painting the fabric, and then laying it out, starting to stitch, adding the bits of fabric." Considering all that, she estimates it takes perhaps a week—probably more than 40 hours—to do a landscape six by sixteen inches.

She explains her creative process this way: "I've got an idea in my head; I can visualize what it's going to be. It doesn't always work out, but most of the time it does. And then it's just getting to that visualization of getting it from up here [her head] onto that fabric. When I start something I get all my fabrics and threads out, in the color ranges, and things that I'm going to be working on. So I've got this whole slew of fabrics, thread, beads, whatever. I've got it all there to work with."

She used to do regular eight-by-ten pictures, but found that longer and narrower ones sold better. Now she does "real skinny ones" about two-and-a-half inches wide that are proving to be her best-selling size. She sells both originals and prints at 18 to 20 art fairs each year, most within a three- to four-hour drive of home. "Sometimes I will get 10 prints made, sometimes 20. Sometimes I have to keep going back and getting more made, especially the fall trees, and certain ones that are very popular."

While prints, which generally are the same size as the original, don't have the same sort of depth as the originals, of course, it is readily apparent the scenes are made with stitches, not brush strokes.

Sometimes Crabtree re-does the same scene. "I can't reproduce exactly, but I can do similar."

She photographs a lot of landscapes, pulls some ideas from other pictures, and makes use of memory and imagination. "There are so many beautiful landscapes and textures and colors," she marvels.

Crabtree has won an impressive list of awards since turning to her talent for embroidery fulltime. Besides the quality of the artisanship, her textured creations attract attention for their stand-apart appearance, for her pictures are unique in this region.

"That's what everyone tells me when they see my work out at shows or galleries or whatever," she says. "They say, 'I haven't seen this before.'"

In the world of art, you have to attract someone's attention before you can sew up a sale.

- *July 6, 2004*

☼

Rug Bug

Margaret Miller ... weaver

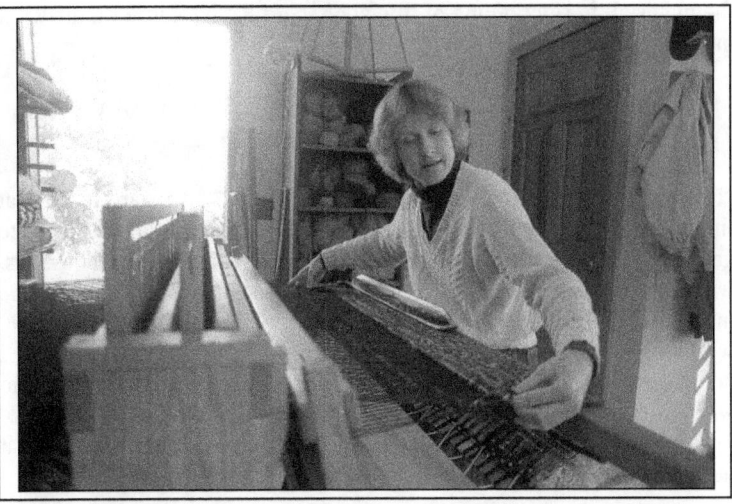

While Margaret Miller lives near the hamlet of West Sweden, in northwestern Wisconsin, her weaving career has a Norwegian thread running through it.

Between her sophomore and junior years of college, in the early 1970s, Miller spent a year in Norway working and studying weaving. She continued taking weaving and design classes upon her return to the University of Minnesota to complete her degree requirements for child psychology. She spent 10 years teaching three-to-five-year-old special education students, in the Twin Cities and Grantsburg, Wisconsin, before deciding to become a fulltime weaver in 1984.

"I didn't become a weaver right away because I was told by so many people that if I became an artist I would starve to death," she says, "so I taught for 10 years and then decided that maybe I would, but I'd give it a try anyway. And it's gone pretty well. I'm really pleased with it."

Miller makes wool area rugs as large as eight-by-twelve feet, some of which sell for "thousands" of dollars at art galleries. She also sells at craft fairs and through home furnishing stores.

"It seems that my more expensive pieces need to go through galleries," she says. "It seems like they do better there than in home furnishing stores, where I'm competing with the overseas market, and they sell things for almost pennies. It's amazing how inexpensive they are. If I was selling my pieces at their prices I wouldn't even be able to pay for the material, to say nothing of my labor. So I have to go for a different market."

Miller currently has woven rugs at galleries in St. Paul, Madison, and Tulsa, Oklahoma.

"I'm trying to get into more galleries," she says. "It's hard to do it at first because the materials for the rugs are so expensive. Most of the galleries, when they're dealing with a price range in the thousands, want to do it on consignment, so I have to put the money into the materials. If I have two or three rugs in a gallery I might have $1,500 worth of materials there, to say nothing of the time. At this point I don't have that much money to have rugs floating around. But I'm working on it, trying to build it up a little bit at a time. So as I make money through the art shows, which is cash and carry, then I can get it done."

She is starting to crack the four annual craft shows the American Craft Council stages in Baltimore, San Francisco, St. Paul, and West Springfield, Massachusetts. She exhibited at the St. Paul show this past April and hopes to be selected as an exhibitor at all four fairs next year. Thousands of artisans—something along the lines of 10,000 to 15,000 according to Miller—apply for the 200 to 300 exhibit spaces available at each five-day show. The shows are open exclusively to wholesale buyers for three days, then to the general public for two days.

"There are people who make $10,000 to $20,000 at each show," Miller says. "You don't have to do too many shows in order to make it then. Although doing the shows is very expensive. It costs at least $1,000 when you add up all the costs. It's worth it if you can get to all of these markets across the nation because everybody comes to you; you don't have to try to get out to all of these buyers. I got several galleries from the last show, so it was very productive."

In addition to heirloom-quality rugs, crafted of top-quality materials, Miller also makes wool rag rugs that cost only about one-third as much. About half of her rugs end up on floors and half are hung on walls. All of her rugs, though, "are made to hold up under foot traffic. They won't fall apart when people walk on them. That has a lot to do with good technique. It requires a good heavy loom and good technique. So I'm able to do that. And I decided at some point that I thought functional art or craft was more important than non-functional, and I like to weave large pieces, so it seemed that rugs were just a good way to express what I want to do. So when I take an eight-by-twelve-foot rug off the loom it's fun. It feels like you've really done something—you really produced something. . . . They're all one-of-a-kind. Because they're handmade they don't come out exactly alike. . . . I get bored very quickly if I have to do the same thing over again." When she makes a pair of matching rugs the second one is not as much fun to make because of that boredom factor.

She has two looms in her home—a large one for making large rugs and a smaller one for smaller rugs. She works at her craft about 10 hours a day. An eight-by-twelve rug takes four to five weeks to weave.

Miller picked up many invaluable techniques during her extended stay in Norway.

"In the Scandinavian countries it's very common for people to have looms," she says. "It seems like almost every home has a loom, so it's very natural for them to be weaving. Most people knew how to weave when I got there, so I got to experiment a lot with their techniques. They have really excellent techniques. Most of the techniques I use they claim as their own. . . . I found that they also are very traditional, generally—very conservative. They like to weave the same designs and the same colors over and over again. That aspect wasn't as appealing to me. But I learned a lot of excellent techniques there. . . . They have some pretty intricate and complicated weaving techniques that they have developed."

Miller believes weaving has become more popular in the United States in recent years, but recognizes she may have a skewed view because of her intense involvement with weaving.

"When I started," she says, "it didn't seem like there were very many people who were weaving. It seems like there are more now, but I'm not sure about that because I am more interested and seek out weavers. I think, though, in general, the crafts in this country are coming of age.

There are so many craft shows; it's just amazing how many craft shows there are. And it didn't seem like 10 or 20 years ago there were very many craft shows at all. Now almost every day in the mail I get applications for craft shows."

Miller traveled to Mexico and Guatemala about eight years ago, which added a Spanish-American influence to her weaving.

"That was a vacation, basically," she says, "but I'm drawn to fibers, so I did a lot of collecting and went to a couple of factories. When you're talking factories in Guatemala you're talking looms similar to (mine). You're not talking mechanized; you're talking hand-operated looms."

Miller uses bold colors and abstract patterns that are more Spanish than Scandinavian.

- *October 5, 1988*

Intimate Curtains

Mary Jackelen ... quilt artist

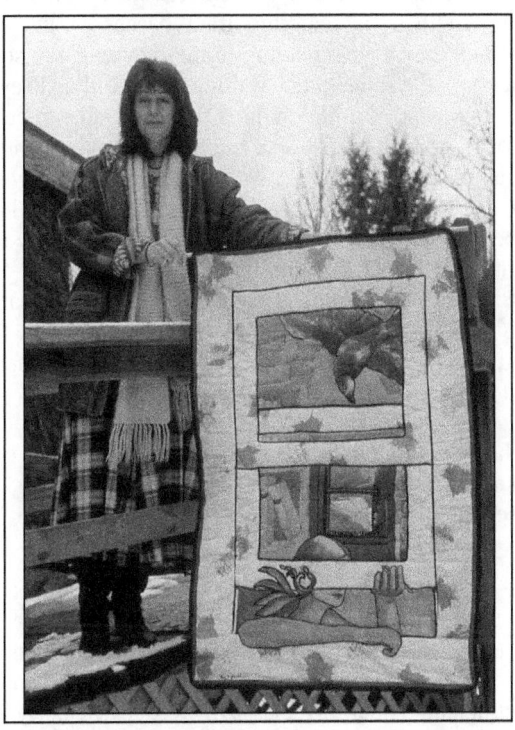

It's an instinct as ancient as the Stone Age and as sentient as New Age. From cave hieroglyphics to the heights of high modern art humans have recorded their stories with symbolic images and figurative pictures. Combining art techniques with a great American traditional craft, Mary Jackelen tells much of the story of her life in intricate, extraordinary, exquisite quilted pictures. To call her creations simply quilts would seem as insulting as calling a masterfully prepared and presented meal "chow." Her quilted pictures are for hanging on walls, not for slinging across beds. They are inspiration for the soul, not cover for the body. They have more to do with wonder than warmth.

They also are expensive, many in the $800 to $900 range.

Jackelen's quilted pictures are a sculpted journal of her life for the past 15 years or so. Rather than record events and express emotions in writing, she sewed together stories and stitched feelings with fabric, thread and visual images.

"They're my experience of times in my life, and they're also sort of consoling," Jackelen says of her quilted artworks. "And so for me to have people see them is real important because I know that if it consoles me and they say something to me they will say something to other people too—the same kinds of things, hopefully. They're kind of like in code, in a way. But the thing is that to be able to communicate the feeling of it, or let it translate to the people looking at it in the way they see it, is important. I think I was always trying to say something, to say a lot, but at the time I started these I didn't have a lot of verbal ability to speak about what I was feeling, so I said it in my quilts. . . . I try to let whatever wants to come through come through, and kind of trust it. And it does seem to happen that a lot of people really relate to the images. It's like a healing kind of thing. I mean them to be healing, and so I want for the people who see them to have a visual healing, and people seem to get that; I think it works."

Ironically, Jackelen now makes her living by talking, as a counselor at the University of Wisconsin—Stout, in Menomonie. She is renting a cabin in Menomonie this winter, but her main residence is in River Falls.

Art classes she took at UW—River Falls in the early 1980s steered her toward her current course as a quilt artist. Art department professors Bill Ammerman (watercolor painting and life drawing classes) and Walter Nottingham (fiber art classes) were particularly influential. Nottingham, "kind of a famous artist in his own right, . . . made a couple of statements that kind of got me on this direction," Jackelen says. He suggested his students should try to bring forward family traditions in their art. Since Jackelen's mother was a seamstress, Jackelen started investigating fabrics and dyes, approaching quilting "from a different direction. I didn't start piecing and quilting until I had done a lot of art first," she says. "I kind of taught myself how to sew by doing that." Things clicked. "It just felt really good to be able to put a couple of different ideas together and come up with these quilted pictures."

A few of her quilted pictures incorporate traditional quilters' blocks. One entitled *Bear Paw*, for instance, uses traditional quilt blocks called

Bear Paw blocks. Jackelen is fascinated by the challenge of combining geometric lines with organic lines. Most of her quilted pictures, though, are as dissimilar from traditional quilts as James Joyce's *Finnegan's Wake* is from traditional narrative writing. There are hidden images, pictures within pictures, metaphysical aspects, cubist and collage influences, unusual perspectives, twists of reality, and other intriguing touches. One entitled *Grandmothers* has a young woman in a Lotus position in the center, with profiled heads of two elderly women on either side of her. These three human figures form the body of a butterfly, which has frogs on its wings, frogs being an old goddess symbol for feminine fertility. In nature, frogs are mysteriously dying and have permeable skin that Jackelen likens to curtains. "They're very sensitive," she says, "and I think of myself as very sensitive. . . . My field around me is like a frog's skin. And the tree frogs I just think are wonderful. I just think the tree frog is darling. Who would have ever thought of frogs in trees? I just love that idea that there are such neat surprises in nature. . . . The way I started that one was: If frogs could pray for humans, what would it look like?"

Her business card, for her art, is headed *Tree Hopper Images*; it features a line drawing of a spread-legged frog atop a circle and a leaf.

Musician/composer Manfred Schonauer says *Grandmothers* is "so unbelievable" that he almost fell out of his chair the first time Jackelen showed it to him. He was so impressed with Jackeleln's quilted pictures that he asked her to display them at the Pipe Dream Center, an old two-room country schoolhouse west of Cumberland Manfred and his wife, Truan, transformed into a performance space for Manfred's music. The four-day exhibit of 16 quilted pictures at the Pipe Dream Center was built around one of Manfred's monthly concerts.

"She's the only person who does this particular kind of work," says Truan Schonauer. "I've never seen anything like it. Some people came in through the door thinking they were quilt quilts, like you would see the Amish quilts, and they were stunned. It was fun to see the reaction on people's faces. We advertised it as a story quilt show, but people still came in through the door thinking it would be the wedding rings and the blocks and schoolhouses. People would walk in and go 'ooohh!' They couldn't believe it. . . . A couple of men actually pulled a chair in front of their favorite quilts and stared at them. I thought that was amazing, for men. . . . There was a little kid here, only eight or nine years old, who stood under one of them and said, 'Mom, I'm going to die if I don't have this quilt.' An $800 quilt. A little kid. But there were children in it and he liked it. There was something about it that pulled into him. . . . Two women had tears running down their faces. I got a box of Kleenex and I said to one of them who I knew pretty well, 'Are you okay?' She said, 'I have been there.' That was the appeal to some of the women, that they could see themselves in the story of the quilt, because these things happen to people."

The Pipe Dream Center is one of the few places Jackelen has publicly displayed her quilted pictures. "She's so unassuming," Truan says. "She's not an out-front person." Some of the quilted picture images likely will be featured on limited edition art prints, and possibly on postcards as well.

"Her artwork should be exposed," Manfred says. ". . . Whatever she had going, she always magnified and focused it and brought it out in her artwork—whatever happened to her in her life."

Jackelen says "it is a little bit intimidating to bring them out" because they are so personal, but since "experiences are better if they're shared" it is important to her that other people see the quilted pictures. Anyway, she quips, she is "pretty sure that most people don't know what's going on" as far as understanding how they specifically relate to Jackelen's life.

The title of one of the quilted pictures, *Intimate Curtains*, is an appropriate term to describe all of them, for they are at once intimate stories from Jackelen's life and translucent curtains that keep details hidden with symbol and code. Jackelen admits she doesn't fully understand every quilt painting, some of which incorporate surprising, optically illusory elements. "I just sort of draw into it, and I don't quite get it," she says. ". . . There's always little things I put in there, and I don't know why. They're just kind of for goofiness. Little birds show up, and that kind of thing."

In addition to experimenting with various styles of art, she also experiments with a variety of fabrics and dyes, and makes use of stones, snail shells, beads, sequins, embroidery, textile inks, trapunto drawing, and other objects and techniques.

Occasionally her intuition leads to a pleasing coincidence. In *Soul Travel*, for example, trees are seen from the perspective of someone lying on the ground looking up toward the sky, conveying a sense of space. A hawk flying in an open area above the trees in the center of the scene is symbolic of a guide. It is meant to convey the message that even when we feel sad, isolated and forlorn, which is how Jackelen felt at the time, if we look at our situation from a new perspective and be quiet, and have patience, we will be guided to a happier, more hopeful stage of life. Jackelen later learned hawks are considered messengers and symbols by some Native American tribes. "There is, for me, when I look at it, a sense of isolation to it, and a lot of space," she says. "Also, it's kind of a circle within a square. I started coming to that, and I really liked the sense of mandalas. . . . And again I'm doing geometric shapes with organic shapes. I just love doing that."

Colors have their own symbolism. "I think the darker colored ones are more when I'm sad and the lighter color ones are the ones when I'm feeling pretty happy. I use dye colors a lot."

Jackelen's quilted pictures not only take a lot of time to make, but require a lot of thought and vision as well. "I do a lot of processing—thinking," she says. Most of the time that starts when she sets up a mental challenge to herself. "It's the mood I'm in right when I'm doing it—whatever is going on in my life at the time," she says. She looks for images that appeal to her, takes photographs, and starts playing with the images on paper. The selection of fabrics and dyes follows.

"Some of it's planned, some of it's not," she explains. "The basic plan is on paper. I have a life-size pattern for it, then I get a light-box and get a magic marker and start sketching it on the fabric. As I'm doing that I'm thinking about what else I want to do on it. It kind of builds."

She doesn't know how many hours of work went into each quilted picture, which vary in size from 27 by 30 inches to 48 by 60 inches and larger. She estimates some may have gone into the three-digit range—in other words, more than 100 hours. If anyone else creates the same sort of quilted pictures, Jackelen is unaware of it. "I've seen other people treat fabric and do different things with fabric," she says, "but not like this."

The symbolic nature of the art leads to highly subjective reactions from viewers. "Some people will be really, really affected by something that I myself am not all that affected by," Jackelen says.

Some people, she adds, "don't like this art, because it's personal. Some people find that threatening. . . . So I've had strong negative reactions too. I go: Okay; that's okay, as long as you get a reaction." Positive reactions such as "Wow!" and "Unbelievable!" far outnumber negative reactions, though.

Truan Schonauer says the first time Jackelen brought a bunch of quilted pictures to the Pipe Dream Center and unrolled them on the floor in the concert room "it was almost like somebody unrolling the Dead Sea Scrolls. You almost felt like you were in a biblical presence; they're that fantastic. We were walking around them like you can't even walk on sacred spots. I knew I had seen something special."

- *November 18, 1995*

Millions Of Stitches In Time

Jean Judd ... quilt artist

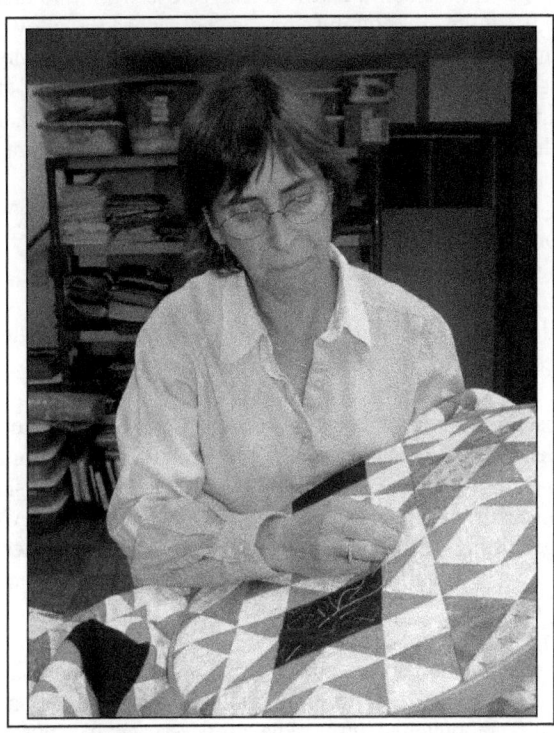

Something old, something new... If that's a good formula for a wedding, why not for quilts? It is, at any rate, the practicing principle Jean Judd has used with increasing frequency in creating quilts intended for wall display rather than bed covering.

Judd, who lives between St. Croix Falls and Grantsburg, in northwest Wisconsin, still hand-stitches quilts in this machine stitch age, but more often than not works in the realm of contemporary abstract art when it comes to fabric and quilt design.

"You can go to quilt shows, and a lot of people have very traditional-looking quilts," she says. ". . . There's probably 20 million quilters in the U.S. alone. So that puts you in a very big pool, whereas this more abstract quilting, and still doing it by hand, with the hand stitch, puts me in a much smaller pool and makes it more artistic. Quilts that are the more traditional ones are probably not going to be accepted well in the art world as art because it's too reminiscent of grandma's quilt."

Judd prefers to call herself a textile artist. She is willing to make traditional-design quilts on commission, as her schedule allows, but is drawn as much to the art side as the craft side of quilting. Most of her quilts that are publicly exhibited are exhibited in general fine arts exhibits rather than in traditional quilt shows. That makes admittance into an exhibit more competitive, but also more rewarding; it also gives the pieces a longer exposure.

Because of the hand stitching, her quilts are more expensive than most quilts, ranging between $800 and $20,000.

"The hand-quilting takes time, the design takes time, the dying of the fabric takes time. All of that works into it," she says.

Judd keeps track of the labor time devoted to each quilt to help set prices. Generally it takes her some 400 to 500 hours to hand-quilt a traditional-design quilt measuring 100 by 100 inches. Often she has 20 or more pieces in progress in her spacious basement studio, which has both a large cutting table and a full-sized pool table covered with pieces of fabric. There hasn't been a game of pool played on the table in about seven years.

"I always start in the center and work my way out," Judd says of her hand-quilting process. "Part of that is to keep it so that the back of the quilt doesn't get bunched up." She uses very small—number 10—needles and stitches for up to three hours at a stretch before taking a break to rest her fingers. "I think the most I've ever done is probably eight or nine hours a day. But that's been extreme. And that would be from 6:30 in the morning to 10 at night."

A quilt consists of three layers—a top, a center batting, and a back. Judd uses unbleached muslin for her backs, a traditional material with a long quilting heritage.

"It makes it so that my stitches show," she says about the muslin. "A lot of the machine quilters use a patterned back of commercial-type fabric so that the stitching on the back doesn't show through and you don't see the starts and stops and things like that. I always have used muslin on the back. I figure if I'm putting all this work in, my stitching better show so that people can see my effort. . . . It's what sets my work apart, the hand stitching. I've gotten awards for hand workmanship."

Most years, Judd demonstrates hand stitching at the annual exhibit staged by a local Mixed Sampler quilters' guild.

In this area, Judd says, most quilters switched from hand stitching to machine stitching in the mid-1990s. At the time Mixed Sampler members discussed whether or not machine stitched quilts should be permitted in the annual show. Judd estimates 90 percent of the show's quilts are now machine stitched.

"I see the benefits of it because it makes it so you get your quilts done faster," Judd says. "What takes me four or five months, they can do in a week with a machine. . . . But you can definitely tell the difference. . . What shows in machine quilting is a steady stream, one stitch right after the other, whereas with the hand quilting there is a definite gap in between. Each one is not identical to the next. But a sign of true workmanship is that it's darn close. Many people cannot believe that this is actually done by hand because it's so uniform. If you got into a micrometer measurement there probably would be a teeny difference between each one, but I don't think you can see anything."

Inspired by a quilting show on public TV, as well as by an Amish cooking program that featured two quilts at the end of each episode, Judd borrowed a quilting book from a library and put together her first quilts in 1990 and 1991.

"I devised my own patterns," she says. "I've never followed anyone else's pattern. I've just kind of designed my own work and went with the flow. The only thing that's very traditional about my quilts is that all of my quilts are hand-quilted. I've never used my sewing machine to actually quilt my quilts. I have used it to sew the little pieces together to make a quilt top, but I've never used it to actually do the quilting, which would be joining the three layers of fabric together."

Judd sold the third quilt she made. Now she does mostly commission work, and also sells through galleries in San Francisco and Scottsdale, Arizona, as well as her own website, which she maintains herself.

"When I first started quilting all of my material was commercially made fabric," she says. ". . . Now, because I've been making so many quilts, I started buying it by the bolt [40 inches wide by 25 yards long] direct from manufacturers because it's a little less expensive and I can get a wider selection than what's locally available. The fabric stores can't carry everything that's available; it's just physically impossible. New fabric comes out every three to six months, and if they were to try to keep up with that they would just go broke."

Judd also hand-dyes fabric for herself and other quilters. Most of her fabric customers are in Europe, where fabric is much more expensive than it is in the United States. Generally three or four quilters order a batch of fabric—24 yards, 24 different, mottled colors—and divide it amongst themselves. The fabric is priced at $24 per yard, which adds up to more than $500 for a bundle. "But you're getting a full bundle, and it was specifically dyed for you," Judd notes. "Because of measurements, no two bundles are identical in color value; they're either a little bit darker or a little bit lighter than the previous one. Humidity affects how that works for me too. If I'm dying in the summer I might get more intense colors than when I'm dying in the middle of winter when the air [indoors] is drier from heat and things like that. So it makes it as though everybody's getting a very unique item when they do order some."

Dying fabric is time-consuming and requires a lot of space. It also involves the use of potentially hazardous chemicals. Because of that, Judd wears a full lab coat, a respirator and gloves when dying fabric.

"It's kind of funny," she says, "because when quilting made its resurgence in the '70s there was very little commercial fabric. Now we have thousands and thousands of options in commercial fabric at quilt shops and that, and people are getting back into wanting hand-dyed fabric because they're colors that are not achieved in the commercial fabric. Commercial fabrics are all pretty much based on the current trend in clothing. And people are now starting to see that there are different colors that you get from the dying process. You get shades that you won't see in the clothing line types of colors."

Sometimes clients find unexpected images in the hand-dyed fabrics. They have reported finding imprints of human faces, hands, leaves, feathers, butterflies, flowers, Indian headdresses, Mardi Gras masks, cave drawings, birds, shoe treads, and other likenesses. "One client," Judd reported on her website, "says that it feels like she is on a treasure hunt each time a new order arrives, and she spends hours going over the pieces looking for surprises in the fabric." Judd is so focused on getting orders sent out when she irons the fabric that she generally does not take time to search for serendipitous images herself.

It takes about 24 hours to hand-dye a piece of fabric. Judd has figured out a way to paint fabric with dye, with free-form painting, which leaves the fabric soft and washable.

Currently, she also is deep into experimenting with "rusting" fabric with rusty architectural ironwork, iron filings, steel wool, copper wire, and other items. The rusting process takes anywhere from 24 to 72 hours. That process originated in Japan in the late 1980s when two artists draped plain fabric over a pile of junkyard scrap and left it there for months. The rusty junk left impressions on the pieces of fabric—and also wore holes in spots because the rusting wasn't controlled. Some quilt artists now are experimenting with the process, devising their own techniques and routines. Judd's technique is to set a piece of architectural ironwork on a table, place fabric over the item, then shake salt onto the fabric and spray the fabric with water every couple of hours. The fabric takes on the ironwork imprint within 24 hours.

"It's all just kind of an experimental process and seeing what materializes out of the whole process," Judd says.

Many potential buyers like the rusted look because it's different. "They also like the hand-dyed fabrics that are not a solid color," Judd adds, "which is kind of what most of my fabrics are—not a solid color. They don't look like something you would buy in a store. A lot of my commission work is actually more of the traditional where there's a lot more piecing in it, but more art-looking quilting in it (too), I guess is the only way to explain it. When you look through my portfolio you will see that a lot of the commission work was more traditional looking, but you can see that the hand-quilting stands out a lot where the hand-quilting is not blending in; it's there as part of the design process."

Most often, someone commissioning a quilt will request a couple of specific elements but not have an entire design concept in mind. "They will say: 'I need to have blue in it, and it needs to be this size, and I want it to be traditional quilt blocks—more traditional.' . . . A lot of these people I hear back from year to year to year. (One) lady sends me a Christmas card every year: 'We still enjoy getting the quilt out, that you made for us, every year.'"

Judd generally likes to have a design come together as she works on a quilt rather than begin with a complete image in mind. With one piece in her ongoing "contaminated water" series, for instance, she used iron filings to add rusting to a piece of fabric that wasn't quite what she wanted it to be. To her eye, the iron filings produced what looked like suspended particles of sand in water. She liked the look, started thinking about water, and used circular stitching to create rings of ripples like those produced by a rock tossed into water.

"They all just kind of come about as I'm doing it," she says. "I don't pre-plan what I'm going to stitch before I get started. It's: sit down and look at it. . . . I just kind of let the fabric and the design that's already there tell me what else it needs."

Judd has participated in exhibits since 2006. Usually fewer than 15 percent of submitted works are admitted into a juried fine arts show. There are cash awards at most of the shows, and entry fees and shipping costs for all. "My art quilts are hanging along(side) an oil painting, an acrylic painting, a couple of sculptures, and things along that line," she says. "I'm really not sending my work out to traditional quilt shows. My stuff is pretty much going to fine art exhibits, which makes it even more of a competition because I'm not always competing against anyone else who happens to be working in fabric but all of the other media." The fine art exhibitions last between 45 and 60 days, whereas most traditional quilt shows are two- or three-day affairs. "If I'm going to spend $40 to ship my quilts they might as well be on exhibit for 45 to 60 days," Judd reasons. "And for myself, I have found that the people that are art collectors are more likely to be at the art centers and gallery shows than they are to be at a quilt show. A lot of quilt shows don't allow purchasing of quilts. So this way I have the opportunity to have my work seen by more serious collectors."

As with wood sculpture, people viewing quilts tend to step closer, which they don't do with oil paintings. Often they reach out a hand to try to touch an exhibited quilt before remembering the "no touching" restriction. As Judd wrote on her website, people "want to feel the texture of the hand stitching, feel the fabric, get closer to the piece. Viewers are naturally drawn to textile art."

When Judd does "dense echo quilting," as in her Scribble Quilt series, there are 168 stitches in each square inch. A 100 by 100 inch quilt with such dense quilting would have 1,680,000 stitches. That is handwork with an emphasis on both hand and work. – *Oct 18, 2011* ☼

Sheer Artistry

Marge Lindemann ... silk artist

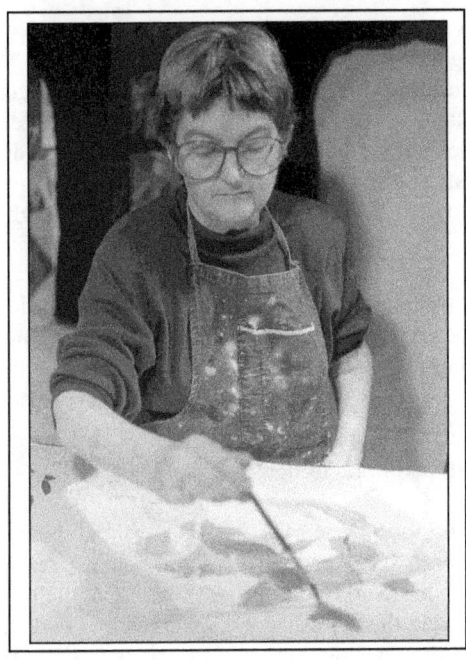

I first interviewed Marge Lindemann November 27, 1992, then a second time July 10, 1995.

Silk. The very word is synonymous with sensuousness, high style and elegance. Apply the art of dyeing to showy silk and the vibrant colors and the smooth, shimmery fabric produce something as eye-catching as a curlicue stairway.

While silk art includes decorative wall hangings, most silk art artists, such as Marge Lindemann, devote most of their time and artistic energy to creating one-of-a-kind scarves, jackets, ties, vests, and other items of clothing.

Silk art clothing is "definitely a luxury item," says Lindemann, a Cumberland, Wisconsin, resident who teaches high school art in Shell Lake and drifted into silk art in the late 1980s. "People who buy this are looking for something classic and long-lasting."

Lindemann's unique 35-inch-square scarves sell for $58 to $68 at several craft galleries and clothing boutiques in northern Wisconsin and the Minneapolis-St. Paul area. More dramatic 45-inch-square ones are in the $75 to $100 range. Hip- or knee-length reversible jackets are priced as high as $350.

"One of the biggest problems is how to price," she says. "Now that I'm in more galleries and I've had a better chance to price-compare things that are on a same par with mine I have a little better idea of what to charge.... I don't price according to the time I put in; I do it according to how successful I think that piece is. If that's a really good piece, and it's something that I think is pretty valuable, then I might put a better price on."

While she "still want(s) to make it a paying business," Lindemann likes the fact she doesn't need to rely on her art as her sole means of financial support. This affords her the luxury of more artistic freedom.

Some of Lindemann's silk art clothing features abstract designs, others of it more traditional floral designs.

"I work back and forth," she says. "If I do abstract things for a while I feel a need to go back and do something more realistic and less abstract. I like that working back and forth. One helps the other. If you do abstract and then go back and do something realistic you can be guaranteed that the realistic thing will be arranged a little better. Your negative space will just turn out a little better because you've been working in nothing but that and your mind is in that mode where you do a better job of balancing your composition and so on."

Given that her husband is an avid gardener who tends several flower beds, Lindemann needs to look no further than her yard for inspiration for her floral patterns. "Flowers are transparent, usually," she points out, "and it was exciting to find that silk was such a good medium to carry that color and sheerness of flowers. So most of the time my stuff is floral. And it's really fun in the summertime, when I really concentrate on this and do a lot of it. I run out and pick whatever one of the 50 or 60 choices I have out there, bring it back in and hold it in my hand and go to town on it. Then I get the very nicest design, when you have the real thing in front of you."

Just as her designs vary, Lindemann's creative process involves a variety of techniques.

"There are all kinds of different ways to get that dye onto the silk, in some kind of a pattern," she says. Lindemann brushes it on, pushes thickened dye through silk screens, applies salt to wet dye to pull the colors into a pattern, and bleeds colors into each other with milk or syrup.

Of the different types of dye available, she prefers a French dye especially made for silk and wool, which she thins with water. "There's a long line of colors, but I basically stick to the basic, primary colors—a couple reds, a couple of greens, and yellow—and everything else comes from that. . . . The real fun is watching what happens when you touch the silk. The dye runs until it hits a resist spot. . . . It's always a matter of finding a resist, and combining that, somehow, with the dye. Most of the time you use this Gutta resist [a gummy substance]. But it can be wax, it can by syrup, it can be milk—it can be anything you can think of that you can put on the silk that will resist the dye. . . . I do anything I can think of that will manipulate the fabric surface. And then when I'm done I do anything I can think of to put those pieces of fabric together to make another design.

Dyed silk is allowed to dry for 24 hours before it is placed in a steamer for 30 minutes to an hour to set the colors. Rinsing then softens the pigmented fabric.

While Lindemann buys hemmed scarf blanks, the pieces she sews together to make jackets, vests, and other garments are cut from large pieces of dyed fabric. "I can dye two-and-a-half yards at a time," she says. "I dye some pieces that I think are going to go together and then hang them in my workroom for weeks at a time until the relationship between the fabric texture and color and overall design becomes clear to me. That is a process of time. All of a sudden I'll know that I want this to go with that, and a piece of this over here, and so on. That's how I work on jackets. They really are a piece of art, as much as any painting or collage or anything else that you create."

Cumberland seamstress Kay Ritchie does most of the sewing for Lindemann. "She's been really fun to work with," Lindemann says. "She doesn't have any kind of a background in art, but she has a good eye for design." Scraps left over from projects are used to decorate the fronts of T-shirts, which are priced at $34 to $38 each. "The T-shirts turned out to be more fun than I thought they would be," Lindemann says. "I kind of turned my nose up at sweatshirts and T-shirts."

Lindemann doesn't pay much attention to sizing when designing a garment, but she does "put a lot of thought into planning something that's going to enhance the human body because, after all, if it is a garment that's its main job."

She generally tries to "make something that will fit a lot of people. More than anything else, the size of the piece of the material that I dye dictates it."

Since "wearing things loosely is certainly a trend" with today's women, she says, "you're better off to always have something that flows and swings and is big. Small women can wear those, but so can bigger women."

Lindemann does a lot of custom work for people too. "They may see something they like, but they want it in a different size or a different color," she says. "If they say, 'I really like that one with the roses on it,' or whatever, I'll try to do something similar. But because I don't use any pattern, ever, I couldn't duplicate if I wanted to, which is good. It keeps me interested, and people are getting a real original."

While she has an art degree from the University of Wisconsin—Stout, Lindemann says she is mainly self-taught as a silk art artist, having learned through trial and error and some workshops. "Once you know how to handle two or three kinds of art materials it pretty well carries over into other stuff," she says.

Silk art, with its flowing nature, most closely resembles watercolor painting. "I really have always admired watercolor," Lindemann says. "That's always been the medium that I wished I had mastered, but I never felt that I had mastered it."

With silk art, she has "stuck to one technique long enough" to develop something she takes pride in. "I tended to look back on pieces [in other mediums] that I had done years ago and flinch," she says. "But I see these [silk art pieces] around—even ones I did three years ago—and think: 'That's pretty nice.'"

☼

A Sewer Of Sails, A Catcher Of Wind

Judy Tepley ... sailmaker

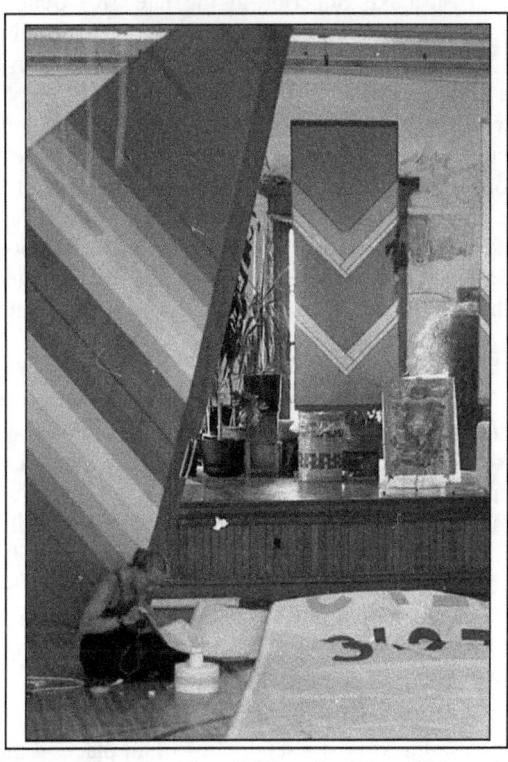

As described by Captain Alan Villiers in *Men, Ships, And The Sea,* Early Man "saw the upturned edges of drifting leaves catch the wind and drive upon the water. He raised leafy boughs for the same effect and contrived sails from matted reeds. . . . Slowly he learned to use skins, mats, and woven cloth for his sails."

Many millenniums after men drifting on crude watercraft held up the first leafy sails for wind-powered propulsion, there lives in Duluth,

MN, a young woman named Judy Tepley who makes and repairs space-age synthetic sails for the sleek, streamlined sailboats that cruise the western end of Lake Superior. She is the only sailmaker in the Twin Ports, and for some distance around.

"There's a woman who still does some small repair in Bayfield," Tepley reports. "There were two sailmakers there up until this past season, but they are no longer in business."

According to Canal Park Marine Museum Director Patrick Labadie, "This has never been much of a port for sailing craft." The first sailing ships appeared on Lake Superior in the late 18th Century. Those belonged to the North West Company, the large fur-trading concern. "Details are really obscure," Labadie says, but there is evidence that two or three small schooners, fifty to sixty feet long, may have been built on Lake Superior in 1796 or 1797. The first sailing ship known to have been built on Lake Superior, however, was a vessel called the *Recovery*, constructed at the North West Company base at Grand Portage in 1802. Only fifteen to twenty sailing ships have ever been built in and around Duluth-Superior. Historical information about previous Twin Ports sailmakers is sketchy too, though it can be stated with certainty that there have not been many, what with the relatively small number of boats to service.

Despite the lack of competition, Tepley, a Twin Cities native who moved to Duluth to get out of life's fast lane, cannot rely on sail work as her sole source of income. She presently also weatherizes houses for the Community Action Program. That means she essentially has two fulltime jobs during the mid-May to mid-September sailing season, since she often works on sails from the time she returns home in the afternoon until midnight or later, as well as on weekends. She also is a fabric artist, and has started making items such as banners out of sailcloth. That might be a way to supplement her sailmaking/sail repair income while working in the same medium year round.

Tepley learned sailmaking at a school in—of all places—Indiana. The couple that runs the school fled Los Angeles for a more tranquil environment. For four years previous to her sailmaking studies she was a well-paid porter, steward, and second cook on Great Lakes ore boats, which allowed her to sock away a nice nestegg. Rather than buy a new car or other material objects, she decided to buy herself a new skill.

She took the first part of the sailmaking course by correspondence to sort of test the water rather than dive headfirst into an unfamiliar area.

She quickly discovered that sailmaking combined many skills she already possessed in mathematics, design, fabric art, and architectural and mechanical drawing. She then traveled to the school, which is located in a converted barn loft, and studied intensively for six weeks. She was the only student there at the time. "I got lots of individualized training, which was just wonderful," she says. ". . . I'd been working with cloth and doing large artwork out of canvas and fabric for a very long time, so I was used to working large. . . . In the course of that six weeks I did almost a full set of sails for a boat called a Tiana 42, which is a really large boat. All the sails on that boat are really big, so it was a real good experience for me to actually have to handle and design larger sails, as well as some smaller ones that were projects that I brought with me for boats for people here in town. . . . So far it has proved to have been a really good decision. I'm not making lots and lots of money at it, but I really enjoy it. I enjoy doing sail work, along with my art work, more than any other things that I've done."

Tepley blends a Bohemian casualness and capriciousness (six years of college left her nowhere near a degree, she changed majors so often) with a dedication to hard, honest work that would put a Puritan to shame. She operates her three-year-old Wind Catcher Sails business out of a small second floor gym of an old school building—the Irving School—in West Duluth.

A sail is an airfoil, just as airplane wings, hang glider wings and kites are airfoils. It is cut in a certain way to allow for maximum sailing performance, depending on how the boat for which it is designed will be used.

"Usually when a boat is designed, a sail plan is also designed with it, so that there's an adequate amount of square feet," Tepley explains. "And then the sail shape, or the actual physical shape of the sail itself, is left to the sailmaker. The sailmaker, with assistance from the boat owners—kind of with a list of needs that they have, and ways in which they use the boat—comes up with a sail plan. There are certain formulas for designing the airfoil that the sail is." On the water, a boat's sails are "trimmed" for performance shaping. "You do that by how tight you pull the different sides of the sail, and where you put tension on," Tepley says. "All those adjustments that you make once you're on the water change the shape of that airfoil so that it meets the needs of the boat, whether the boat is sailing into the wind or the boat is going downwind. You need to change the shape of the sail in order for it to be the most efficient. . . . That's kind of the test of a good sailor, is working with your boat enough, and really knowing how to read the wind and look at the shape of your sails in order to make the boat do what you want it to do."

Good sailors are made, not born. Sailing techniques must be learned by on-the-water experience, in all types of conditions.

The same sort of practical experience is required to become a good sailmaker as well. "You go to sailmaker's school and learn what you need to know about designing airfoils," Tepley says, "and then you have to take that information back with you, and then sail enough and be able to talk to people enough about what their needs are to put both those areas together. . . . I feel like I know a lot about designing sails, but I don't know very much about sailing in wind conditions and trimming, so I need a lot more experience to be a better sailmaker. I need to sail more and more, and see sails get trimmed, and do that myself, and understand how to get the boat to do what it needs to do no matter where the wind is. And it takes going out on the water and exposing myself to that over and over again, and making decisions about it. . . . Sailing is recreation, and it's just really a delight, and at the same time I have to look at it kind of as work too because I do need to learn, and that's a real pleasurable way to get more education."

Tepley has done most of her sailing on a catamaran, which is a twin-hulled boat. She has been sailing on larger boats in keel club races more recently.

While the lure of sailing is still basically a primal instinct for adventure, and Man's desire to test himself against the forces of Nature, sailboats and sails have entered a space-age era the famous explorers of centuries past never could have imagined. According to the *Encyclopedia International*, "Since 1950 Dacron has almost entirely supplanted natural fibers in sails. Properly woven and treated, Dacron cloth has practically no drawbacks. It has negligible stretch, an imperviousness to sunlight, low water absorption, and strength." Nylon is another favorite material for modern sails.

"Traditionally," Tepley says, "sails were done out of cotton canvas, or Egyptian cotton, or flax cloth. And one of the things that happened with those original cloths is that they had a lot of their own stretch, so you didn't have to actually build an airfoil. Most natural fiber sails were built very flat, and then when they were sailed on the boat the wind stretched that cloth into the airfoil that was needed. But with the modern cloths, especially the Dacrons, the cloth is made in such a way that the weave is very tight no matter what the weight of the cloth, and then there's a resin that's coated on both sides, and it's kind of pressed through rollers, so the cloth is very stiff; it almost feels paper-like. The reason they're built that way is because it cuts down on kind of a diagonal stretch. And there's a way to calculate how much stretch there will be. So in designing sails out of Dacron, in order to build an airfoil into that shape you actually cut the panel to a certain shape and then bring those seams together, and then it makes an airfoil that is always there. The Dacron is very dimensionally stable. It's pretty tear-resistant. It's not as much subject to mildew. In all natural fiber sails mildew is really a problem."

Many racing yachts now use Kevlar- and Mylar-laminated sails that are even more lightweight than Dacron sails—and considerably more expensive.

Most boat owners still want traditional white sails, but now and then Tepley manages to persuade a customer to add some color, which adds another element of challenge and excitement to the designing.

"The striped sailcloth is really exciting to work with," she says. "That's a really small sail, but there's kind of a variety of shapes the sail itself can take, depending on the skill of the person on the board, depending on their height and weight. The board changes for their height and weight, and the sail needs change for their height and weight too. There are kind of regular everyday sails for a sailboard, and then there are ones that are much smaller in square feet for bigger winds so that you're still able to control the board. Design features change on those too."

Three-fourths of Tepley's work is sail repair. While she finds enough satisfaction in that to always do her conscientious best, it does not compare to the pleasure and fulfillment of the creative process of designing a new sail.

Sails need repair for a variety of reasons. They chaff against the mast or some other part of the boat, causing abrasion. Ultraviolet sunrays weaken the thread where the three-foot-wide panels of cloth are stitched together. Cigarettes and battery acid burn holes in them. People rip holes in them by stepping on them. Rips also occur when a sail catches on something while being pulled down hurriedly. "Some of them are real nuisance things and some of them are just wear," Tepley says. ". . . What ages a sail more than anything is its exposure to ultraviolet light. Of all the things that happen to sails, that's what's the hardest on them."

Tepley uses thread made of Dacron, which is resistant to ultraviolet light and less stretchy than other thread. That is important "because the cloth is made so that stretch is controlled. It's really important to also use a thread where the stretch is controlled. . . . The thread actually has a core of polyester fiber, and then the Dacron thread is spirally wound around it, so it's real strong. And it comes in a variety of weights because for every different weight of sailcloth you need an appropriate weight of thread. . . . If you undersize your thread, the wind is so powerful that it just splits a seam right open."

Tepley charges $20 per hour for repair work. A lot of repairs take only 15 to 30 minutes, so she needs to do many to make money at it.

For a new sail, she uses a calculator and mathematical formulas to estimate how many square feet of sailcloth she will need. That gives her a good idea of how many hours of labor will be involved, and the amount of hardware required.

While she cannot yet—and perhaps never will be able to—rely on her sail business for all of her income, the business has grown gradually, with many repeat customers supplying her with steady work during the summertime.

"It's increasing all the time," she says. "What I've found is that it's really a word-of-mouth business. I can't find anyone who's responded to very much of the advertising I've done. So business from the Duluth Keel Club and people who keep their boats at Barker's Island, and some who work from up the North Shore too, all has come pretty much from word-of-mouth."

In other words, it is taking a while for sailors to get wind of her.

- *July 25, 1984*

☼

Subterranean Simplicity

Don Karsky ... weaver

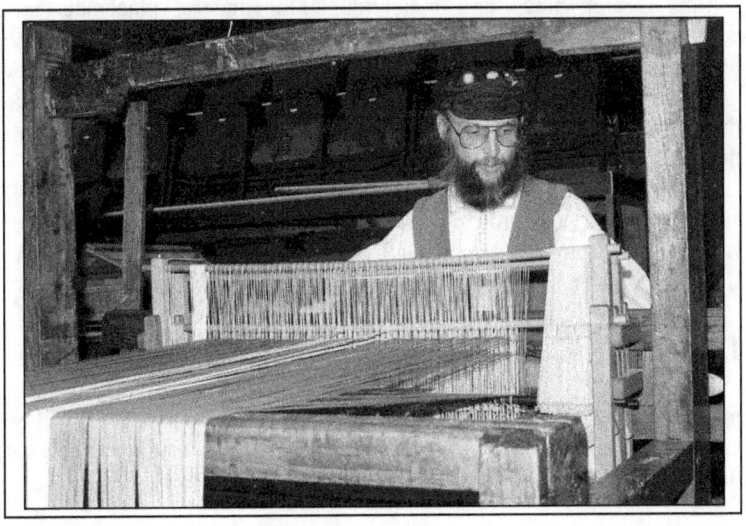

Interviews from November 6, 1989...May 21, 1993...June 11, 1993...and February 22, 1995 went into this profile.

Enter Don and Julie Karsky's driveway, a few miles north of St. Croix Falls, Wisconsin, and the first thing you notice is a basement garage squeezed between two earthen banks. So far things appear fairly normal. You sense something unusual, though. Then it occurs to you: Where's the rest of the house? All that is visible is a small semi-circular structure above and behind the garage entrance, with some sort of white frame structure on top of it. You walk up some free-form concrete steps to the left of the garage and find yourself on a carpet of crushed limestone on the flat garage roof. Eight 10-inch-diameter white plastic pipes poke through the garage roof, most curiously. There is a small, rough wooden door in front of you that is somewhat remindful of a cave entrance, for it leads into another flat-topped hill.

Welcome to one of Wisconsin's most unusual houses—a two-story earth-sheltered house built of silo blocks, concrete and rebar.

Inside, you likely will find Don weaving at a loom and Julie washing lengths of fabric Don has woven—to pre-shrink it—at a hand-operated washing machine.

For the past five years this forty-something couple has been entirely self-supporting, operating a cottage industry that involves weaving and selling foreign flags and matching table runners, placemats and coasters. Call their lifestyle subterranean simplicity. Their unique house has no telephone, furnace, TV set, or piped-in electricity. They grow much of their own food in a moated circular garden, and make their own wine, beer and root beer. Their refrigerator is a four-foot-deep hole in a kitchen wall, 17 feet below ground level.

Julie invented a word to help define their simplified existence: LaQuistada. It means, according to Julie, "the being you are from the lifestyle you live."

Don and Julie made a deliberate choice about the lifestyle they wanted to lead. "Lead" is the key word in that sentence, for when they decided to simplify their home environment they weren't trying to follow anyone else's lifestyle, but rather lead the lifestyle they felt was best for them.

Before building their self-designed underground, or earth-sheltered, house they lived in a self-built A-frame house in Almelund, MN, that had all the modern conveniences most American homes have.

"There was just some drive that told us that wasn't us," Julie says. "We needed to do something more simple—cut our own wood and bake our own bread and light our own lamps. It was the mid-1970s and the price of fuel oil, gas, and everything skyrocketed. That was one of the major reasons for us."

Don and Julie are not escapists. They do not want to be completely separate from the rest of the world. They do, however, want to have as much control as possible over their own lives so that they have more choices of their own degree of community involvement.

"We're just as dependent [on the outside world]; we're just dependent on different things," Don says. "If people stop buying our stuff it's all over. That's total dependency, one way or another. But I wouldn't work this hard for someone else, even though I would probably make more money if I worked this hard for someone else."

Don does nearly all of the weaving, specializing in the flag designs of the five Scandinavian countries—Norway, Sweden, Finland, Denmark and Iceland. Norwegian items are far and away the best sellers. The flags of Poland, Germany, France, Italy and Ireland account for most remaining sales. It is not possible to weave the American flag and most other national flags. "It can't be woven," Don explains to the many people who ask about buying a woven United States flag.

Julie sews the ends of the flag-patterned items, pre-shrinks the all-cotton fabric by washing and drying it, irons on labels, and does the pricing. They both load goods into their two vans and sell their hand-crafted wares at more than 30 arts-and-crafts shows each year in Wisconsin, Minnesota, Iowa, North Dakota, and South Dakota. They also stage an annual five-weekend holiday home show.

Before weaving became their sole source of income, Don was a drummer with a string of bands for 22 years, playing everything from hard rock to polka. Julie was everything from an airline attendant (she quit after three weeks because she couldn't stand living in New York City) to a cocktail waitress. For three or four years, when weaving provided a part-time income, they scraped and painted a lot of houses to make ends meet.

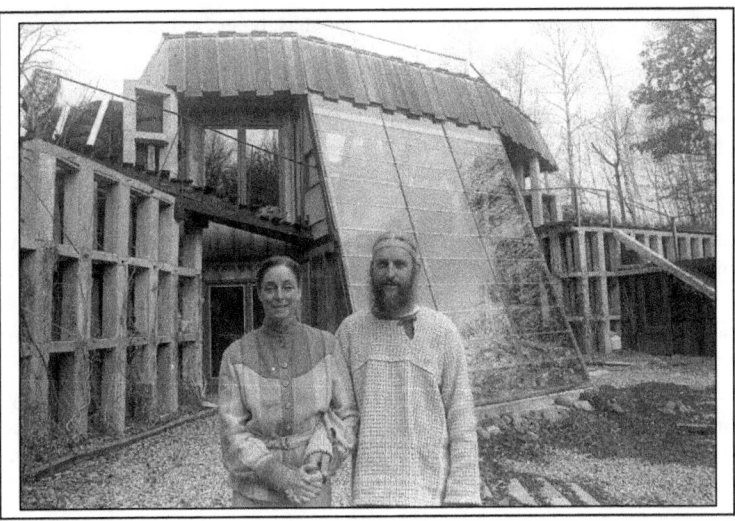

Anyone witnessing Don's swift, assured movements at a loom would be surprised to learn he has no technical training. Except for picking the brains of other weavers he chanced to meet, he is self-taught.

He owned a loom for more than 10 years before he began weaving, having bought a boxed circa 1850 antique loom at an auction for $2.50 in 1972. When he first pieced together the parts of it in about 1983 he had never even seen a loom set up. Wear marks and common sense guided him in the assembly. Within a year he was building small "lap" looms and weaving scarves, shawls, belts, and wall hangings to sell. In 1988 a friend of Swedish heritage asked him to weave her a yellow and blue scarf, yellow and blue being the colors of the Swedish flag. With a lot of yellow and blue string left over from that project, Julie suggested to Don that he weave the Swedish flag to display at a show. "Then we had to please the Norwegians and the Danes and the Finns," Julie says. Now Don's output is nearly all flags and flag-patterned items; he does some beige and brown "Earth tones" and a red, white and green Christmas pattern.

"As we got to know the business better and things started selling," Don says, "the more we could refine it and get it down to a point where we could style an item that nobody else is doing—a flag. There are a lot of weavers, but no one was weaving flags, flag placemats and runners. So we narrowed ourselves right down to where nobody else was doing anything—and just like people told us, it took us five years to learn it."

Their cottage industry, Karsky's Kraft, has been "a banner business" ever since.

There are 13 looms active in the operation, including the original antique loom and a replica of that. There are three different loom sizes for three sizes of fabric. "What we end up doing is building a loom to fit the job that we're going to do," Don explains. Commercial looms on the market are more complicated than Don needs, so he makes his own looms to suit his own needs.

Whereas he used to design patterns of material, Don now designs more productive weaving methods and loom set-ups so that less effort is required to turn out the same quantity of goods, at the same quality. While his inventions would be too complicated to try to explain, suffice it to say that the word clever—or "klever"—comes immediately to mind.

That same cleverness is in evidence nearly everywhere you look in their house, which is heated by a wood-burning stove and the sun (a glass-walled south side lets in a flood of sunlight). There are tables and chairs made from split burls and hollow tree trunks. Shelves made of thin strips of wood glued together follow the curvature of the walls. A car radio looks almost like a built-in appliance.

The 1,600-square-foot [or perhaps that should be round feet] house consists of four circular sections on each floor. The foot-thick concrete roof of the upper level is covered with four feet of dirt, black plastic, and crushed limestone. A six-foot-diameter skylight illuminates one section. There also are six 10-inch-diameter skylights, with the two in the bathroom vented. Electrical generators in the attached garage are used to pump up water pressure and provide juice for power tools. Low-wattage direct-current overhead lights provide nighttime illumination, but not enough for reading or weaving.

The building was so experimental when it was constructed that advice Don and Julie received from people they considered construction experts proved to lead them into problems. "We accepted advice to be true, and it turned out no one knew what they were doing," Don says, "so the ventilation and things like that are not as well done as they should be in this house. We get all the ventilation we need from above-ground, but that carries humidity in the summer, where if we brought our ventilation in below-ground we could cool and dehumidify the air using the cool of the earth, and just the principle of hot air rises."

"It's mostly like a basement in most homes, if you treat it as that," Julie says. "If you work with Momma Nature and what you have available inside you can work a balance."

"The upper floor is always like a regular house, I would say," Don continues. "We never get too much humidity upstairs, though. . . the upstairs is still four feet underground."

Don and Julie designed the shape of the rooms, the number of windows, layout angles, and other details, and had an engineer determine the rebar bone structure, concrete thickness, and other structural needs.

"The walls being silo block, all the walls are round, so there doesn't have to be reinforcement rod in the walls proper," Julie says. "That's just in-place, tongue-in-groove silo block. But the floors—the bottom floor and the middle floor—and the roof all had to be poured in place, so that, of course, took a lot of rebar, to reinforce the concrete for the two floating concrete slabs."

Don and Julie reasoned a circular underground structure would be better able to withstand natural pressure.

"The study of building underground and trying to save energy led to other ways of saving energy that were much more conventionally accepted," Don points out. Those things included super-insulated houses, better-insulated windows, thicker walls, and greater popularity for heat pumps. "You weren't underground, but you were saving just as much energy by investing in those devices as you would be by digging a great big hole and burying the thing. . . . In that sense, people don't have to change their lifestyle at all. It isn't a big lifestyle change to be underground, but you can't just build on."

They selected the building site because a hill there "was just perfect for digging to make a house in it facing south into the woods," Don notes.

Consignment sales have never worked for Don and Julie. What does generate sales is demonstrating their craft at shows, which seems to authenticate the products for people. They take along a loom to every show, and generally dress in generic Scandinavian costumes to further attract attention. In fact, costumes are virtually required at some Scandinavian festivals.

"I love the demonstration," Don says, noting there is a new audience every five minutes. "The demonstration of it, I think, is the real selling point. It's a quality item, but if we didn't demonstrate, if we hung a quality item in a store, it doesn't sell."

While their unique house is unlike any cottage described in any Grimms fairy tale, in a sense there is something of a fairy tale quality to their life because the self-contained cottage industry they have created allows Don and Julie a freedom most people only dream about, and a blissful togetherness that makes "and they lived happily ever after" seem like an appropriate ending.

☼

A Lens Of Place

Bob Olsgard ... photographer

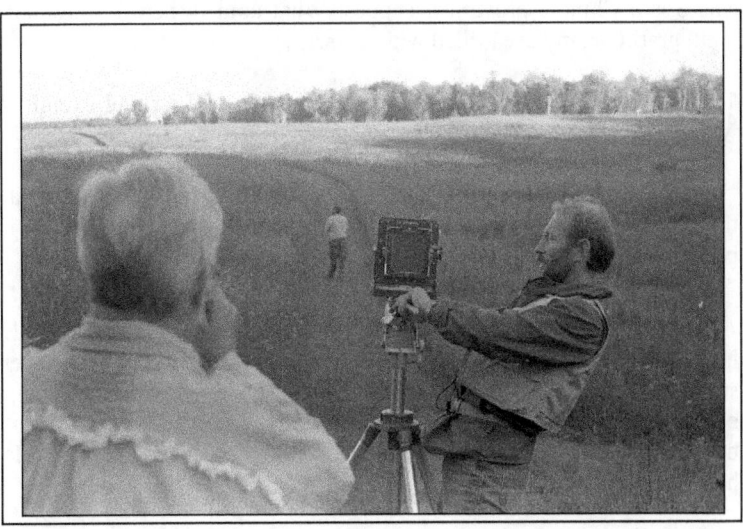

"A lot of times," Bob Olsgard says, "you will take a picture that really is striking and you don't know why. You usually do know how. But if you knew why you could probably make another one more easily."

Olsgard, a commercial photographer who lives in the Sarona, Wisconsin, area, has developed a workshop called "A Sense of Place" to try to help people understand more about the why of photography, particularly nature photography. Noting that there are a lot of excellent books about the technical and compositional aspects of photography, Olsgard says: "I'm trying to hone in on what they don't tell you in the books, and how to get into that part of it. It's more of a philosophical, artistic approach—more of the why and less of the how."

While Olsgard developed—is developing—the program for gifted and talented high school students, his first opportunity to present the program came at a recent week-long "Nature And The Arts" session at the Hunt Hill Audubon Sanctuary, attended mainly by adults.

"The reason I call this 'A Sense of Place,'" he told those at the Hunt Hill session, "is that usually—especially when you've made a picture when you've gone to some place, or even here—you have this wonderful feeling of this place, a sense that there's something unique happening here, and it's happening in your senses. And how on earth do you get three dimensions, quad sound, and all the smells and touches and feelings that happen out there into a picture? It's all important. Maybe we can work with some things and get a little closer to that."

There is a Chinese proverb that goes: What abideth here I know not. With gratitude, my eyes filled with tears.

The Sense of Place program combines viewing and writing exercises with actual picture taking to try to achieve Olsgard's elusive goal.

"It combines a lot of sessions that I've done as parts of other courses at the advanced level, but I've never tried to incorporate writing into it before," he says.

Although Olsgard has lived only five miles from Hunt Hill since 1981, he didn't know of the facility's existence until he read a newspaper story about the National Audubon Society suspending its ecology camp operation there in 1986. "It was just a dumb oversight on my part because they put it here for the same reason I moved here," he says. He has high praise for Hunt Hill as a natural and spiritual preserve.

"A friend of mine was volunteering over here, and I came over to help paint the dormitory one day," Olsgard says. "I got talking to the art coordinator, Judie Balderson, and I never did get around to painting that day at all. We just talked for a couple of hours about what I wanted to do with the Sense of Place workshop. She said, 'We have to have you here, at least for our Nature And The Arts week.'"

Olsgard, who has a studio next to his house, specializes in photographing objects rather than people. "What I do for money is commercial photography," he says. "It's magazine ads, newspaper ads, brochures, catalogs. In my spare time I can make the pictures that I want to make."

At the moment, his major personal project is a photographic study of the Lake Superior watershed. He has traveled throughout northern Wisconsin and northeastern Minnesota, as well as to Michigan's Upper

Peninsula and Canada, to capture images for what he hopes will turn out to be a book. He plans to start looking for a publisher this winter.

Don't expect a standard coffee table book full of pretty pictures, though. For one thing, Olsgard prefers black and white film to color film. "I just don't feel that I can get as close to what I was after as I can in black and white," he says. Secondly, he doesn't hold to the popular belief that nature is something perfect and distant, something separate from humankind.

"I love being out among the trees and the flowers and all that, but we use nature so strangely, just as an idea," he says. "We use it as kind of a way of separating ourselves from the trees and the flowers and the lakes, and we're really not separate. As long as we have the idea of nature as something separate then we don't have to look at the landfill in Sarona and say, 'Well, how does that fit in with nature?' It ought to. It can. I think it goes back to the 18th Century. We had the philosophers who (spoke of) the Noble Savage. They had this vision of nature as something perfect and distant, and then they were imperfect and full of the worldly wants which make Man an imperfect being."

He says that if a label must be put on his Lake Superior watershed project something such as "social ecology" or "visual ecology" comes closest to what he is trying to accomplish. Far from being pristine, the watershed area is "a place where you've had mining and logging and a lot of human activity for well over a century, maybe two centuries." Even before that, he points out, Native Americans were mining copper.

"I'm real excited about it," he says. "I'm not sure that anyone has ever approached it in quite the way I have. . . . They're real compelling images; it's just that the approach is ecology."

Olsgard, who taught photography courses at Inver Hills Community College, in the Twin Cities area, for five years, will present his Sense of Place program at Minong High School next spring, as an artist in residence. He is not working through the Wisconsin Art Board's artist in residence program, though. "I've kind of shied away from that because of the administrative difficulty," he says. ". . . I think it's neat to be able to expose people to different ideas through the medium of photography, and through writing. You're exposing people to your way of looking at the world. Somehow I haven't been able to get that to work with the state Arts Board yet. I wouldn't rule that out. But you have a stack of forms that would scare an Internal Revenue agent, and it's not like they pay you that well." - *July 30, 1990* ☼

Guided By The Light

Dianne Bryant ... photographer

The light that permeates the photograph is as bright and rich as butter. What is most remarkable about Dianne Bryant's "Golden Pond" photo is that the golden glow is as natural as nitrogen. "People will not believe that's not a filter," says Bryant, a St. Croix Falls, Wisconsin, nurse who has made photography a part-time business. "But it is natural light—a golden light."

The "Golden Pond" photo is one of Bryant's best achievements as a light chaser, which is a major element in her quest to capture images of nature and the landscape at their magical and even mystical best. She captured the image at sunset in central Minnesota. "I really became a student of sunsets and sunrises," she says. "It's really fun to study the cloud formations and the environmental elements that really give a sense of if it's going to be a good sunset or sunrise. On this particular evening I was driving up by Itasca State Park and it was raining, and I could see the sky. It was like you were looking through a foggy glass. And it started turning more golden, and I knew it was going to be just an exceptional sunset, and I knew I wanted it over water, so I drove like a maniac to try to find a body of water within a mile or two. I came to a sign that said 'Landing,' so I turned my vehicle in real quick, barreled down the road, saw the neat composition with the trees, and got off three frames and it was gone. That's how quick it happens. Timing is everything, especially with your light."

Light, she says, "will make or break a photograph. . . . With photography you have to be real persistent and go back until you get the right light." One award-winning shot called "Morning Tranquility" required a visit to the same boat landing on three mornings before the right elements—light, fog and other factors—fell into aesthetic place. "The third morning back I knew I had what I wanted—my mental vision of the surreal river effect that I wanted to portray. . . . I knew I had the right light, the right mist and everything—the right elements to make a really great photo."

Bryant has been a photography buff since about sixth grade, when she won an inexpensive Kodak camera in a school contest. "My brother was overseas in the service at the time," she says, "and said he could get me a really nice camera really reasonable. So then I started shooting 35-millimeter when I was in high school, I think. I just loved getting out and shooting. I'm basically self-taught. I do a lot of reading in magazines and books. In the last 10 years I've probably taken a half-dozen different one-day seminars to learn more of the technical aspects. But I don't have any formal training. I just love going out. It puts me in a different world."

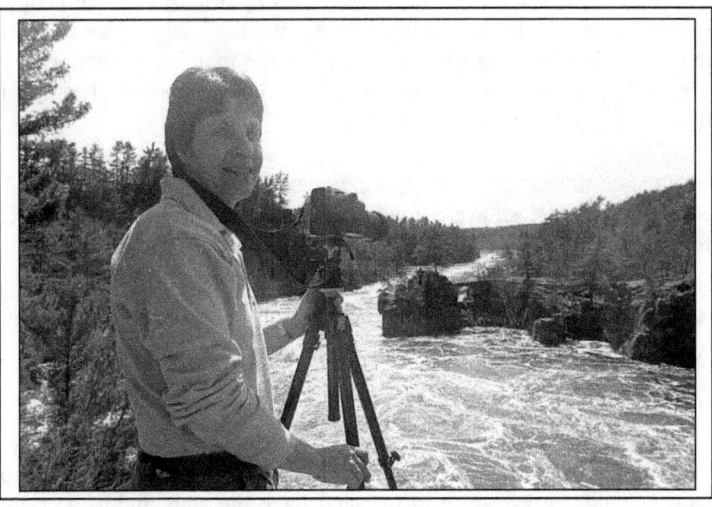

While she enjoys traveling to take nature and landscape photos, her favorite places to photograph are the St. Croix River and its environs, including Interstate State Park. "I spend a lot of time in the park with my camera, in all different seasons," she says. "It provides a respite for me." A 20 by 30 inch print of her signature "Morning Tranquility" photo is on display at the Polk County Information Center in St. Croix Falls.

Bryant sells photocards and enlargements of her color photos and does custom matting and framing under the banner of Photographic Journeys, a moonlighting business she started two years ago. The Journeys part of the name has a double meaning; it means both physical travel and a sort of spiritual travel.

"When I'm out with my camera I get totally absorbed in nature," she says. "I've always been an outdoor person. I was the tomboy of the neighborhood growing up, and I've always been outdoors with my brothers. I just love nature. I'm very inspired by nature, and through my photography I feel I can really share that with people—the beauty of nature, the magnificence. It's just real calming to me. That's how I came up with Journeys—in travels, and transcending me into a different realm. . . . I enjoy traveling back roads and scoping out different spots that I can go back to. When everything comes together, that's when you end up with a really nice photograph. . . . It's a study of nature, too, basically is what it is. It's a combination of studying nature, being in tune with the climatic factors, and patience. . . . My nature photography enables me to really share with everybody the beauty that I see, and I guess that's why I really am excited that people enjoy my photography and really like my work. I don't plan on ever being a millionaire or anything, but it's nice that I can support my hobby selling some of my prints, and by really sharing the beauty of nature with people through my photography."

Many of her floral cards are quite popular. "I love my wildflowers," she says. "I actually have a four-year degree in horticulture science, before my nursing degree."

Bryant attempts to create works of art with her camera, a Canon Elan II with a versatile Tamron 28-300 mm lens.

"I don't just go and take snapshots," she says. "I like to compose. Like the shot with this tree down the river. . . It took me three trips to get what I wanted. But I had this mental image of what I wanted to portray. I like to do nature justice and have the right light, the right composition, to really make an exceptional photo, not just a picture. . . . I don't use filters, basically. I will use a polarizer in the fall for the fall colors. But I don't like to distort nature. I want to use the [natural] special lighting that's out there."

Patience and persistence are two of a good photographer's most important qualities. After spotting one place near Dresser she wanted to photograph at sunset, she waited several weeks "for the right elements to come together." On New Year's Day evening, she looked out a window and thought: "Tonight's the night." She collected her camera gear, jumped in her van, and buzzed down to the site. "Sure enough, I got what I wanted," she says.

Bryant has been sea kayaking, mostly on Lake Superior's south side, for six years. "I love water. I love paddling. So it just puts me in really neat places to photograph. . . . I've gotten some nice shots out of my kayak, in quiet areas, of wildlife."

The first print she sold, around 1994, was a shot of a sunrise over Lake Superior.

"I basically started doing it [photography] out of my own enjoyment," she says, "and then when people wanted to purchase my photos I thought: *Gee, this is really neat.* It's basically a hobby of love. . . . I sell a lot of eight-by-tens, matted into 11 by 14s. And then a fair number of 11 by 14s [matted] into 16 by 20s. It's whatever the customer wants. I can go up to 20 by 30 is my biggest. People wanting to buy my work just automatically got me into the framing and matting business because they wanted a finished product. And I've always enjoyed working with my hands. My brothers and I would spend hours in my dad's workshop building birdhouses and stuff. I buy oak by the thousand-foot run, and make all my own frames, and do all the matting. It's really relaxing for me to be doing matting and framing in the evening. It really enhances the pictures, and it's really allowed me to market my work a lot better because people want the finished product. So it's created a small business for me, which I really enjoy doing."

Bryant spends 15 to 20 hours a week on her Photographic Journeys business. She also exhibits and sells at summer art shows.

Currently, a Stillwater, MN, lab processes her photos. "You need a decent lab," she says, "a custom lab so that things aren't batch-printed, so that they're going to look at each print and print for the saturation or contrast that there should be."

One of Bryant's photos was included in a *Minnesota Weather Guide* calendar (another is now in the final selection process), a few of her St. Croix River photos were published in a national magazine called *Rivers*, two of her photos were included in an annual international "best of" photography book, and she does some work for tourism brochures a local publisher puts together.

"Nature photography is a real competitive business," she says. "The key is marketing. You have to really have the time to market your work. . . . I've got to get out and do some marketing. It's a time element. But you can only sell your work if you spend some time marketing. That time element is one reason why Bryant would like Photographic Journeys to be a fulltime business eventually. "It's where my heart is," she says. "It's so inspiring and so rewarding for me."

- April 27, 2001   ☼

Blind Intention

Bill Kinney ... wildlife photographer

For someone who "didn't know anything about photography" five years ago and sold his first photo barely a year ago, Bill Kinney is doing quite well, thank you. Five of his big-game animal photographs have appeared on the covers of outdoor magazines and he is being published enough that he recently quit his carpentry job to devote all of his time to making a living as a wildlife photographer.

Kinney, a bearded, curly haired 27-year-old River Falls, Wisconsin, resident, has had more than 30 photos published in magazines since his first published photo, of a small boy fishing, appeared in the March 1987 issue of *Wisconsin Trails* magazine. *Outdoor Life, Oregon Fins & Feathers,* the *1988 Sportsman Deer Yearbook,* and *Archery World* have used his photos on their covers. In fact, he was on the cover of *Archery World* two consecutive issues. Many of his other published photos have appeared as full-page photos, used to illustrate articles written by other people.

" It was kind of fun, because probably the first 10 times I got published they were all full-page pictures before I ever had a smaller one published," Kinney says.

Kinney has been serious about wildlife photography for less than two years. He learned the basics about photography and photographic equipment by managing a River Falls photo shop for three years after graduating from the University of Wisconsin—River Falls in 1983. In August of 1986 he quit his job at the photo shop, bought a 300 mm 2.8f lens and 100 rolls of film, and drove out West to spend four months photographing animals in the Rocky Mountains.

"When I was out West I learned how to take wildlife pictures," he says, "because I did it for four months. All I did was fished and took pictures of wildlife. I shot 260 rolls of film out there and maybe a total of 30 rolls were good enough to actually send in [to magazines]."

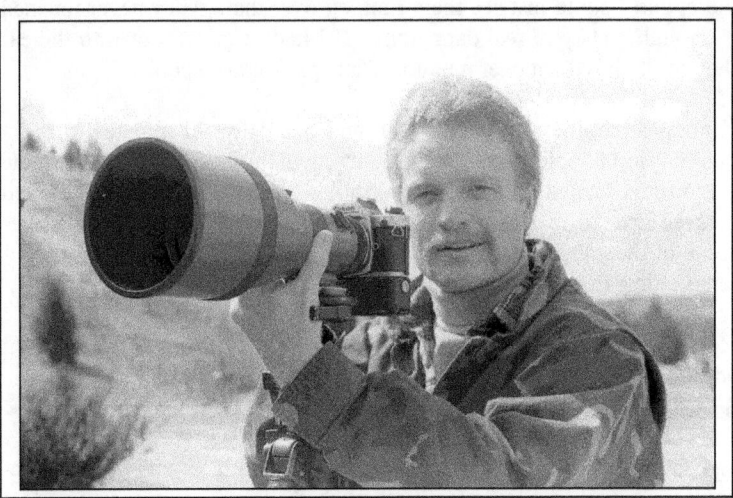

Kinney had taken many photographs of deer before then, but with a 5.6f lens with which he could not use fast shutter speeds most of the time. Most of those shots came out blurry, and thus unsalable, so he tossed them out after returning from his Rocky Mountains trek, which took him from Jackson Hole, Wyoming, at the south side of Yellowstone National Park, to Glacier National Park.

Out West, he photographed mule deer, elk, bears, big horn sheep, coyotes, and other animals. Once, when he was imitating the call of a bull elk to try to draw elk close to him, a bull elk charged and chased him up a tree. "That was kind of exciting," he says. "It came up to the tree and rubbed the tree for a while."

He made sure he was always near a tree when photographing potentially dangerous animals, if possible. Occasionally he found himself in a dangerous situation unexpectedly, though, as he relates about one precarious predicament: "I was up in the Lamar Valley [of Yellowstone National Park]. I was on a hillside photographing some mule deer, and there was a high bridge going across the Yellowstone River, and I heard a thundering noise, and I couldn't figure out what it was because it was the dead of winter, in December, and it was really cold out—about zero degrees. I looked, and here were about 30 buffalo running across that bridge. I was parked probably a hundred yards down the hill from where I was actually standing photographing. By the time I turned around they were so close that there was nothing I could do. I just ran for the car and left my camera sitting there. All 30 of them ran right by it, less than 10 feet away. I had my big lens on there, and I could just see them running over that. They never touched it, though. They're real dangerous. If I hadn't gotten down to the car they might have run over me too. That was kind of spooky."

Kinney sometimes arose at 3 a.m. and hiked for 90 minutes to be in position to take pictures of animals at dawn. While he uses a portable camouflage canvas blind with portholes, out West he usually found natural cover in which to hide. In Yellowstone Park and other places some of the animals were so accustomed to people that it was no problem getting close enough to them for his purposes.

He generally carries two Nikon camera bodies with him in the field. In addition to his 300mm lens, he also makes a lot of use of an 80-200mm 2.8f zoom lens. Converters increase the power of his lenses.

His favorite film is Fujichrome 50. He does black-and-white photography as well, but not nearly as much as color. "You can sell five times as many black-and-whites as you can color," he says, "but you get into a nice scene and you see all that good color there and you think, 'Well, I could get a cover photo out of that.' You hate to turn down a cover photo [possibility] to shoot some black-and-white. There are people who shoot a lot of black-and-white and they make good money just shooting that." Payment is higher for color photos, though, of course. A cover photo can bring as much as $1,500. Kinney received $800 for his *Outdoor Life* cover.

He always uses a tripod to steady his camera. A motor drive allows him to snap off a series of pictures quickly.

He photographed some ducks and geese last spring, but has concentrated on big-game animals so far. "To do birds, I should have at least a 400mm 2.8 lens," he says. "I'm going to set up and do some drumming grouse this spring. I've got a good spot picked out for that. And then I'm going to work on pheasants and turkeys too. I'd like to get some good cardinal shots and that, but I can't sell them."

Kinney uses a shotgun approach in marketing his material to magazines. After querying a magazine to find out if it is interested in seeing some of his photos, he sends scores of slides there if he receives a green light. He sent out more than 3,000 slides this winter and spring, including 1,700 shots of whitetail deer he took last fall. "You have to hit each magazine with a bunch of stuff and let them decide what they want out of there, because there are so many people doing it," Kinney says. "It's really super-competitive."

Some magazines keep a few slides in their files for possible use and return the rest. Some keep 30 or 40. Others hold everything submitted indefinitely. Others return everything if they find nothing of use to them in a batch.

"I did real well this year because I shot a lot of stuff in heavy snow, and other photographers weren't doing that," he appraises. "It adds a lot of drama to the photo. Now I see this year a lot of people got out and shot in the snow. I was the only one doing it before."

Kinney also has turned a few of his photos into posters, which he sells at sportsman shows. He also is trying to persuade some discount chain stores to carry posters. He would like to have "a full line of posters" published, of many different animal species.

He also does commissioned dog portraits, sells some slides to wildlife artists, who use the slides for reference, and serves as a sales representative for manufacturers of other outdoor-related products.

This fall he plans to head West again for at least three months for another picture-taking barrage.

- *March 29, 1988*

Visions Of Francene

Fran Hart ... watercolor artist

Two interviews formed this profile—the first from March 12, 1990 and the second from September 23, 1997.

The term artistic vision is tossed around as cavalierly as a Las Vegas high roller tosses tip money to hotel and casino employees. Painters who slap childlike stick figures on canvases, sculptors who assemble common objects just so, and filmmakers who splice together scenes in seemingly random sequence are all said to have artistic vision. This devaluation of the term is something of an insult to artists who have true artistic vision, which is what Francene Hart has.

Hart, a Webster, Wisconsin, area resident, not only has an artistic vision; her watercolor paintings and pen-and-ink drawings are best described as visionary creations. By combining elements of realism, abstractionism, symbolism, and graphic design, Hart produces something of a surreal, spiritual world that envisions mystical dimensions of both the natural world and humankind. The earthy and the ethereal meet and meld in Hart's visionary world.

"It is my intention," she wrote in an artist's statement, "to create paintings that are an expression of the multi-faceted connectedness between spirit and nature."

In one of Hart's paintings forest trees form an arched cathedral. In another three spectral sleeping women symbolize the connectedness of sand, sea and sky. In another a rainbow of light radiates from an otherwise medical book-mundane female form. In another slender arms reach both skyward and earthward across layered, stylized land and sky images.

"Francene Hart is an artist and designer who has a reverence for the natural environment," Anita Carlson, executive director of the Duluth Art Institute, commented in 1993, when Hart had an exhibit at her gallery. "Her roots to northern Wisconsin are expressed in the complex representational relationships which compose her works. A wondrous array of plants, animals and goddess figures inhabit a metaphorical world of healing, continuity and transformation. The spiritual content evoked in her two-dimensional water media images create a strong sense of fusion, connecting earthly and heavenly realms."

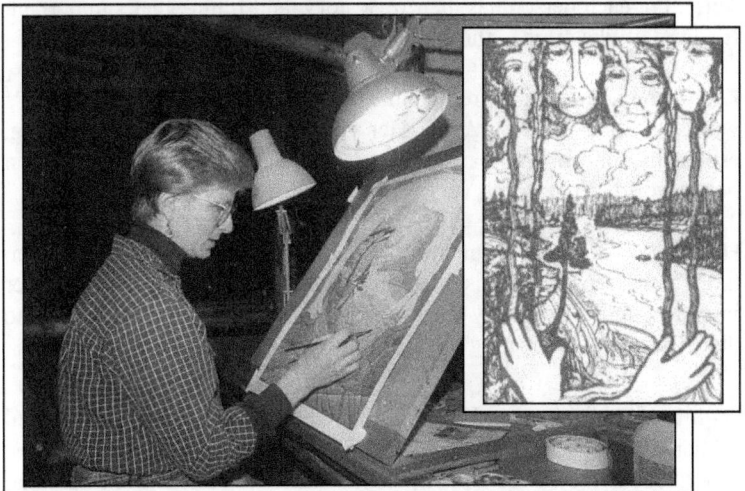

Hart, who lives in a woods-surrounded country log home, confirms that her first influence is the natural world. "More recently things have been getting more and more complicated, and watercolor is perfect for what I'm doing because essentially I'm seeing different aspects of reality, or layers of reality, in the way nature and the way we connect with all those different aspects."

While she has "no answers" to the great mysteries of the universe, she believes the world is more than "a simple three-dimensional reality. . . . One thing that's been happening over the last year in my work is there's been this introduction of a geometric element. It's kind of like a trancelike thing, mostly transparently layering that in with my other images. So some of them have been becoming very complicated. And as I'm kind of pursuing what that might mean I've gotten into a field of study that's called sacred geometry. It is kind of a worldwide study, and it's fascinating because it's cross-cultural and across time and all that. So that's just kind of a new element that's been going on. It's real exciting."

Nature is by no means the only influence on Hart's art. Reading, travel, meditation, and other activities and outside stimuli are all sources of inspiration. "I try to remain open," she says, "so that when inspiration comes I'm ready for it."

Each painting is "a little adventure" for her. "It's real interesting when I go out to see the different kinds of reactions that people have [to the paintings]. Each one is almost like a story. It's my story, in some sense, but each person has their own story, and I think that's important. It's kind of like art is in the eye of the beholder. Well, it's really true."

Larry Dodge, a semi-retired counterculture journalist, describes Hart's work as "kind of New Age. Her paintings have a lot of meaning, especially for women, Native Americans, and for the whole idea of a better world. They speak very well."

Hart agrees her work generally appeals more to women than men, though she senses "that is changing somewhat. Some of the brighter images with the geometry and stuff men have been real attracted to, so that's been real interesting for me."

While Hart dislikes the New Age tag many people pin on her, several of her paintings have been reproduced on the covers of books best described as New Age—books about such subjects as nontraditional healing and consciousness raising.

"A number of different types of healers—massage therapists, psychotherapists, people like that—are now putting my work in their offices," she says, noting that her art is "a little more personal" than art found in most corporate offices. "And some people were writing me checks with 'Healing Art' written on them [in the memo space]. That's kind of nice. That's not something that I have advertised, that people are telling me how they have in some sense received some sort of healing from it."

Publishers generally use pre-existing paintings as book covers rather than commission a painting from Hart. Hart prefers this because it allows her to visualize her own images rather than try to satisfy someone else's visualized image. While the New Age label doesn't appeal to her, Visionary Artist does.

This past autumn Hart tried to find a publisher for a journal book she put together called *Blessings,* which features about 20 paintings and a dozen black-and-white drawings, along with a few select quotes relating to gratitude. "If I had the money I would self-publish," she says, "but when you're dealing with color it's very expensive."

She has, however, self-published greeting cards, full-color prints of her paintings, and four coloring books. Although most of the coloring books appear as though they would tax the talent and attention span of teenagers, Hart says kids "really respond to. . . even the more complicated images. I think in some sense kids have a lot more depth than a lot of adults give them credit for."

Her greeting cards—or note cards—are blank inside, with reproduced paintings on the covers and Hart's hand-signed signature on the back. Her 12 by 18 inch prints are printed "a few at a time," she says. "That's why I can have such a large variety. Otherwise I'd have like two."

Except for square or round mandala-type paintings and drawings, Hart works in a vertical format almost exclusively. "It's just what it's come to over the years," she explains.

Creating this visionary art, this art that helps heal, is therapy for the artist as well. Hart cannot imagine life without painting. To her, painting is bliss, and a blessing. "I feel very honored to be allowed to do it," she says.

And as long as she paints there will almost undoubtedly be what poet William Wordsworth called a "visionary gleam" in her eyes and visionary images on paper.

Calendar Man

Louis Raymer ... wildlife artist

It's a significant milestone for an artist or a photographer when a company wants to devote an entire yearly calendar to showcasing his or her work. Wildlife artist Louis Raymer, of rural Webster, Wisconsin, reached that milestone 20 years ago. Since 1967 Raymer has done six paintings each year for a high-quality calendar published by Shedd-Brown, a Minneapolis company that specializes in selling advertising items to businesses throughout the United States.

Raymer works two to three years ahead so that Shedd-Brown salesmen have printed samples to show to potential customers—businesses that have their names printed on the calendars and give the calendars as Christmas gifts to customers and clients. Shedd-Brown also sells many other "business incentives" items such as pens, radios, knives, cushions, and so forth. Raymer receives a flat rate for his work; his financial compensation is not dependent on how many calendars are ordered. He's not even aware of how many are printed.

"I like it that way," he says. "I get pretty good rates. I've had a number of different deals with them, but it seems to work best if they just pay me an outright fee." He says he likes "doing a painting, getting paid, and being done with it."

Raymer's watercolor paintings are reproduced on the top half of the 13 by 17 ½ inch calendar pages, with calendar listings for two months on the bottom half of the page. Shedd-Brown also publishes a smaller 12-page calendar with a Raymer painting on each page. Half of those paintings are from previous years' calendars. Raymer does all of the paintings in a vignette style, in which there is no border. Background settings are sketchy, not detailed. Something of a standard mix of wildlife is represented each year. A typical calendar includes a songbird, a migratory game bird, a big-game animal, a small-game animal or a non-game animal such as a wolf or a raccoon, a fish, and perhaps another bird species. Most bird paintings are of pairs of birds.

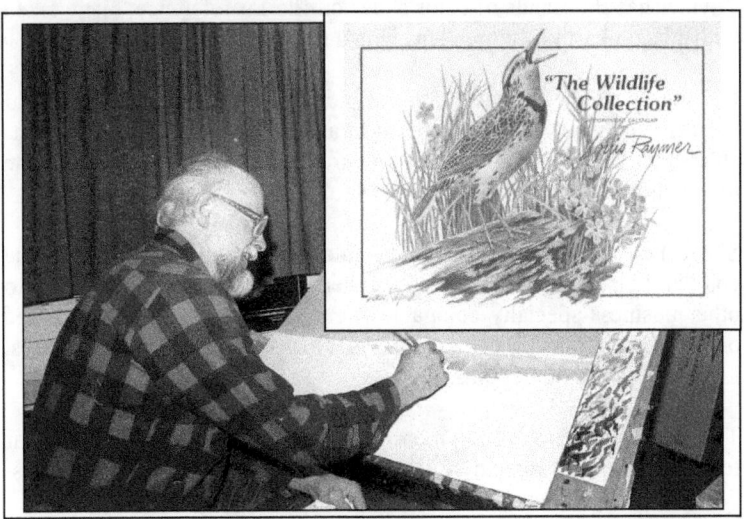

Most of the birds and animals depicted on the calendars are broadly known throughout the United States.

"I just happened to walk in the door at the right time," Raymer says. Shedd-Brown recently had "lost" the artist who had been doing wildlife calendars. Raymer, who carried an impressive background in commercial art, was asked to do a sample painting in the vignette style, and has been painting wildlife images for Shedd-Brown calendars ever since.

There is "a lot of give and take" between Raymer and company representatives as to what birds and animals to include on calendars. "We may select eight or nine subjects as possibles, and then I'll tell them if I have good research on them or not," Raymer says. "I do all my own research, all of my own photography. And if I have good research then I'll paint it. If I don't have good research I won't. It's better to not do something that you're not totally familiar with."

Raymer's lakeside home is only about 10 miles east of the 30,000-acre Crex Meadows Wildlife Area, so he doesn't have to travel far afield for a lot of his research. He prefers to take photographs in the field rather than do location sketches. "You're fighting the elements all the time when you're out sketching," he says. "I do some, but for practice. But I've been painting so many years I don't think I need any practice; I do it eight to 10 hours a day."

Raymer has thousands of color slides on file for reference, many taken with a bazooka-like 400mm lens with a squeeze-focus grip.

In recent years he has taken a lot of pictures from tree stands. "You'd be surprised what you see from up in a tree," he says. "I have a portable stand, and I can climb right up a tree with it. Animals don't relate to you as a human, somehow, when you're up a tree. It's really fun."

Shedd-Brown owns all rights to the calendar paintings. Sometimes the company also uses the images on other products or sells the rights to other business specialty companies. Raymer's images have appeared on note cards, playing cards, ashtrays, clocks, dishes, drinking glasses, ice buckets, and other items.

Through Shedd-Brown, Raymer also paints a "full painting" each year for a calendar published by C. W. Transport, a large Wisconsin Rapids-based trucking company. He has done that for five or six years.

For a few years he also produced a "Lucky Luke" series calendar for Shedd-Brown that allowed him to employ the Norman Rockwell-style facet of his artistic talent. While whimsical scenes of the backwoods rube Lucky Luke proved popular in the Midwest, they didn't go over as well in other regions.

Although best known for his wildlife paintings, Raymer still is involved in commercial art, which gives him the opportunity to paint a variety of subjects, using different styles and techniques, including cartoon designs. Minneapolis-based Spectrum Studios, which does work for advertising agencies as well as contract work directly for large companies, represents Raymer in this realm.

"The reason I like commercial work is that I like to be dared to work," he says. "I had almost three years where I could just sit here and paint, which I thought was my dream. I painted paintings and I sold them. But I got bored. I like somebody to dare me to do something—to challenge me more. I like pressure; I like a deadline. It's probably crazy, but after having done it all my life I can't readjust to the kind of sedentary style of just sitting around painting. That was my eventual dream. I got there and didn't like it."

- *October 22, 1986*

☼

Portraits Of Americana

Christine Mount Kapp ... portrait artist

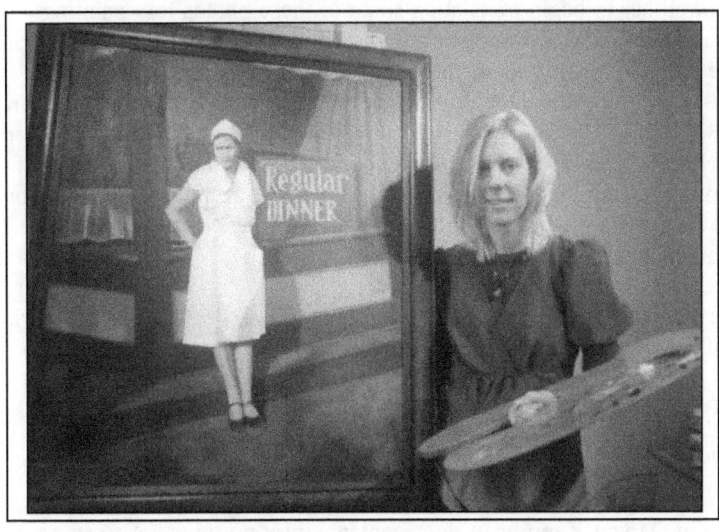

There is a good reason why many of Christine Mount Kapp's paintings resemble posed photographs from the 1930s and 1940s: She often uses vintage photos from that period as base images for portraits. Given her youthfulness, people frequently ask why "that old stuff" inspires her.

"It's a funny, long story how I started doing this," the Cushing, Wisconsin, area resident says. "Several years ago I was visiting the Chicago Art Institute—I love going to the museums, looking at the art. There was one painting in particular I was drawn to. It had people in it, 'cause that's what I like; I like to paint people. It was kind of a country scene. And so I immediately walked across the room and had to go see it. And lo and behold, the artist's name was William Sidney Mount. Mount is my maiden name. It was so weird, like: how funny that I would walk up to this painting, and that I'm here today looking at this, and that out of this whole roomful of paintings this is the one I wanted to walk up to and look at. I just thought that was so strange."

Intrigued, she "had to find out" if William Sidney Mount was part of her family tree, so she "did some genealogy work for several years" and was able to tie the 19th Century portrait painter from Long Island, New York, into her family line. "He was actually one of the first American genre painters painting African-American people in a positive light," she relates.

In the process of the genealogy work, Mount Kapp "found a lot of great compositions" as she dug up family photos. Her love of history inspired her to begin translating some of those photos into paintings—small slices of Americana featuring her own ancestors. One of the first ones she did was of one of her grandmothers wearing a white waitress dress and cap, standing outside an Eau Claire, Wisconsin, diner in 1932, beside a large sign inside a large window which reads "Regular DINNER." With a background in graphic design, Mount Kapp is drawn to using signage in paintings. "When I go out on the road for shows," she says, "people will donate their pictures to me if they have a good one with signage."

Her favorite images are of working class people, dressed in their work clothes and standing in front of their places of work.

"My favorite time period is the Thirties and Forties," she says. "Most of my work is from that time period. But other time periods do come in. I've done some from the Seventies."

Indeed, Mount Kapp even does contemporary portraits. And some of those—one of her own young twin sons, for instance—seem to have a vintage quality about them.

Mount Kapp grew up in the Minneapolis suburb of Apple Valley, when "it was mostly farmland and new housing and wide open fields," and has lived on an old farmstead in northwestern Wisconsin, between St. Croix Falls and Grantsburg, since 2002. She and her husband are in the process of remodeling the hayloft of their small barn into an art studio.

This summer the former school art teacher—she taught in Minneapolis, Grantsburg and Taylors Falls, MN—is reviving an Art Camp experience at her home for children ages eight to 18 the week of August 17-21. She staged two such children's art camps each summer for five years before taking a break from that last year. With three other artists involved, she can accept 32 students, who attend four classes each day and go home each night.

"I get a lot of joy out of teaching kids because they come with an open mind and they're just ready to absorb it all, like a sponge," she says. "It's kind of fun to help mold a new soul. Plus, I can think back and remember all the fun art classes I was able to take in the summer when I was a kid. It really meant a lot to me, so I like to pass that on."

Mount Kapp is "mostly self-taught," though.

She works with oils on canvas, mainly, employing certain methods and techniques she has learned and developed over the years, including using several layers of glazes.

"That's something that's unique about my paintings," she says of the layering technique. "Painters all paint different. Some painters paint with thick, heavy paint. And I can do that too. But I love the effect of the glazes because it's kind of like a stained glass effect. They're very thin, transparent layers. It's like sheets of glass—colors on top of colors. It gives it such a strong luminosity and glow, and that's what gives it the three-dimensionality. It's an Old Masters technique, the glazing. But I don't always work totally in that way."

Mount Kapp does commission work for families, commercial concerns and community organizations. She also participates in six to eight large, juried art shows each year, mainly in Minnesota, Wisconsin and Iowa. Doing art shows generates some of the commissions. Participation in the annual Art-A-Whirl show in Minneapolis, for instance, led to a commission for two large paintings for the Iowa State Bank just outside of Des Moines, Iowa.

The price for an original Mount Kapp painting varies. A 16 by 20 inch painting may sell for $600. Larger paintings can be priced at anywhere from $1,200 to $6,000. She also has limited edition giclee [*zhee-lee*] prints made of many of the paintings—generally an edition size of 500, in three different sizes. Giclee prints are stretched over backing frames to resemble canvas originals. Small prints cost $40. "It makes art accessible to everybody, which I think is a good thing," she says of the prints. "There are a lot of artists that don't do prints, but I don't try to be snotty or anything."

She has begun doing some sepia tone [dark reddish brown] paintings, just as there are sepia tone photographs.

"I do work in charcoals too," she notes. "I just haven't done it for a long time."

In fact, Mount Kapp has an "extremely diverse" painting background. She has experimented with many painting styles. "I can paint very abstractly," she says. "I can paint photo-realistically, which I prefer not to do."

When she first began doing shows about eight years ago she displayed such different artistic sides that some people thought two different artists painted the pictures, since the older ones were signed "Mount" and the newer ones—the more realistic, photo-based ones—"Kapp," this being shortly after she married.

Developing a distinct style is one of the biggest challenges for any artist, and Mount Kapp has conquered that challenge.

"I know a lot of people paint from old photographs," she says, "but just traveling around I hear a lot of people say, 'You're unique in the way you paint.'"

Mount Kapp's paintings have a nostalgic appeal with men as well as with woman, which gratifies her. Her paintings appeal to people for many different reasons. With a painting of a barber, for example, someone's father may have been a barber, or the exterior of the barber shop may be very similar to the barber shop someone patronized in his youth. A sign of a brand name product in the picture might tickle someone's fancy. People may have a family photograph that is similar to a painting.

On the other hand, too much detail, especially in facial features, could be detrimental to sales. Mount Kapp says that selling paintings of "strangers" is one of the most difficult things to do. "That's probably why you don't see a lot of (artists) at art shows with figures in their paintings," she says. She eliminates a lot of detail. Faces of figures in her paintings often are "mushed" to add vagueness to their identity.

In 2007 she won Best of Show awards, and prize money, at both the Wausau Art Festival and the Artstreet show in Green Bay, for the body of work she displayed at the shows. "Both of them had around 200 artists," she notes, "so Best of Show is somebody walking around saying you had the best of the best there, so that's quite a compliment."

She says uniqueness and topnotch execution is what impresses judges.

- April 8, 2009

Expressions Of Love For The Land

Gregg Rochester … landscape artist

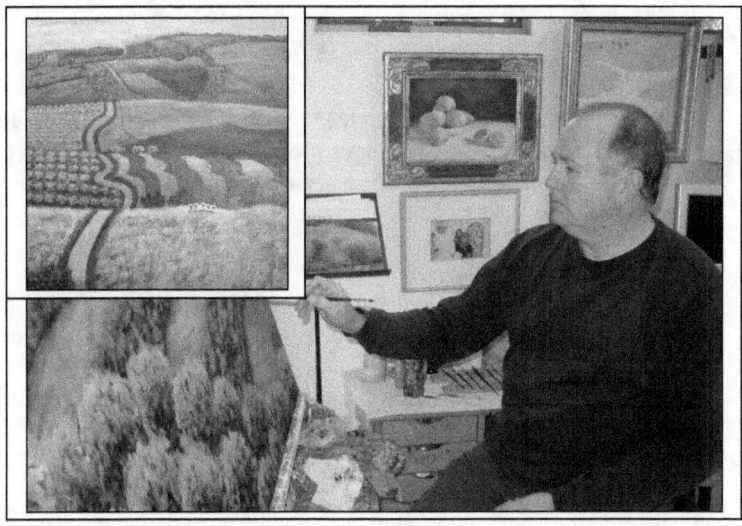

Some of his landscape paintings are playful. Others shimmer with a sense of wonder. Others exude mystery. Whatever mood a painting has, Gregg Rochester hopes they all express his love for the land. This heartland artist, who lives in Amery, Wisconsin, likes to say he has always held the land in his heart.

One of the signature notes of his work is that he never places buildings in his landscapes, even though many of them are farmland scenes obviously impacted by human activity.

"I don't like to put buildings, roads, telephone poles, or any of that in it," he says, though roads are part of some of the oil paintings. "I really try to make it appear as though, in some way, that when you hang one of these paintings on a wall it's like you're looking out a picture window. And most of us, I think, if we had the choice, wouldn't like to be looking at telephone poles and roads. So it's the idea you're looking at an expanse without a lot of human interference."

Having worked as a clinical psychologist before becoming a professional artist, Rochester tries to bring a sense of healing to his paintings. Inspired by the philosophy of contemporary psychologist and writer Thomas Moore, who believes people need regular exposure to natural surroundings to be psychically healthy, Rochester wants his work "to help people have a stronger connection with nature" and "give them a feeling that they can look at one of my paintings and go into it—to leave this room and be going into that place." He knows that looking at one of his landscapes is not a substitute for actually being outdoors, in nature, but believes his paintings can "continue to develop and enhance that connection and that relationship with nature."

Rochester has done about 50 playful "rolling hills" paintings inspired by the Wisconsin landscape that have proved to be popular all over the country. He characterizes those as "kind of exaggerated Wisconsin landscapes." They easily can be seen as collage-like, with their bold colors and piecemeal designs.

"I think maybe the first ones that I did were based a little bit on some places that I saw," he says. "It's where I saw the possibility of them. But from that point on they've become just my imagination, because they're all relatively impossible, as far as being really steep inclines and various things like that. But even though they are impossible, people kind of relate to them anyway."

As with song lyrics of some famous songwriters, some people see deep meaning in the playful images, such as how a painting leads someone through the paths and transitions of life. *Oh, really?* Rochester will think. *I was just having fun with red.*

Besides these "more funky landscapes," Rochester does traditional landscapes, still-lifes and some abstract paintings. His paintings currently can be found at galleries in New York City, Minneapolis, St. Louis, Indianapolis, Scottsdale and Tucson, Arizona, Wisconsin's Door County, and Stillwater, Minnesota.

Many of his landscapes feature tall grasses and patches of prairie. He finds grasses attractive for many reasons. "I like the way air moves through grasses and changes their positions, and the way light moves around them," he says. "I like the many colors grasses can have, especially through their life cycle. Most people are obviously aware of the changes in colors in the trees in autumn, but I'm particularly sensitive to the many color changes grasses go through also, especially in

November. I like the soft feel of grasses, the textures. When I look off into the distance at grasses I often wish I could lay in them."

A 20 by 20 inch painting runs about $1,200. A 48 by 48 inch painting sells for about $5,000. While that is a large painting, Rochester does much larger pieces. In fact, he has made a name for himself as a painter who works in large scale. The largest painting he has done is 72 by 84 inches, for a single canvas; he has done triptych works [a set of three panels] where each panel is a 72-inch square.

Rochester's propensity to paint on square canvases also helps distinguish his art. Since probably nine out of 10 artists work almost exclusively with the rectangle shape, square canvases stand out. "Almost all artists work in rectangle, and almost all artists work small," Rochester notes. "So I knew that if I wanted to get a good market for my work one of the things I should do is paint large, and not always paint rectangle."

Even with the rectangle shape, the vertical format is far less common than the horizontal format, so Rochester tries to exploit the short side there as well. "That's where these rolly-hill paintings are good, because they're vertical. (Someone) may be looking at a lot of art for a project, whether it be a corporate building or a home or whatever, and they have a hard time finding any vertical paintings. So mine become a good grab for that."

Rochester grew up in Wyoming and South Dakota. One of his most gratifying accomplishments is that former United States Senator George McGovern, the 1972 Democratic presidential candidate, personally selected one of Rochester's South Dakota landscape paintings to hang in his office at the George McGovern Library in Mitchell, South Dakota.

Both his mother, Jacqueline Rochester, and one of his grandfathers were professional artists, so Rochester always felt pulled to artistic expression. Those artistic expressions were made with music [woodwinds and classical guitar], pottery and silver-smithing before he turned his attention to painting in any serious way in his late 30s. Meanwhile, he studied psychology at a college in Indiana, did an internship at the Mayo Clinic in—appropriately enough—Rochester, MN, then found a job at the Hibbing, MN, hospital. Eventually he had a private practice there, in Hibbing, which is where he met his wife, Zoe, a seventh grade teacher and bead artist. When Zoe accepted a teaching job in Amery the couple moved to Amery.

While Rochester did some work at the Polk County Adult Development Center in Balsam Lake after the move to Amery, by then he was in the process of shifting gears toward art.

"It eventually got to the point where I needed to go fulltime [with art]," he says, "and I've been fulltime now for 10 or 11 years."

Depending on the sort of work they do, psychologists tend to burn out after about 20 years. Doing intense psychotherapy had Rochester looking for a change.

His mother, who died last spring, never pushed him into art and did not teach him how to paint. She did, however, offer valuable advice about the business side of art. Jacqueline Rochester, who was both a painter and a sculptor, was very well known in the Southwest. She lived in Colorado, New Mexico and Phoenix after Gregg moved away from home. Some of her designs were used for clothing, tile and furniture upholstery.

Rochester followed her path into designs for clothing, since he "was interested in creating interesting images for clothes." He started selling in that area, then "got this big deal going" with a well-known company that had a nationally distributed catalog. "I was very excited about this, thinking I was going to move into the big time," he says. According to Rochester, he was ripped off, however. "That's the point where my mother said, 'You've got to get out of this and just start painting paintings.'"

And that is what he did. He also followed his mother's advice to study with a very good artist. For about two months in 1994 he was the sole student of renowned "tonalist" Michael Workman at the Scottsdale Artists School, honing his landscape painting skills.

"That was a real profound experience," he says. "It's kind of like taking an intensive training with somebody like that, even for a short time, is the same thing as taking years and years of work in classes and that kind of thing. . . . It was a huge influence on me. And I feel that that's when I really started painting, after I did that; I'd been fooling around before that."

Rochester gives his paintings depth with a layering painting technique. "Instead of putting on thick paint," he explains, "I start off with very thin paint and build the colors up from that. You can kind of see it when you look at it; it has a lot of color that comes up, up, up. And you can get the idea there is sort of a base color that starts, and then it works its way up. It's time-consuming to do that. And of course you have to wait for the paint to dry between the layers." Because of that, he generally has four or five paintings in progress.

He occasionally uses a computer in his studio to display photographs that have elements he wants to use in a painting. Sometimes he also takes a photo of a painting he is working on and plays with the colors on the computer. "I can see whether I might want to make some changes to the original while I'm looking at that." Rather than experimenting with the actual painting, he saves time by doing that color experimentation with the computer.

He produces 30 to 40 original paintings a year. Prints of about a dozen of his most popular paintings are available by custom order.

Rochester also draws upon his playful side to hand-paint racing bicycles with theme designs. His Map Bike, for instance, has a fictional road map on one side and a world map on the other side. One bike is all African designs. One he did for his wife has bead designs all over it.

He has an entire exhibit, Le Tour d-Art, that features the painted bikes and bicycle-related paintings—abstract paintings, fantasy bike rides and landscapes as seen from a bicyclist's point of view. The painted bikes often make people laugh with delight and exclaim, "Wow!"

He has painted some of the bikes on commission. Given that it takes 40 to 50 hours to paint one, that work is less profitable than his canvas painting, so he takes on only three or four such commissions a year.

For all of his playfulness, Rochester derives the deepest personal reward from the healing power some of his paintings can have.

"I've been getting a lot of requests to do shows in hospitals, and a lot of my work is purchased for hospitals too," he says. "There are several in Minneapolis that have my work in them, both in public areas as well as in patient rooms and that kind of thing. I think that just encouraging a feeling of calmness and relaxation, (or) the feeling that being around certain colors gives us. . . creates kind of a healing sensation. So I try to have that happen in my work. And that's all connected to my working as a healer."

- November 3, 2010 ☼

Three Directions At Once

Al Servoss ... watercolor artist

When Al Servoss studied art at the University of Montana in the late 1960s his teachers, like those at most colleges at the time, imparted very little information about the business side of art. "It hasn't been until the last eight or 10 years—or actually the last five years, probably more accurately—that they started also giving information to undergraduates about how to make a living at art, the business part of art," he says. "You know: How do you go out and approach a gallery? What do you do? Are you just going to sit in your garret or your studio and create art?"

Unprepared to make his way through the maze of commercial art galleries, Servoss turned to teaching and eventually learned on his own what he needed to do to make a living as a working artist. He taught at a small college in Madison, Wisconsin, for three years, then moved to Australia and taught there a couple of years. "I realized I was just not fulfilling what I wanted to do," he says. "I'd always wanted to be an artist and I wasn't doing it; I was just teaching. . . . I was generally depressed."

When his wife, Gail, was offered a good job in Florida she offered to provide the financial support the couple needed while Al concentrated on creating and developing his art. "We lived there [in Florida] for a year," Servoss says, "and I studied with a couple of very, very fine painters and teachers, and went through periods of depression and joy; you go on the highs and lows. And that's when I started to learn about the business end of it—getting into galleries, and exactly how good I'd have to get, too, as an artist, because the competition was so severe. I guess I just didn't realize what it was like. . . . I painted eight hours a day, five or six days a week. I'd paint in the kitchen; I'd set my stuff up on the kitchen table and I'd work. . . . When I wasn't actually painting I was out seeing exhibitions, talking to other artists. I was really obnoxious, I'm sure, to everybody that was down there because I was always going around and getting information. I was a real parasite, practically, because that's all I wanted to do, and I had the time to do it." He managed to become established with one gallery in Florida.

From Florida, he and Gail moved to Minneapolis. "By that point," he says, "my work was starting to develop a little bit and I fairly quickly got into a gallery in Minneapolis—the Groveland Gallery, which I still show with—and worked myself into another gallery in Stillwater, whom I also still show with—the Tamarack House Gallery."

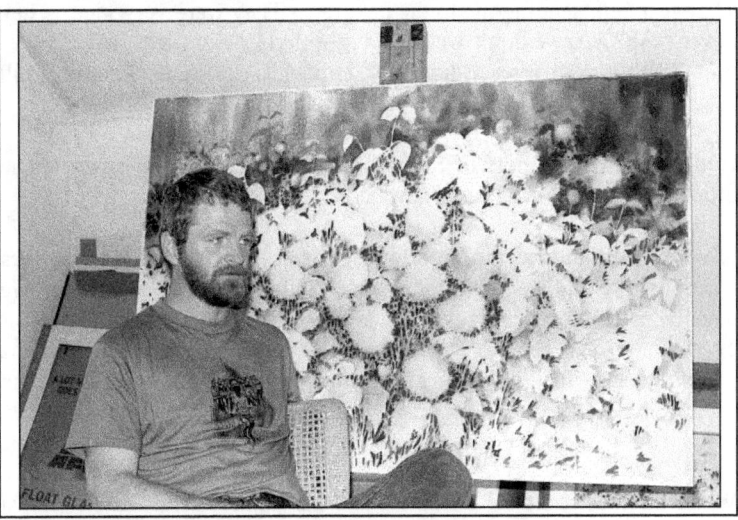

After a year in Minneapolis Servoss and his wife fulfilled a long-held dream by moving to an old house in the country near Chetek, Wisconsin, in 1978. While the birth of a child sent Servoss scurrying back to the financial security of part-time teaching (currently at the Chetek elementary school), he still spends much of his time in a second floor studio working on watercolor paintings for galleries in Chicago, Milwaukee, Minneapolis, and elsewhere.

"(Teaching) is a capsulized part of my life that I can handle very nicely right now," he says. "And it gives me the majority of my time for my family and my art, which is what I want." He and Gail now have two children.

He says "Galleries are interested in two things: They're interested in good work, and work that sells. And I'm not really sure to this day which one they're most interested in. Because it's a business like anything else, I think they have to be interested in what's going to sell. Sometimes excellent work will be in galleries and it won't sell, because then you're talking about a product and its relationship with a consumer, and there's nothing very glamorous about it, as much as you'd like to think there is."

He says "There are more good artists than there are good galleries, so you've gotta be lucky, and you've gotta hang in there. When I first started out, in Florida, I went to Sarasota, which is a real art haven, and I was turned down by five or six galleries in the space of two hours. They just kept sending me to the next one. They were very nice. They never said, 'No, we don't want your work; your work stinks,' or something like this. . . . It's getting better, although it's like walking up a hill in wind at times."

Galleries find that most of Servoss's paintings sell, even when, as he often does, he ventures into a new style.

"I work in about three different directions at once, which is sometimes frustrating to the galleries," he says, "but most of the galleries are usually pretty receptive to what I've been in and find a market for everything I do, pretty much." He feels fortunate to not be pigeonholed. "It's like eating," he says. "You don't want to eat the same thing every day. . . . When I pick something up I never totally leave it behind, but it changes."

While he does some oil paintings, and has painted with acrylics, most of his paintings are in the watercolor medium.

"My training in college was in oil painting and drawing," he says. "I do an awful lot of pen-and-ink drawing. I was lured into watercolor years ago before I ever started painting seriously. I was just fascinated by the spontaneity of watercolor, the fluidity of it. And I have a personality that lends itself very well to the medium. There's an immediacy, for me, about watercolor that I can't achieve with oil painting. Now, I know of oil painters who can also achieve that immediacy, and they can't do it with watercolors. You find yourself feeling more flexible in one medium, for some reason, and I think a lot of it has to do just with personality. So I had no training when I started painting, basically, in watercolors. That's why I went to workshops. I still go to workshops occasionally. I try to go to one at least every other year, if not every year, because I think it's good to go to other artists no matter what direction you work or where you are with your own painting. No matter how good you are, I think you can always learn from your peers. You get a different slant and a different viewpoint."

Servoss also presents workshops himself. He has given an annual three-day workshop at his home, for between 12 and 20 students, for the last six years. He also has given workshops in St. Paul, Minneapolis, and elsewhere, and also will give one in Montana this summer. "I really enjoy doing workshops," he says. "They're fun. The people are there because they want to be there. It's not like public education where they're kind of channeled into a room and told, 'Okay, this is where you're going this period.' The people come, and they've paid their money, so you know they want to be there. And you've gotta give them their money's worth too, or they won't come back."

He advises workshop participants to paint subjects with which they are familiar.

"I've lived here for six years now, and most of the work I do is a reflection of things that I've seen right here on the land," he says. "These logs and stuff," he goes on, pointing to a painting in his studio, "or something like that, are laying down in the woods. These are things that I've seen right around here, close by."

Servoss works basically from memory, after doing numerous sketches on field trips. Only about ten percent of the sketches are transformed into paintings, however.

"When you do a lot of drawing you familiarize yourself with an object, and then you can find yourself working from memory better," he says. "It takes a long time to develop this. . . . One of the nice things about painting from memory is that memory is selective. You select what's important and you leave out the stuff that isn't, in your memory."

Lately Servoss has painted a lot of forest scenes that have a highly luminous quality, as though the viewer is looking at something in a brightly lit glass case. He also has been doing larger and larger paintings, in part because there is a demand for them. The Chicago area gallery where his work is displayed, for example, has many corporate clients who want very large paintings.

"There's a technical challenge to doing something large, as opposed to something of a smaller scale," he says. "When you're working smaller you can see what you've got; when you're working large it almost becomes a trick to just pull the thing off, to get it to work for you, just because it's so big."

He has found that spontaneity often produces better results than a piece he labors over and possibly over-thinks. "Sometimes those spontaneous things that happen quickly are the best," he says, "because it's almost like an electrical thing that happens between the artist and the paper." If he is dissatisfied with the result, less time has been wasted if, as often happens, he decides to scrap something.

Some of his large paintings sell for as much as $1,000. Most of the smaller ones are priced in the $500 to $600 range. Gallery owners feel they could be selling the paintings at higher prices, but they want to raise the prices by moderate increments so as not to antagonize patrons. "It's much easier to raise your prices slowly," Servoss notes. "I would rather sell my work and get it out than to have it sitting around the studio."

While most of Servoss's paintings are realistic, or representational, he does some abstract paintings as well. He finds those generally are slower to sell, though most do eventually sell. "It depends on where you're selling your work," he says. ". . . It's funny, because people like them—they say they do, and I think they do. The galleries certainly have been fond of them. But, again, it's what moves and what doesn't move. And I have found that, basically, over a period of time, for the general public representational art is selling better. But I try not to let it keep me from doing the abstract paintings, which I want to do and feel a necessity to do. I enjoy doing them a great deal."

- *June 5, 1984*

☼

Frame Of Mind

Jeff Hile ... painter, potter, sculptor

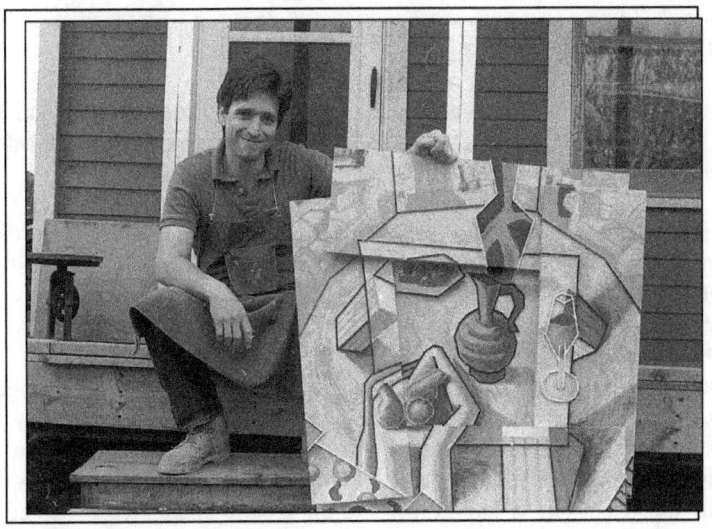

When asked the standard "What do you do?" question, Jeff Hile has a difficult time describing what he does. "What I say is that I do paintings on wood constructions," the Cumberland, Wisconsin, area artist says. "Which really doesn't necessarily tell you a lot unless you're actually looking at them because that could be a lot of different things, I guess."

Hile's off-the-wall—both literally and figuratively—painted wood creations are sort of a cross between painting and sculpture, with a certain sense of collage in the mix. He paints on hollow-core mahogany doors which he cuts up, then overlaps the pieces in a skewed, non-square design. "It has to do with an idea of motion, trying to capture a sense of things not being exactly solid, or just a little bit askew," Hile, 35, says of the lopsided edges. "There's something a little bit uncomfortable, I hope, about that. I think it forces you to look at things in a little different way...."

"There are a lot of people who really appreciate seeing something done in a new way—looking at things in a new way. Those people, I think, tend to enjoy the paintings whether they buy them or not. They like the kind of game that's played and try to figure out why it's like that. Others just have a real tough time because it doesn't fit that image that already is in their heads [of what shape a painting should have]. That's pretty challenging. But I guess I'm not trying to appeal to that audience as much. I'm really trying to appeal to those who are interested in change and a progression of knowledge, and I would say moving ahead. I guess there are those who would disagree with whether or not it's moving ahead. But anyway, moving someplace."

Hile counts Van Gough, Gauguin, Cezanne, Picasso and Matisse among the artists who have influenced him, along with such latter-day artists as Frank Stella, David Hockney and Elizabeth Murray.

His boldly exuberant—a lone adjective would not suffice in this instance—paintings, which could be best described as impressionistic, probably, have no frames, in the traditional sense. After years of doing traditional watercolors, for which the selection of a matte and a frame was nearly as important as the painting itself, Hile wanted to have a complete work when he finished painting. "I didn't want any changes to take place after I was finished," he says, "because there really is sometimes a surprising change when a frame gets put around something. So first I started to put the frame on and paint that. Pretty soon the frame got bigger and bigger and the picture plane area got smaller and smaller. Now I kind of see this as the frame and the painting all being part of the whole."

He likes to work on a three-dimensional surface because then the painting "is" something rather than "about" something. "I think it's an object in a different way than a traditional painting is. It has a kind of physical presence that's different."

He also likes that "something about a spiral keeps showing up" when he overlaps pieces of a piece, as it were. He sees them as "spinning in infinity, sort of. . . . I'm trying to show that, somehow, without giving up entirely on what would be the traditional format. . . . I don't think I'm really breaking ground, to speak of, but I think I am participating in what the trends are today rather than do some new version of something from the past. This is participating in what's going on today in art."

Hile's current style evolved over the last two to three years. He says it owes a lot to his experience as a set builder/designer for area stage plays. "I'm using kind of the same materials I use when I build sets, in many cases."

Most of his paintings have bright colors and bold, stylized images and designs that almost leap out at the viewer. The ornamental ceramic pots and vessels he makes have the same sort of bright, sunny, playful quality. When much "serious" modern art focuses on degradation and despair, this may make Hile look like Mr. Sunshine. While he is not exactly that, for sinister images do show up in some of his paintings, he does have a generally optimistic philosophy of life.

"I think it would be profitable to present the positive side of things, for all of us," he says. "Maybe it's the teacher in me, I don't know." [Hile taught junior and senior high school art at Cumberland for 10 years, until last year.] "But people are more likely to listen and learn something, I think, if they can find some pleasure in what they're viewing rather than being pounded over the head with another statement about how bad things are and how we're all going to hell in a handbasket and all that. There is a real strong strain like that in art right now. It's really very pessimistic. Maybe we should be pessimistic, but I'm not choosing that."

Hile generally starts a painting by making a pastel drawing. Sometimes a "vision" comes together in this pastel form, other times there is more of a re-evaluation when the work is transferred to a three-dimensional construction.

"Some decisions have to be made before you make a construction," he says. "It's different from painting on a flat surface where you can kind of make decisions as you go along a little bit more. It's more difficult to just kind of throw all these pieces together because they have to hold together, for one thing. And all of that form has to be put on before paint is applied. I can make changes later, but generally I have to have a pretty solid idea when I do the initial part."

Hile fills in the sides of the pieces of mahogany doors he cuts up, then adds "strips of things over the top, too, for some texture."

He uses acrylic paint for several reasons. Acrylic paint is less toxic than oil paint, it makes brushes easier to clean, and it works well with his preferred painting method. "I work fast—kind of dashing things off," he says. "That's kind of the point, I guess. I think I want something of that kind of flurry of activity to show in the painting, so acrylic suits me pretty well because you really have to work fast if you're going to do any blending or anything because it dries out fast."

As he explained in an artist's statement: "I believe. . . . that my work is the result of a struggle to consolidate and order two differing disciplines—ceramics and painting. The tension between them represents much of what I'm working on—the relationship between two dimensions and three, and the relationship between the exterior boundaries of three-dimensional objects and the rectangular 'window' of the traditional painting canvas."

Hile's work can be found at several galleries in Minneapolis and northwestern Wisconsin. "I'm really kind of at the beginning of trying to expand my market," he says. "For a long time I did art fairs and shows and that kind of thing in the summer. The work that I'm doing now just isn't marketable in that way."

Now that he has enough financial security to paint for himself rather than try to please the tastes of others he seems at least as concerned about creative satisfaction as he is about sales.

As for the future, he anticipates his painting will continue to evolve and change.

"You couldn't (necessarily) go up to something on a wall and say, 'Oh, I know whose that is' in a year or two," he says. "I think change is important for an aspect of what I'm doing. It probably isn't the best marketing strategy, however."

- *April 8, 1991*

☼

Ornamental Art

Eugene Kraskiewicz ... ornament artist

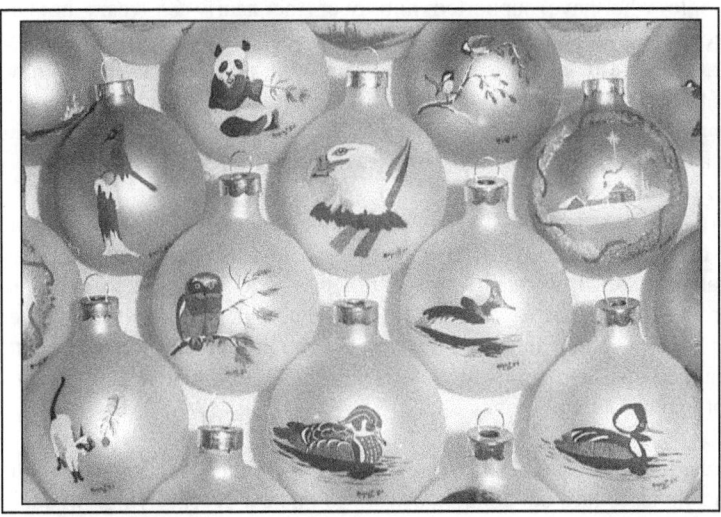

I interviewed Eugene Kraskiewicz five times over a 10-year period: Sept. 12, 1984 ... Feb. 28, 1985 ... Dec. 6, 1985 ... Dec. 2, 1989 ... Dec. 1, 1994

Like Santa Claus, Eugene Kraskiewicz is preoccupied with Christmas all year round. While Santa and his elves are busy making toys to leave under Christmas trees, Kraskiewicz creates decorations to hang *on* Christmas trees. Every year the Rice Lake, Wisconsin, wildlife artist hand-paints thousands of ball-ornaments with detailed designs of songbirds, game birds, rustic outdoor scenes, farm scenes, cartoon characters, and other images—one image to each ball. They are sold as "Art by August," his middle name of August being more euphonious and easier to remember than his alphabet-soup last name.

Given that the hundreds of gift shops and galleries in 38 states and four other countries [England, France, Australia and the Bahamas] that display his ornaments start putting out their Christmas items in late September or early October, Art by August has something of a double meaning, for most of those outlets want Christmas items in hand by August.

Scores of celebrities and prominent politicians have purchased the ornaments, and some have hung on the White House Christmas tree and the Christmas tree in the U.S. Capitol rotunda. Kraskiewicz values every customer equally, though, whether it be a governor or a game warden, a movie star or a social worker. He doesn't want to charge prices that would put the ornaments out of reach of most people—people who have supported him over the nearly 25 years he has decorated Christmas ball-ornaments. "Whether a person pays $5 or $2,000 for a painting, I want him to enjoy it, and I want him to know that I did my best for that piece," Kraskiewicz says. Purchased directly from Kraskiewicz, the ornaments cost $11 each. The price is higher in retail shops.

"An ornament is not that expensive, but yet a person has something that is original that he will have for years," says Kraskiewicz, who has many awards from such organizations as Ducks Unlimited and The Grouse Society displayed on a wall in the basement studio of his home. "It takes a good hour or hour-and-ten-minutes to do one ornament. Maybe when you come down to it you make minimum wage. You're not making a lot of money."

Kraskiewicz works 14 to 16 hours nearly every day of the year, without vacations, to turn out enough artwork to make a decent living. In addition to hand-painting Christmas ornaments, he also decorates animal antlers, antler slices for various items of jewelry and other products, wooden Easter eggs, and turns out all sizes of watercolor paintings. Some of the images he creates are reproduced on T-shirts and sweatshirts sold in such stores as Shopco, K-Mart and Wal-Mart. All told, he does 7,500 to 8,000 pieces of artwork each year. This year Christmas ornaments accounted for about half of that output; he decorated more than 3,800 ball-ornaments. One year he painted 7,200 ornaments—and did little else that year.

Demand exceeds supply for the ornaments. "I could have had probably close to 10,000 [this year], but you can only do so much, and I want to break away," he says. "I want to start doing more paintings. . . . It's going to come to a point where I'll do maybe 500 limited-edition [ornaments] a year and that's it."

While painting Christmas ornaments may not be as creatively satisfying as full-scale paintings, Kraskiewicz still derives a large measure of satisfaction from the ornament painting. "It's fun doing, really," he says. "And it's neat to get letters from people from almost all over the world. Last year we got letters from people in Australia and New Zealand ordering and saying how they appreciate the ornaments. So it makes you feel good. . . . We've gotten letters from granddaughters saying that they received a dozen ornaments from their grandparents, and the grandparents said 'When you put your Christmas tree up 25 years from now you will remember your first Christmas.' So it really makes it nice. You have a nice feeling."

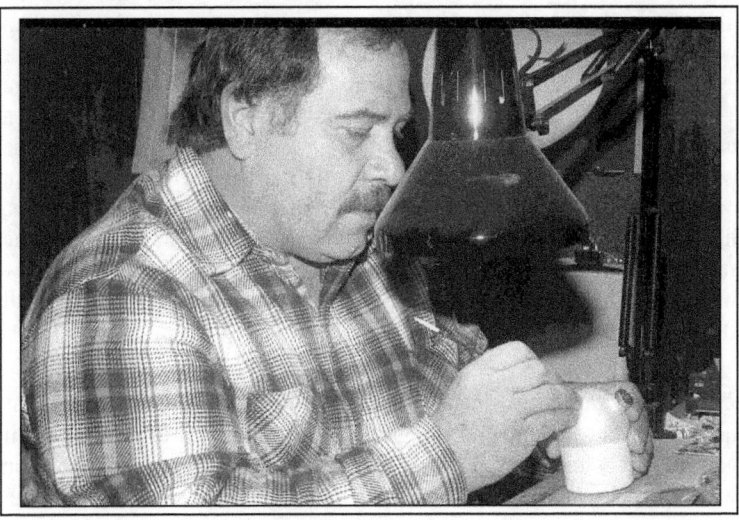

Kraskiewicz hosts a one-day home show the first Saturday of December every year. That event now attracts more than 3,500 people, a few of whom fly in from other states. To many people, buying some new "August" Christmas ornaments is a yearly rite as traditional as cutting their own Christmas tree.

While each Christmas ornament is a hand-painted original, Kraskiewicz says some near-duplication of design is inevitable "because you can only do a mallard in flight a certain way; there are maybe five different positions, or so."

All of the ornaments are painted with acrylic paint, with bird images the most popular. Even at this small of a scale, he says, "You've really gotta know birds" to make them look right, with proper coloring and proportion. "If you're out in the outdoors you almost pick it up [naturally]," he says. "Like a carpenter or a mechanic or whatever, if you do it every day of your life you can almost put a car together probably blindfolded. It's the same thing with painting birds and that. The more you paint them the more you understand them and get detail. . . . The detail has gotta be there. And usually when you work on them eight, ten, twelve hours a day, it's really hard on you," he says about eye strain.

He preferred painting on satin—or matte—finish ornaments because they were not quite as eye-straining and took paint better, but those are no longer available, which leaves him with mirror-like shiny ornaments. "They're hard to paint because you've got that constant glare from the light beating back up at you," he says. "And then when you use those jeweler glasses you even increase the light back in your eyes; it's really terrible. . . . But I do enjoy it. I think it's really fun. There aren't too many guys who can paint in miniature. . . . If I do a painting, like 24 by 36 [inches], and you're doing like a farm scene with the barn and the detail, I think it's hard doing a big one. But overall I think it's more time-consuming and harder on the small ones, like the ornaments and the eggs and stuff like that. . . . It seems like the smaller the stuff is, the finer the detail, the better it sells. I don't know why, but it just does. . . . I'll sell 20 or 30 times the amount of small stuff as I will the big pieces."

Kraskiewicz uses picture references for birds with which he is less familiar. With "loons and things like that," though, "after a while, if you know the anatomy, you can just about put it in any position you want. And I usually sketch on paper first before I put something on an ornament. . . It takes about three coats of paint because when you use a water-base paint and you put it on a smooth surface the first two coats are almost transparent, so you have to let each coat dry. So I usually work on three or four dozen. One [dozen] I'll be penciling out, the second dozen I'll be putting (on) the first coat of paint, the third dozen the second coat of paint. So you can usually put out maybe two-and-a-half to three dozen a day, if you're lucky. And that's on a 14-hour day, so it's a long day."

The ornament company from which he buys "blank" ornaments generally produces three or four different colors of ornaments each year. "One of the big sellers about the ornaments, too, is [some] people want a different color every year in their collection," Kraskiewicz says. ". . . It seems like people still like the white and the dark blue and the gold. The blue looks nice with snow scenes; it really brings out the winter. And then the white looks nice for the game birds, and the gold looks nice with silhouettes. I do some research, like on skiers. If I want to do downhill or cross-country [skiers] I'll get some skiing magazines. You have to have something to go by, because I'm not really a skier, and I don't have the time to take pictures. But on the animals and that, I have a 35-millimeter camera and I shoot my own pictures."

Since "everybody and their brother is doing wildlife art today," as Kraskiewicz puts it, a good marketing strategy is as important as talent to an artist. "You have to be on your toes because there are so many terrific artists out there," he says. "That's why seven or eight years ago I started touching on the mountain men and Indian things. Now with *Dances With Wolves* and a couple of the other big productions about the Old West—*Wyatt Earp* and all those—Western and Indian art is just going crazy...

"I've come out with a lot of different things the past couple of years. I have so many new ideas about what I want to do. I'm working now with another artist who I think is going to go places. He's been doing carvings and miniatures, and we're using those as remarks in my paintings. He does carved feathers and little Indian war shields and things. We're knocking the socks off the market."

Kraskiewicz generally avoids Western and Indian subjects when it comes to Christmas ornaments because he would have a tendency to spend more time adding details, which would either deflate his income or inflate the value of the ornaments. "When you get to a point where you start detailing out so much it's not worth $11 anymore; it's worth $35 to $40, and nobody wants to buy an ornament for $35 or $40."

The time/selling price factor also caused Kraskiewicz to cut back on the number of limited-edition ornament sets he turns out. In past years he hand-painted 50 or 60 copies of four different sets—for instance: a set of waterfowl, a set of upland game birds, a set of big-game animals and a set of eagles. This year he hand-painted 25 copies of a set of four loon-image ornaments. He points out that since the oak display case costs $87 and the specially-coated large ornaments $7.50, he isn't making much profit by selling the sets for $150.

"It's sort of like an heirloom," he says of the ornaments. "If the artist makes it... big somehow, that little ornament that they paid maybe six or seven bucks for in 1982 might be worth $150 to $200 down the road if the guy [artist] makes it. So that's another way of thinking about an investment—and it's a cheap one."

☼

Leaves Of Class

Laurie Paulson ... leaf painter

You could say that Laurie Paulson turned over a new leaf four and a half years ago. Almost literally. Considering what she could handcraft as a birthday present for her adult artist daughter, the idea of painting a cardinal [bird] on a large pressed leaf popped into her head. Her daughter, Teresa Christensen, loved the framed result so much she encouraged her mother to do more leaf paintings and try to sell them. In fact, she had Paulson paint a duplicate of her birthday gift painting, sold that, and returned with seven orders.

"She got so enthused about it," Paulson says. "She was really animated, and she was just insistent I do this. She just knew that it was something that was going to be successful. Then my husband jumped on the bandwagon, and together they kept prodding me to do this. Every one I did sold right away. And it's just kind of mushroomed from there."

With no previous artistic training or experience, the Balsam Lake, Wisconsin, resident suddenly found herself, at age 56, a late blooming professional artist. Two years later a national magazine, *Birds And Blooms*, published a one-page feature about her unusual artistic creations and she began painting nearly every waking minute to fill orders flooding in from around the country.

"It's been a fairy tale world," Paulson says of the experience of the last few years. "I'm Cinderella."

Paulson's success is not only a Cinderella story, but also a story about making lemonade when life hands you lemons. That first leaf painting—and a large percentage of her leaf paintings since then—was done on a heart-shaped leaf from a Mexican bamboo plant in her back yard. Paulson tried to kill the invasive bush more than once, without success. Now, of course, she's glad it survived. It is her version of the golden goose.

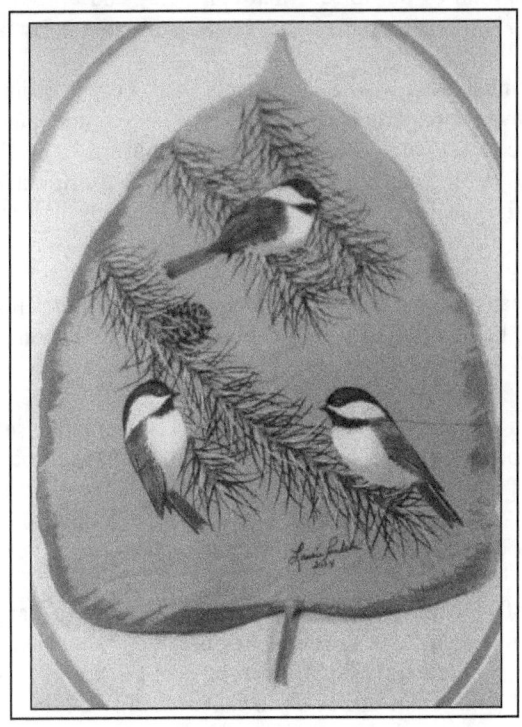

An obvious question is: Aren't pressed, dried leaves rather perishable canvases?

"Once they're in the frame they're protected by the glass," Paulson says. "Once they're in the frame they're there to stay, and they'll be fine."

Paulson tried various methods of preservation before deciding that simply pressing and drying leaves was sufficient. She keeps them, sorted by size, in plastic storage bins, where "they'll stay [intact] for years," she says. "I put something over them to keep them flat, otherwise they do want to curl up."

While all paintings are sensitive to sunlight, leaf paintings are vampire-sensitive. Paulson no longer participates in outdoor art shows because of problems with sunlight, humidity and other elements. Even when protected from sunlight, green leaves turn color. "Once the chlorophyll is gone the green is gone," Paulson explains. She uses leaves from throughout the growth stages, from late spring through fall. Within a couple of years green leaves "turn to some shade of tan or beige or brown. It's kind of fun to see what color they end up." If there is a way to keep leaves green, she hasn't come across that information.

Besides bamboo leaves, she also paints, with acrylic paint, on other types of leaves, including such large leaves as sycamore and sea-grape leaves she collects when she and her husband, Merrill, travel South for the winter. "I can't use all leaves; they just don't turn out," she says. She learned what leaves lend themselves to serving as canvases and which don't through trial and error.

The first year or two she painted birds, then added butterflies, animals and finally, beginning last year, people. "I'm in the learning process," she says. "I still have a lot to learn."

She needs a visual reference for most subjects—a picture in a book or magazine, or on a postcard or greeting card. "I have a lot of books," she says. "I have many, many bird books, with all the different types of birds. . . . A lot of time the only thing I use the visual for is the bird itself; the background might be something totally different each time."

Paintings of chickadees are most popular, which is a happy coincidence, for it is Paulson's favorite bird to paint. "I've always thought they were the cutest little birds," she says. ". . . Now I've painted so many that I paint them out of my head." Cardinals, loons and eagles follow chickadees on the popularity scale.

Paulson doesn't restrict herself to leaf paintings. She also paints on regular canvas—and sells prints of those paintings—and on small wood slabs. Those paintings sell well too, but not as well as her leaf paintings, most of which range in price from $39 to $99.

She does her own mounting, matting and framing, putting most of the leaf paintings into standard five-by-seven, eight-by-ten, eleven-by-fourteen, and fourteen-by-eighteen frames. "If I see a frame that catches my eye, as soon as I see the frame I know exactly what I'm painting for it," she says. "The frame almost tells me what kind of a leaf to put in it."

Some leaves appear to have been trimmed to fit into frames. That isn't the case, though. Paulson gathers many imperfect, flawed leaves rather than search only for full, perfectly formed leaves. She believes malformed leaves "look more authentic."

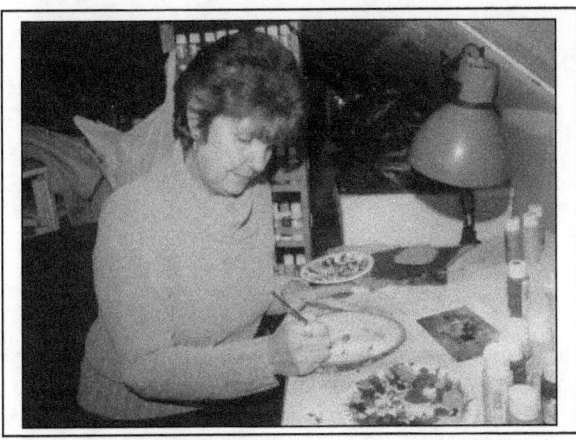

While the popularity of her leaf paintings has made Paulson feel like Cinderella, it was an iconic toy character, Barbie, that first brought her success in the realm of arts and crafts. She and Merrill have made miniature Barbie doll furniture for more than 13 years. Since the best market for the furniture is their website, they have shipped orders to such remote, far-flung areas as the Arctic Circle, Siberia and the Australian outback. Japan is a major market.

"From September to December, a lot of our sales are generated through the Internet," Paulson says. "We work on it all year to stock up for the fall, and then the orders come in fast and furious."

Laurie makes the dining and living room furniture, Merrill the bedroom and deck/patio furniture—such items as swings and Adirondack chairs. Some sample prices: sofa, $14.95; full bed, $26.95; coffee table, $8.95; pair of table lamps, $7.95. The Paulsons work with both wood and plastic, and more than 100 fabric designs.

The Barbie furniture website also includes some information about Paulson's leaf paintings, which take two to three hours each, on average, with animals generally requiring more time than birds. "It used to take me a lot longer," she says. "But I'm learning as I go, and one of the things I'm learning is how to speed up a little. I'm sure everybody goes through that part of the art."

Money doesn't grow on trees? It does, in a way, for Laurie Paulson.

- *December 7, 2004*

Becoming Mary Pettis

Mary Pettis ... landscape artist

Bob Dylan, whose chameleonic character has been part and parcel of his enigmatic identity for fifty years, once said that an artist should forever be in the process of becoming—to be always "busy being born," to quote a famous phrase from one of his masterpiece songs ("It's Alright, Ma"). I call this series of profiles Becoming Mary Pettis *because Mary seems to be one of those seekers who is always learning and striving to better her art, probing her soul in a lifelong quest for elusive perfection. The first profile of the series is from an August 29, 1984 interview.*

As famed commercial pitchman John Houseman might growl, Mary Pettis learned to draw and paint the old-fashioned way—through painstakingly perfected classical craftsmanship. She is now teaching others the techniques of classical realism at her own "atelier," or studio-school, in her country home a few miles southeast of Osceola, Wisconsin. Currently there is room for only two full-time students in a small second-floor studio next to Pettis's own studio. "Right now," she says, "I've had (other) people who have wanted to (study) full-time to really get a full training, and it's just impossible."

The return to classical realism is one of the major art movements of the 1980s. Atelier systems where small groups of students work almost in apprenticeship fashion with skilled art masters are becoming increasingly popular on the East and West Coasts, and elsewhere.

"All of a sudden everyone's trying to paint this way, and very few people know how," says Pettis, who studied under one of the major figures in the movement, Richard Lack, of Minneapolis, who has operated an atelier for 15 years. Pettis became interested in studying with Lack through a magazine article she read about him in 1971, while still a college student. After several interviews, Lack accepted her as a student on a trial basis, then as one of his first two full-time female students.

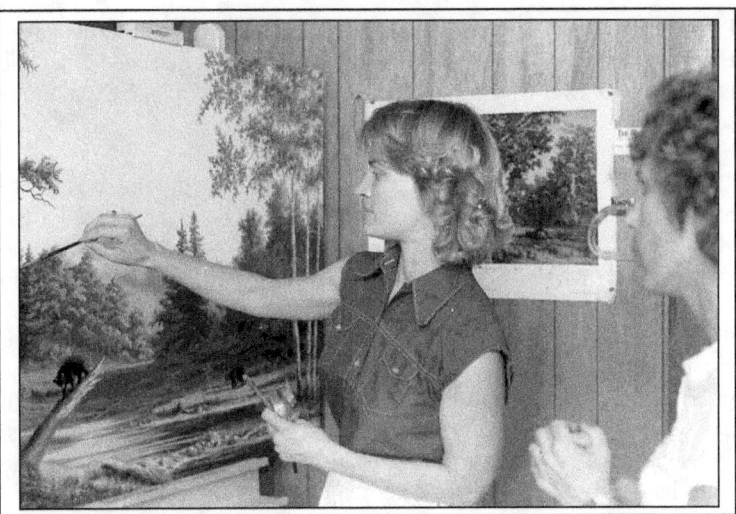

"In the late '60s and early '70s the majority of the art being done was highly abstract," says Pettis [left in above photo], "and much of what we were taught in college was more how to express one's self, or more on a psychological level. If you could explain well enough what you were working on it really didn't matter how it was done; the technique or the degree of competency wasn't all that important. So it was quite a shock to see that article on Richard Lack. Immediately I thought: I would give anything to be able to paint like that."

Pettis studied under Lack for three years, one year less than most students do.

"That was very good training," she says. "It was incredible. We did figures every morning in pencil and charcoal, and did casts of antique sculpture in the afternoon. After we did several casts—like after a year or so—we were allowed to hold a paintbrush and paint a cast in black and white. From there we went on to simple still-lifes, to more complex still-lifes, to portrait work and painted figures and whatnot, depending on our level of development. We had our individual projects in the afternoon, but in the morning everyone worked together around a model. So that was a tremendous education. I learned how to draw and I learned a lot that I really didn't assimilate until a couple of years after I had left him on color and composition and laying paint. I learned how to *see*, which in itself is quite an accomplishment for an artist."

Pettis later took copperplate etching classes from an artist from Florence, Italy, and has also found much success in that medium. She is best known as a wildlife painter, though, with some of her paintings selling for as much as $3,500.

"In college," she says, "everyone had told me, 'Well, you're going to have to decide if you want to be a fine artist or be a commercial artist and do wildlife, but there's no way you can do wildlife and be a fine artist.' That was the first question I asked Richard Lack, is: 'What do you think of wildlife art?' And he was quite emphatic in saying that it's not what you paint, it's how you paint it. It's whether or not you incorporate the elements of fine art, which are balance, harmony, unity, (and) beautiful color, and hopefully the subject matter you chose will have some inherent beauty or significance. I feel that wildlife does, and so I feel I have something special to offer. So that's kind of the bent that I chose. Plus, there's no denying that doing wildlife art I can charge about seven times as much as I could on a landscape, although now that's changing."

She has pursued wildlife art with a passion the last three or four years, in addition to her etchings.

Teaching had long been in the back of her mind. "I thought once I got some of my ideas together that I had gotten from reading various books and from training that I would like to pass it on. It's kind of like a desire to be a parent, I guess. There was kind of a desire to be a teacher too, to pass on some of the really good stuff that I knew. But I never really solicited students; I just waited and people came to me asking if I taught, and if they showed enough of an interest. . . . I guess I ended up teaching just kind of by word of mouth. People would come in once a week." A few local women still attend a weekly class on Tuesdays. Pettis also turned a small room in her house into a studio for a couple of full-time students, believing "really the only way to teach is to have someone on a full-time basis." Her first student was Darrell Wirkkula, who came from Hibbing, Minnesota, to study with Pettis after spending seven years trying to teach himself how to paint in the classical style without making much headway. "Then I came and studied with Mary," he says, "and in three months I learned more than I did in all the seven years I'd spent trying to teach myself." He ended up marrying Pettis and sharing studio space with her. Currently Pettis has two full-time students, Doug Berg, from Osceola, and Joyce Staley, of St. Croix Falls.

Comparing some of the paintings Berg did before he started studying with Pettis about six months ago with what he has accomplished under Pettis's tutelage makes the value of Pettis's method quite obvious. The difference between the then-and-now paintings is as great as the difference between someone pounding out a two-finger rendition of "Chopsticks" on a piano and an advanced piano student performing a classical sonata.

"I can see an improvement each three to six months," Staley says of her own work. She has studied with Pettis for nearly two years, spending six hours a day at Pettis's house three days a week. Berg is there five days a week. "There are so many things to learn," Staley says, "and she keeps telling me the same things over and over and over again, and one day it clicks. Then you've taken another step."

Staley, who began painting five years ago, took lessons from a few other teachers before finding Pettis. "There are a lot of art teachers out there, but it's very hard for them to teach you the way they teach," she says. "They get up there and they're doing their thing, and you're just following what they're doing, and you really don't learn from that."

Despite the revived interest in the classic style of art, many bigwigs in the modern art establishment still consider classic realism too commercial or too unimaginative to be on the same exalted plane as avant-garde or cutting edge art.

"The impression I get," Wirkkula says, "is that people don't teach it, and they kind of revile it, because they don't know how to do it. There are things in masterpieces that there's no way anyone would be able to figure out how they got certain effects that they did, or how they laid the paint to get a surface. You can see softly blended edges, but the colors are so luminous that it's hard to understand how they did it, and the technique for doing that has been lost, by and large. . . . The people who come out of art schools can't draw hands, let alone an entire figure. It takes a lot of time to learn how to draw a figure." As Pettis points out: "Drawing is not mere imitation, it's an expressive use of lines."

Expression explores the essence of a person, place or object.

"There aren't any formulas," Wirkkula says. "A friend of mine up in Hibbing wrote me letters asking what colors I used for the lights and shadows of trees. I wrote back and told him, 'Do you have any trees outside your house? Look at them. Those are the colors you use.'"

While emphasizing the same basic principles, Pettis doesn't follow the same program Richard Lack uses. She doesn't have her students first become as proficient as possible in drawing before having them learn how to paint, for example.

"That's a bit more academic than what we're doing here," she says. "I think it's important to carry along the method like paint handling. I think paint handling is something you can start on an elementary level, along with starting drawing on an elementary level, and learn how to paint. There's a method of laying paint. There's a method of seeing color. And maybe drawing is (a student's) strength and maybe color is his strength. I don't think it necessarily has to follow the progression that you do this first, and then that, and then that. . . . I think it's refreshing, and I think it's pertinent, to carry all the separate disciplines side by side as you progress up to getting technical competence. I don't have the track record here that Richard Lack has, so maybe I'm wrong. But the thing is, too: we're trying to make a living on our art here too, so we have to kind of try to figure out ways that we can speed up the process. Even if you're selling pictures for $30 to $60, at least it's enough to pay the gas to and from here. So it's nice to have things that are short-term projects. . . . A lot of purists would say, well, you're compromising by not spending as much time as you could, or by not painting subjects that are the most noble subjects to paint or something. But there are a lot of masters who would prove them wrong."

Drawing remains the cornerstone of Pettis's atelier program.

"If you can draw a [human] figure you can draw anything," she says. "It's more difficult to paint a beautiful figure than anything else in existence, I think. The reason why is because we all know what a figure should look like. We've lived with people and we've really looked at people, and ourselves, more than anything around us. So you can goof up on a limb of a tree and it'll still look like a tree. But you goof up on the length of an elbow from the shoulder and everybody's going to call you on it—or eyes being too close together, or cockeyed or something. People will notice that."

Another invaluable tool is "a sense for masses and shapes." By studying and understanding clouds, for instance, an artist is able to have clouds do what the artist wants the clouds to do. That way, Pettis says, "you don't have to wait for the perfect day and have your paints sitting right in front of you. That's, I think, where we depart a little bit from some of the little bit more academic schools, although when we get the space we will do more academic work."

Despite the restrictions of space, logistics and time that have forced Pettis to take some teaching shortcuts and alter some goals, she is fairly satisfied at the progress her students have made.

"There are all kinds of things in daily living that get in the way," she says. "If we were hermits we'd probably be able to reach those ideals. But I think we're doing pretty well. We're working within limitations, and still we're, I think, going to come close to reaching our goals."

- 0000000 –

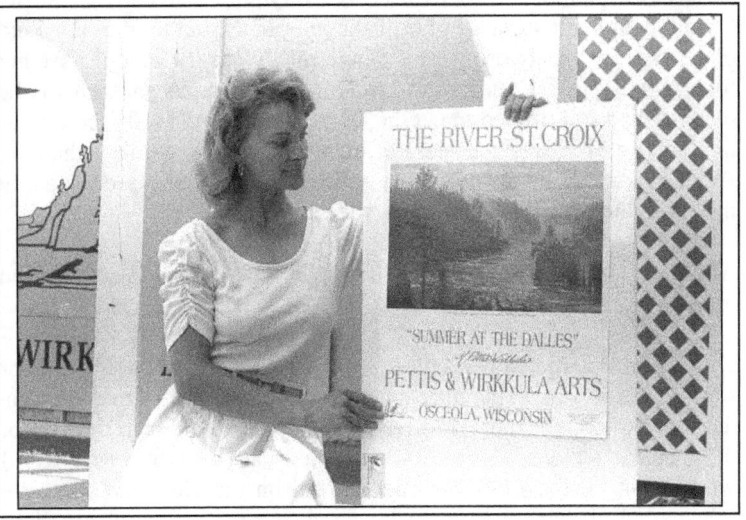

My second interview with Mary, on June 7, 1991, concerned a four seasons set of paintings of the St. Croix River Dalles, the focal point of the Minnesota and Wisconsin Interstate State Parks. She operated an art gallery in Osceola at the time.

While the St. Croix River Valley has been a popular subject for artists for 150 years, there is no painter, past or present, whose name conjures an instant association with the region. Osceola area resident Mary Pettis is making something of a bid to be "the St. Croix Valley artist" with her recently completed four seasons posters of the St. Croix River Dalles and other locally oriented work. Pettis's posters depict different scenic views of the Dalles—the steep-walled rock gorge at Minnesota and Wisconsin Interstate State Parks—during the four different seasons of the year, at different times of the day. The spring painting is set at sunrise, summer at midday, autumn at sunset, and winter on a moonlit night.

Dalles House restaurant owner Bob Clark commissioned Pettis to do the four paintings that were made into posters. The original paintings, which measure approximately four by five feet, hang on a wall in the Dalles House's main dining room. It took Pettis eight to ten weeks to complete each painting.

"I started with the summer picture because I had done numerous paintings of that spot," she says. "So I had a lot of color studies and mental sketches and whatnot.

"The spring picture was tricky because everything is so dark at sunrise. Usually you don't see a lot of brilliant color in the morning; it just kind of depends on the atmosphere. One morning I was out scouting around for a good spot. I knew I wanted to get landmarks in each of the pictures, and so I wanted to get the Devil's Chair [a natural rock formation] in. And it was the most brilliant orange sunrise, so I thought, 'Well, I saw it.' It was nice because it reflected in the water, and still there was the mist coming down in the valley."

Angle Rock and The Old Man of the Dalles rock formation are featured in two other paintings.

"If I haven't painted a particular spot before, then I have to do a color study," Pettis says, explaining her working method. "I have to sit on the spot and do the colors on a really small scale. And then for each of the pictures I did an 18 by 24 color study also. That was where I worked out all the problems and decided on the view and the color scheme. And then I presented it to Bob [Clark] for his okay. If he wanted something one way or the other he gave me a little input on each of the 18 by 24 color studies."

Pettis decided to make posters rather than limited edition prints from the paintings so more people could afford the pictures. "We printed them on the same quality paper, and we're using the same process and everything as the limited edition prints," she says. "It's just that they're not signed and numbered. But I think that they're really high quality, and we're real pleased with them. . . . I think they'll be really nice for visitors in the area here, to come and take back mementos that are nice and frame-able and not that expensive."

She adds that the posters may serve to promote the area and attract more visitors.

Pettis estimates she has done approximately 80 on-the-spot paintings between Osceola Landing and the north end of St. Croix Falls.

"It would be real exciting to see a whole show of everything all put together that I've done of the area," she says. "But I'll probably never see that because I've done so many that have just gone out to different parts of the country. . . . I've done quite a few of Cascade Falls [a waterfall at Osceola]. And then I've done a number of them at Interstate Park—just tons. We kind of live there in the summer. We camp, and the kids will fish and I'll paint. . . . I'd love to have a poster of Cascade Falls. That would probably be one of the ones I would do next if we were to do one—and maybe a couple of panoramic ones. Just Osceola itself is beautiful, with Cascade Falls and Cascade Creek and the Upper Mill Pond, and then the scenic bluffs."

She has put out one other poster made from a painting she did of a St. Croix River island just north of the Highway 243 bridge at Osceola. "Everybody has a story about that island," she notes. "Most of the local people, and the people that come back home to visit relatives, come in the gallery and they like that island. And anyone who canoes the river has usually pulled over on it and camped there and eaten there or something."

That island poster was done about two years ago, about the time her gallery opened.

"I could spend my whole life painting the river valley," Pettis says. "It's just the most incredible place. When I first moved here I was so reminded of the Hudson River Valley, which I wasn't tremendously familiar with; I had passed through it. And I had studied the art of the Hudson River painters. All through school they were my favorites. And when I moved here I was just struck by the beauty of it."

Pettis, of course, was not the first person to notice similarities between the Hudson and St. Croix river valleys. Hudson, Wisconsin, was not given its name by happenstance; it reminded founders of the Hudson River Valley, in New York state.

"From what I could see, there wasn't a St. Croix River painter," Pettis continues. "There are several Duluth painters, and there are some Lake Superior shore painters. But I came to the river valley here and no one knew of anyone who was the river valley painter. I just see the St. Croix having the potential of being just like the Hudson River Valley because the foliage and the type of vegetation is really varied. You get the northern pines and the southern elms and maples and all that. And the gorge is incredible, and it's majestic. And just two miles away you've got pastoral scenes. And then the lakes. It's just an artist's dream here. I think I could paint the rest of my life. I could paint thousands of pictures within ten miles of Osceola. It's all here. It's really fantastic here. It's a fantastic area for an artist."

- 0000000 –

By the next time I interviewed Mary, on October 15, 2001, she had moved to an historic hilltop home in Taylors Falls and her artistic journey had taken a new path.

"Chiang, this world isn't heaven at all, is it?"
The Elder smiled in the moonlight. "You are learning again, Jonathan Seagull," he said.
  - *from* Jonathan Livingston Seagull, *by Richard Bach*

Her detailed representational paintings made Mary Pettis one of the most, if not *the* most, popular artists in the entire St. Croix River Valley. A large part of the public loved her work, publishers clamored for print rights to her wildlife paintings, and prestigious commemorative commissions came her way. She had her own galleries in Osceola (1991-1993) and Taylors Falls (1996-1998). After being a devotee of detail for 25 years, though, Pettis is now following her artistic muse down a different path.

"My whole philosophy on art has changed so much," she says, struggling for the right words to explain herself. "I'm not painting leaves and feathers anymore. I guess... If I were to say what's going on with me artistically right now, I would have to say it's powerfully humbling to realize after 25 years that it's not about being technically proficient. But you have to be technically proficient in order to come to that realization. . . . So now I'm at this place where I realize that it's not about capturing a place or telling a story with detail, . . . and that it's not about how much time you put into a picture to get it to say all the little things. . . . I'm right at the threshold, and I realize that I'm just a beginner at this now, after 25 years. Now I'm at this place, and now I see how far I have to go. . . . I don't know how else to say it other than it's so humbling to realize that I'm just a beginner. I'm not very good at it yet. I'm starting to understand what I want to do with my art, and it's about making a connection. It's synthesizing not the stuff I see but the emotions that I feel when I'm out there capturing the mood, and the time—the moment—and being able to synthesize it to the point where you eliminate all the trivial stuff and only render, as accurately as you can, the visual effect that contributes to that emotion."

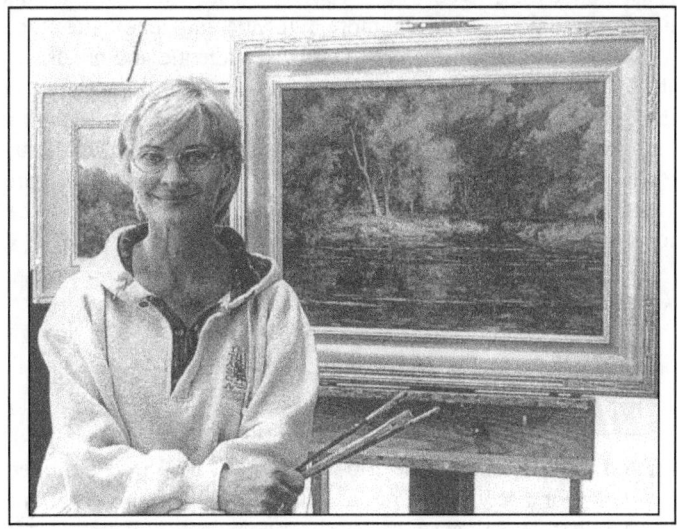

Pettis, who lived in the Osceola area during most of the 1980s and 1990s and now lives in Taylors Falls, is about a year into a five-year plan of trying to become what she calls a master painter, in the "alla prima," or "plein air," style. She still does representational art, but it is representational art with a large measure of expressionism to it. Alla prima means painting from life. It is "direct painting," on site, generally done start to finish in one session. In a book about the alla prima style, Vermont artist Richard Schmid wrote that he considers the style "to be the ultimate in representational art because it is about real experience and demands the highest level of skill." To Schmidt, the three most important aspects of painting are knowing why you want to paint a certain subject, "an analytical grasp of what you see," and "the skill to control the process of painting." A great painting will emanate self-expression.

Pettis has studied plein air and alla prima painting with such masters as Jim Wilcox, Zhang Wen Xin, and Robert Duncan in Jackson, Wyoming, and Stapleton Kearns in Rockport, Massachusetts.

"The greatest artists are self-expressive," Pettis says. "I've been rolling that off my tongue for 20 years, but I never really understood. The older I get and the better I get the more I realize that what that means is that you bring all your life experience to the table when you get to that level. And it makes you very vulnerable. But it's heartening too, because everything counts. And nobody can make art like I can because nobody has lived what I've lived. That's what will ultimately make my art unique. And the more authentic and honest I can be with who I am in my life experiences the more authentic and honest my art will be, and the greater I will be as an artist. That boggles my mind, that that's the way it works as an artist. I hope I live long enough to be able to say what I'm finally learning how to say. . ." Her voice strains; she seems near tears. "That's where I'm at. . . . If you could figure out how to put that into words in a cohesive way, that would just be really a wonderful gift for me."

Take what you have gathered from coincidence. – Bob Dylan

In 1995 a late-19th Century painting of a St. Croix River Dalles scene done by E.E. Edwards was used on a poster celebrating the centennial of Minnesota Interstate State Park. Last year Pettis was commissioned to paint a Dalles scene for the 100th anniversary of Wisconsin Interstate State Park, for a commemorative print celebrating the centennial of Wisconsin's state park system. By sheer coincidence, Pettis lives in the historic Taylors Falls house Edwards and his family occupied for two relatively short stretches.

"I had been a fan of E.E. Edwards ever since I was a member of the historical society in Osceola," Pettis says, "and Ward Moberg was talking about E.E. Edwards' work and how they were having a retrospecttive show of his [elsewhere in the Midwest]. . . . I had no idea until after I was living here that E.E. Edwards had actually lived in this house and looked at that view [of the St. Croix River]."

Pettis's husband, Randy Pearson, whom she married in 1997, has owned the house since 1984.

Besides being an artist, Elijah Evan Edwards also was a Methodist minister and educator. According to a catalog for a 1990 retrospective exhibition at Hudson's Phipps Center For The Arts called *Vision and Imagination in the St. Croix Valley*, "he is credited with being one of the first resident artists to paint St. Croix River scenes." The catalog author quoted Edwards as writing, in 1896: "I have been a wanderer on the face of the earth, but have not found any landscape rivaling the one shut in amongst (our) own green hills. It is a combination of that which is loveliest in many land-scapes."

Edwards's paintings, writings and lectures—again according to the exhibition catalog—helped in the creation of the two Interstate State Parks.

"I thought he captured the mood of the river," Pettis says of Edwards. "You could tell that he loved the river, the emotion of it. And it's perfect for documentary interest. I thought that was interesting too—showing the logs where they were piled up on Angle Rock, . . . and the little boats that the people were riding in, . . . and how the area had been logged off in a lot of areas in his pictures. I've only seen a few, but I thought that was interesting—how between that time and ours the valley has regenerated. It's now forested again."

A Minnesota Historical Society art curator, Tom O'Sullivan, said during a lecture given in conjunction with the 1990 Phipps exhibition that early river valley artists displayed a "documentary urge" to record the human activity that took place within the river valley. Fellow lecturer Kurt Leichtle, a University of Wisconsin—River Falls history professor, said those artists "wanted to emphasize another side of the St. Croix—the side of the St. Croix that worked, that was industrious."

Pettis cites artistic maturity, restlessness and other factors as reasons for her artistic re-evaluation.

"In the same way that a novel isn't a better novel just because it has more words, . . . or a melody isn't a better melody if it has more notes," she says a painting packed with detail is not necessarily better than a less-detailed painting. In one recent landscape painting focusing on a few white-pine trees, for instance, she attempted to capture on canvas "all the feelings that blustery October brings to us"—the chill in the air, the sense of the season to come, the memories of past Octobers and fleeting summer, and the sensation of autumn color. She says sheer detail could not communicate all of that, that a detailed painting "would be just an illustration of *stuff*, and I wouldn't get that emotion. If it's done right you get the same emotion when it's upside down. It's the abstract elements, and how they play off of each other, that gives you that feel."

While "the quality of light is a lot of it," she explains, it has more to do with tonality. "All the things that make music great is the same stuff that makes art great," she says. "And you can't see music. It has to do with tone and rhythm and balance and harmony and how they all interact with each other to make a whole—how they play off each other. Tonality is the range of value in a picture." Staying with the music analogy, she goes on: "The effect of light would be like a one-line melody in a symphony. But how dark do you make your darks? How colorful do you make your darks? How colorful do you make your lights? If your darks are colorful, are your lights going to be pumped with color or are they going to be more muted? It's subtle stuff. . . .

"The sad thing is that your audience diminishes as maybe you get a little more sophisticated in some ways. My friend Marcie, who paints with me, read in a book—or else she had a teacher or something who once said: As soon as you get to the point where your family doesn't like your pictures anymore you know you're on the right track. I wouldn't say it's necessarily that, but. . ."

Borrowing a phrase from sports parlance, Pettis speaks of her new direction as trying to take her art to another level. To test her progress, she entered St. Croix River paintings in three national competitions this year. She had work accepted into shows related to all three competitions. One was the annual Arts For The Parks competition the National Academy of the Arts created 15 years ago in cooperation with the National Park Foundation. Pettis made the Top 100 of the competition, meaning her *Punctuation* painting of a wild, flood-swollen Dalles scene is part of the traveling exhibition being shown at seven or eight sites. Another of her new paintings is currently on display at the National Arts Club in New York City. That show is a fundraising event for the Metropolitan Museum of Art. In November a Pettis painting will be part of the American Artists Professional League 73rd Grand National Exhibition at the Salmagundi Club in New York. Pettis says it is "a great thrill" to have her work shown at such prestigious places so rich in history.

While she turns out fewer finished paintings now than when she was a "leaves and feathers" artist, she does "ten times the work" by doing repeated small color studies in preparation for the larger paintings she wants to do. Those small studies help her understand what's going on with light when the sun is in a certain position in the sky and solve various problems the painting might pose. "And then I take my big one down there and try to capture the effect before the light changes," she says. "But I know where I'm headed [with the painting]. On the larger piece, I'll start an hour before and have the whole composition in, and then right when the light gets the way it is then I try to freeze the light effect, with the shadows, in the accurate places, and then hit those color notes that only last for a few minutes. It's a rush!"

Okay. But isn't using the outdoors as a studio during wintertime difficult to do around here?

"Yes," Pettis admits, "but I just bought a new coat. I just got myself a down-filled parka that goes all the way down to my ankles. So I paint outside year round. It's a little tough on old hands that are getting more arthritic all the time, but that's okay. All things yield to effort. . . . The more you paint on location the more you're able to paint away from the location too. In order to get good at that, at this style of painting, you have to do it a lot before you go back to the studio again."

There are no prints of Pettis's new paintings. While the company that publishes prints of her older work continues to sell those, that company "wouldn't be the least bit interested in any of this stuff," Pettis says.

She understands that her audience may well grow smaller in one sense, and possibly larger in another sense, as she gains more national recognition, as her art becomes "maybe a little more sophisticated in some way." Moving away from what has brought success is a tough decision for an artist to make. "For me," she says, "that was doing highly detailed renderings of subjects that are popular subjects. And now I'm painting one single tree in the middle of a field. But I think that when I get better at this—better at doing this the way I want to do it—I think the single tree will speak to my audience too. . . . An audience for art, a lot of times, is interested in the way an artist looks at things, so what you kind of do is elevate the commonplace. Then it helps your viewer go out and look at nature in a completely different way, or a blustery October day in a different way."

Besides changing her approach to art, Pettis now also looks at her art in a different way in that making a living as an artist is no longer her main concern. "I'm very grateful—abundantly grateful—that I was able to do that," she says. "I'm grateful to the people that have bought my work over the years, and that I touched a chord with, and I helped them see how much they loved the valley through my work. . . . There are thousands and thousands of my pictures out there, if you count the prints and etchings. And I'm very grateful for the people that love my work and have followed my work over the years. But the path that I'm on now is a different path than when I was trying to make a living as an artist and get better and better at drawing and painting *stuff*. The path that I'm on now is I'm hoping to become a master painter, and I'm only a beginner on that path."

- 0000000 –

Given that I wanted my book Polk County Places *to not only explore places but also explore how places shape us and how we relate to certain places, on September 12, 2007, I was with Mary for about two hours as she selected a St. Croix River backwater scene to paint and translated the scene onto canvas in the field. The resulting portrait of a painter at work is one of the longest and most significant pieces in that book. The book simply would not have the same balance and weight without it.*

"Oh, look at this," Mary Pettis says as we walk along railroad tracks to the east side of the swing bridge across the St. Croix River three miles south of Osceola. "Isn't this lovely? Oh! I was thinking another spot."

The scene before us is a river backwater to the south side of the tracks, not the main river channel. Mary, a former Osceola area resident who now lives in Taylors Falls, is an artist of national renown. She did an on-scene painting at this place yesterday, and is back to paint another.

"I kind of squint down and look at kind of the structural rhythms," she explains. "I like this Y," she points out. "That's a strong armature for a nice painting. I played on that a little bit yesterday. But now, when I squint down I don't. . . The darks really aren't connected as much. So I could zero in or I could go up to my second stop. This *is* pretty neat. I always like looking into the light."

"Looking into it, huh?" I say, somewhat surprised, thinking about capturing the scene photographically.

"I know it's not as good for my eyes," she says, "but I just love that back-lighting and the rim-lighting."

She proceeds to another potential spot. Here she likes the touches of blue in the calm backwater. "I love doing the water lilies too." This spot is "really cool" as well.

We continue walking along the railroad tracks so Mary can check out another spot. "Oh, this is nice too," she says as we reach that place. "That's just intriguing, where the sky comes through. I like the water lilies better in shadow, and then to come out into the sun; I like that a lot. And the tree overhanging this way is an interesting. . . Oh, that's really cool!" She contemplates her options. "Yeah, I like that. I'll probably end up doing that. That's just magical down there; I just love that. And then I can zero in just a little more. And then there's just a little glint of light back—just the ribbon that would keep that touch of infinity, or an indication of infinity. I like that."

It seems as though she has made a decision. First, though, she wants to visit one more spot a little closer to the bridge, on the north side of the tracks. She thinks that one is probably a little more intriguing in evening light. "It's all kind of just washed out now," she says. Which is to say it looks flat and lacks emotional impact. "About six o'clock in the evening this is just magical—unbelievable." Obviously she has been here before, and studied the scene. One evening this week she hopes to return to paint it. This mid-morning in mid-September her choice will be one of the other spots.

"Usually I just look for something that makes my heart skip a beat," she says. "Emerson called it that gleam of light." That little flash in her psyche is "like a metaphor for something else. And for me right now that's that touch of blue in the shadow. I love that, how the lily pads come out from the shadow into the light."

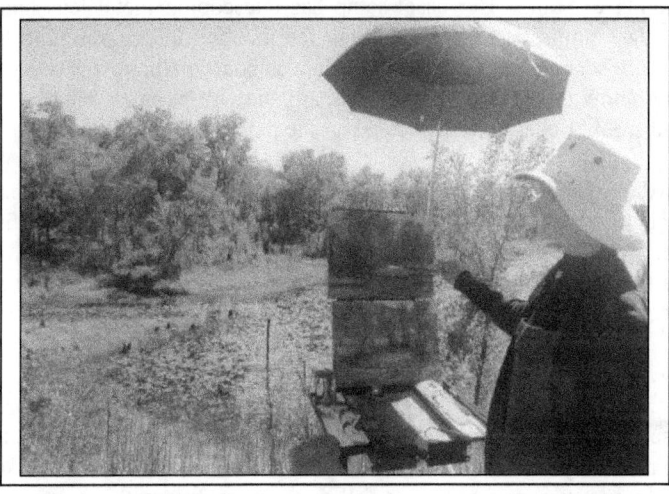

The second most important element of her decision-making is more analytical. She asks herself: *Does it have a structural rhythm? Can I connect the darks in a way that will make a nice painting, rather than just a portrait?* "I used to just paint portraits of things, but now—I think just because I'm a more mature artist—I'm looking for rhythms in the landscape, rhythms of the darks and how that will connect to the light. Can I put the scene in a format that will attract my viewer's eye from a distance and communicate that same feeling that I'm feeling when I'm looking at it? That has to be done kind of not on the emotional level but on the intellectual level. Can I combine the darks so that they'll form a nice pattern? So I squint down usually to do that. So here I see that I have an entrance, with this blue sweep. And then it disappears into the shadow and goes underneath that tree trunk. That's really cool. And then my eye will follow the sweep of the tree trunk up and toward me, which is a tricky artistic thing." The more she analyzes the scene the more she seems to like it, for its various elements. It has a "beautiful structural rhythm," to her artist's eye. This will be the spot, she decides. She walks back to the first stop to retrieve her briefcase-like painting case, then returns and starts setting up, a few feet off the south side of the tracks, which are perhaps ten or twelve feet above the level of the lily-rich backwater.

Mary is tall and slender, wears thin-rim glasses, and has relatively short, straight blond hair. Today she is wearing a jaunty, wide-brimmed white hat, faded blue jeans, black sandals, and a black jacket-shirt over a black turtleneck sweater. She also slips on a burgundy apron with pockets, where she keeps wipes to clean her palette, before beginning to paint. Her easel setup has telescoping metal legs and a small dark umbrella that shades both the painting in progress and her face. She sets up the 12-by-16-inch canvas board painting she did yesterday below the same-size canvas board she will paint on today. She has no stool or chair; she will stand as she paints.

"Nowdays," she says while setting up, "I try to quit as soon as I think I've captured that feeling that's inspired me to paint a place in the first place. And whoever gets it, fine. And if they don't, then they're not my audience for that particular painting. That's kind of a cockiness that comes with maturity, I guess, too, as a painter."

Mary developed a well-earned reputation as one of the best artists in the St. Croix Valley, largely on the quality of her detailed wildlife and landscape paintings. Just as Jonathan Livingston Seagull intuited that there are many levels of learning, in the late 1990s Mary left her comfortable, secure career behind to follow a new artistic path toward what seemed to be a higher level.

"It's a subtle difference, but it's there," she says. "I was painting for the market more—painting for people, just painting what I thought people wanted to see. I decided to take the leap and follow my muse instead. I kind of thought I was walking away from my market, and what ended up happening was that I ended up expanding my market in a big way. I would have never dreamt that I would have been as successful and had the following that I've ended up with, and a broader, national audience, when here I thought I was walking away from the recognition. It's ended up being a really good thing for me to follow my muse. So now I teach people: Go for it. You just don't know where it's going to lead."

Mary is a classically trained artist who now paints in the "plein air," or "alla prima," style. Paintings are done at the scene, outdoors, generally in one session. Her paintings still are representational art, but it is representational art with a large measure of expressionism.

"You try to get the right stroke in the right place," she says. "If you do that, then by the time the canvas is covered your painting should be done. It just has a different pressure. And the paint is thicker and the brushwork is more expressive. It doesn't have that noodled look—it doesn't have that belabored look—of a more finished classical landscape that's been filtered through the intellect. It's more intuitive. . . . It's taken me a few decades to be able to edit the landscape to only those elements that add to the emotions I'm trying to portray and eliminating all the superfluous aspects. But it takes a while to figure that all out—what is essential and what is superfluous. It's like I'm doing poetry instead of novels."

Just as audience members are not supposed to think about the years of practice it took a dancer to perfect a ballet movement, plein air paintings should appear effortless. "It has to go beyond," Mary says. "It has to transform the technique because painting is a language, above all, and it doesn't matter how good you are at speaking the language." If an eloquent preacher has nothing much worth saying, she poses, how eloquent is he, actually?

"I love making connections among all the arts because the more knowledgeable I become on all the artistic disciplines the more I see that they're all the same. They all deal with rhythm and balance and harmony. . . . So that's what I look for usually while I'm setting up my setup like this. Usually I'm thinking about those abstract elements of rhythm and balance and harmony so that once I actually begin painting I can turn off that left brain and just let it flow from the right brain."

Mary begins painting by "toning" the canvas with a light-brownish color. She likes to tone with a color that won't be part of the visible painting. "I never know what color I'm going to tone the canvas with until I get there," she says. "Color is such a fascinating thing. We respond differently to different colors, and so I look for kind of a sense of warmth and depth. While I'm toning the canvas I kind of design it in my head, deciding what's going to be in light and what's going to be in shadow, and where my areas of focus will be."

After those decisions are made it's a matter of deciding what the "skeleton" of the scene, on which the painting will be fleshed out, will be. She scratches some basic skeletal shapes for tree trunks and large branches on the canvas. While she has "a whole slew of brushes" with, she generally uses only one brush for a painting. Most of the time she challenges herself to complete a painting—or nearly complete it—in two to two-and-a-half hours. "Actually, I try to have it in the first fifteen minutes, where I can see where I'm headed with it, where I can see the finished product—in my head, at least. I should be just in love with it after the first fifteen minutes. And if I'm not, then I'll go back to the drawing board and change my design."

A sandhill crane croaks off to the south, and other critter sounds are audible as well. "I love this. Isn't it wonderful?" Mary says of the setting and the whole peaceful atmosphere.

"Nowdays when I paint like this I don't think so much about: *What are trees? What's water?* I think patterns. We're drawn to patterns. Like this shadow, for example, just forms a beautiful pattern. It just follows right up and goes up this tree. It's reaching—reaching toward the sky. Now I look at trees as having personalities, with relationships and connections. When I think about it like that, then it kind of comes through in the art. I think this tree has a connection to this one that's bending this way, like one's the old man and the other's the young guy. They have a spirit and a personality, and they're all connected, and springing from this sumptuous undergrowth."

"Do you prefer days when the sun is out, or are cloudy days good too?" I ask her.

"Oh, I like it all," Mary says. "The reason that the Impressionists loved cloudy days is because the light stayed the same. So I like any mood. But if you're going to paint in the sun it takes a lot of knowledge to freeze the light effect so that it doesn't look like part of the painting was done (at a different time)."

As she paints, Mary tells me about some of the galleries where her work is displayed—in Maui; Kirkland, Washington; Couer d' Alene; Idaho, and elsewhere—and how she has taken painting trips to Tuscany, southern France, Hawaii and elsewhere in recent years. She is invited to "paint outs" with other big-time plein air artists. I ask if a landscape scene of this area would sell in the Lahaina gallery.

"No, it's all local scenes," she says. "In [Kirkland,] Washington, though, it's interesting; I sell a lot of things that remind people of the Midwest, and of their home. I do some European scenes. But most of the ones that I've sold are paintings of spots like this."

She now is about fifteen minutes into the painting, the point at which she tries to have her shadow areas almost completely filled in. "So how is it looking to you?" I ask.

"Good," she says. "I love it. And I'm pleased with the rhythm that I'm going to have here. It's an interesting entrance here, and that kind of a nice sweep here. I can edit that just a little bit. . . . And then this light area will be in here. . . . Yup, I'm just about home free." She paints more, trying to capture "the warm glow" of what is underneath the blue reflection.

"I kind of work where you start out of focus and then gradually put things in deep focus. And I used to work from light to dark, but now with this method I work from dark to light. It's so different from when I was doing the classical method way back when you very first met me. Ironically, it doesn't always seem like it, but all my classical training comes to bear when I paint like this. . . . All our life experiences, and everything we've learned, and all the circuitous routes we've taken in life, it all comes to the easel when we are painting. . . . My gut reaction to a place says as much about who I am as it does about the place I'm painting. And that's why who the artist is makes a difference. That's why I tell people who start in their later years it's not too late to start painting because everything counts; you know, it all counts. You bring it all to the work. When your heart is in the right place in a creative endeavor like this it comes through."

She is cleaning off her palette, which seems to indicate she is entering another stage of the painting. "Yup," she confirms. "I'm done with the shadows and I'm going to go into the lights, and I don't want the two families to get mixed up—the light family and the shadow family." She also cleans her brush well.

"I like working with an umbrella," she explains, "not because of the paint or anything, but because our eyes will dilate and contract, depending on the amount of light that's getting in there. Just like a camera, we see light better when our pupils are wider; we see color better when the lens is wider." A broad-brimmed hat helps with that too.

"Now I start judging whether or not the light and dark relationships are accurate, and the colors that I want," she says as she starts applying paint from the light family. "I try to work from where my darkest dark is, and my lightest light, which is usually right in the area of focus—that area that's going to be the most intriguing. . . . And then if my area of highest contrast is in here that will help me judge this green over here, for example, which has a lot more white in it. If I dart my eye back and forth I can judge all colors by the relative intensity and the chromacity. So I can kick this up to where it looks like it's too bright. But if I judge everything else relatively in its chromacity. . . it should read as bright sunlight. . . . The more you do it the more you know the little rules, like the value of the light usually stays the same, but the color will change. It will be the same degree of lightness and darkness, but the color will cool as it recedes and warm as it comes closer to us. Things like that just kind of become automatic. And then I'm always looking to see that there's a nice rhythm, like the lights have a nice rhythm and they're playing off of the darks. I want to keep that rhythm."

It's time to put in the blue of the water and the sky, for blue is another part of the story, another color that connects to all of the other colors and shapes. Mary has learned to trust that if she paints what she sees everything will look right in its context. "I remember when I was watching my favorite painter, Zhang Wen Xin, paint," she says. "He would put a color down on this white canvas, and I just couldn't believe that that would be the right color. And I tried to see it, and tried to see it, and just couldn't see it. And then by the time he got all the other colors in in relationship to it it was perfect; it was just the perfect color."

Which is not to say Mary is recording the scene as a camera would. She is taking out a middle section that doesn't contribute to the scene, borrowing a small overhanging tree trunk from a short distance away because she likes the touch of light in it.

"An artist can move mountains," she says. "When I first started I just did everything a literal transcription, exactly what I saw, because at that time I believed that truth was beauty"—she laughs heartily at her former belief—"and I've since. . . I've done a lot of studying on especially the author and English critic [John] Ruskin, and this was a huge debate that was going on at the time of the transcendentalists—and since the Greeks, of course: Is truth beauty? Is beauty truth? . . . It's interesting, because that very thing was a debate that a lot of artists in my circle were having. Is truth of the fact of what you see a higher truth, and is that what we should be after? Or should we be after truth as of capturing how this place is affecting us? And Ruskin said that both are truth; there's the truth of the facts—the truth of the representation, just to make an honest representation—and then there's the truth of sentiment. And he said that truth of sentiment is a far higher truth, and much more difficult—that it's a higher form of art to capture. But truth isn't just the end in art either."

Mary is gauging her progress as she paints. She wants the painting to have "a complete, finished look" after about an hour and fifteen minutes. Then she will spend another hour "pulling it together." She tells me this is a pretty complex scene. "In what way?" I ask.

"If you were to take a photograph of it it would just look really busy," she says. True. If I had been looking for scenic photo settings I probably would not have snapped a shot of this particular scene. "There's so much stuff. There are *so* many trees; there are hundreds of trees. How do I pick and choose which ones so it just doesn't look like a jumble of trees? How do I pick the ones that are going to be the most expressive and emphasize them, and still have that look of dappled light, and yet have a breadth and a resonance? . . . I'll go after that inner warmth, so I'll grab warm colors here. I kind of squint my eyes down and see like a warmer green than the other green. It's just a sense of warmth that I'm getting from the side of that tree."

Several times she has stepped back to the other side of the railroad tracks to view her painting. When she does it again I ask what she is looking for. "I'm looking to see if the painting is hanging together as a whole, if it has what I was talking about," she says.

"So you're looking more at the painting rather than the actual scene?"

"Both. I start out by looking more at the scene, and then as I get further along I look more at the painting to see if it's capturing what I set out to capture about the scene."

She uses a reducing glass—the opposite of a magnifying glass—to do the same thing. "If I'm sitting, then I don't have to back up so much," she says about that tool.

She asks me to step back beside her for a look. I do. "See how it's starting to have a sense of place?" she says. "That's what I'm after—

just a sense of place, the sense of light, and whether or not those rhythms that I'm talking about are hanging together, and try to keep that warmth, that warm feeling that I felt when I first chose this spot. As soon as I get that all, then it's time to quit; I'm done—instead of going in and adding more words, ya' know."

This time the step-back view tells her she needs to continue connecting her light colors in a sweep. "You want to design the painting in such a way that the eye will keep moving around in the painting. . . . The eye always follows the light." The idea, she expands, "is to keep your viewer in the painting a long time, and keep your viewer's eye moving around the different areas. And we're always drawn to the light, and the eye is drawn to warmth, and it's drawn to detail. And it will linger over really hot areas—your areas of intense color—and it will just glide over areas that are more green or have less chromacity. . . . So that's the kind of thing that I decide when I go back."

Mary has been painting for slightly longer than one hour, and is on pace. A complicated scene such as this generally takes her a little longer than two hours to finish, and she tries to balance breadth and detail to maintain a certain melody, the melody being the big, strong relationship of the darks.

"Where in the world would a person rather be than right here right now?" she says, relishing the day, the place and her passion for painting. "I can't imagine where it could be. What a privilege. It's just a privilege to be in the face of nature like this, and then just to see the subtleties. I love this time of the year because the greens are no longer green." Actually, I would have guessed this time of September, this transition time between summer and autumn, would not excite artists. Leaves no longer are gorged with green, and yet there is only a tinge of autumn's coming colorama. The landscape has something of a faded look about it. To Mary, though, each tree limb has its own personality. "Some are warm, or some are cooler. Some greens are more yellow, some are magenta. Just all that character. And then the different trees have different types of leaves that reflect the sky differently, and different growth patterns. It's just awesome. There's all that variety, and yet there's a unity to it." She compares it to the way there is a binding unity to all of humanity at the same time each person is defined by an individual character.

"A philosopher-painter, huh?" I say a bit teasingly, while impressed by the analogy.

Mary laughs. "I don't think you can paint for thirty-five years, especially out in nature, and not be a philosopher. It comes from too much time alone listening to yourself think, I imagine."

After more time elapses she picks up another philosophical thread. "Ruskin said all great art is praise. When I first read that twenty years ago I thought: *Well, yeah*. . . But I didn't really get it. But now I get it. When you stop trying to make a finished picture and just try to express what you love, that reverence that accompanies trying to get at the heart of stuff that we love, it becomes easier to see. It's creating art out of love for what that is, not my own glory or 'look what I can do.' It isn't about 'look what I can do' anymore. . . . I say it's kind of like painting adverbs instead of nouns. It's painting the flow of the vine, and warmth, and the outreaching stretch of the branches. It's more about that. It's just a more spiritual thing. Unless you're looking broadly you don't see that; you just see the little individual leaves. . . . I've always been a lover of detail, so it's been hard because I love detail so much. It's always been hard for me to grasp the whole, and I never knew how to portray that until I started trying to paint it fast and capture the essence in plein air painting. When I knew I didn't have time to fill it all then I had to start really using a different approach, just really thinking about what I was looking at. Then I started realizing that the art that I was most drawn to was art that had all these beautiful abstract elements."

She paints more, then steps back and lets out an "Oh, yeah!"

"What are you liking here—just the rhythm of it?" I ask.

"Yeah," Mary says, "that it's starting to have that sense of mystery now. Everything is starting to just plunk into place. It's twice the painting of this one [the one she did yesterday] already, because of that. Yeah. If I were in a gallery and that (was) framed and on the wall across the room there's no way I couldn't walk up to it. The one on the bottom I probably would have a ho-hum attitude about; it wouldn't pull me in. But the one on top, there's no way I wouldn't go up to see it closer. Now I have to be careful not to destroy that; I love that feeling."

Given that I'm still not clear if she is painting a finished canvas or a study she will try to perfect later, I ask if she sells paintings this size. "Yeah," she answers. "This is a fifteen-hundred-dollar painting. Can you believe that? Is that nuts? But the ones that I sold around Maui were even more than that."

"But do you sometimes use these to do bigger ones?" I ask.

"Yeah, I use 'em as studies," she says. "And that was my intent when I did this one here [yesterday's]. But it takes a little while. This was the first painting I've ever done in this spot, and I really started to get a sense of place." A gust of wind blew over her setup yesterday before she was really finished with that painting. While the painting miraculously clung to the easel by two clips, Mary took the act of nature as a signal to stop painting. She says she plans to use the unfinished painting sort of as notes to herself for a larger painting. As it is, "it lacks that harmony and that breadth of effect."

Our conversation returns to what paintings sell where. From what she says, it seems that for the most part people like to buy landscapes of what they see in their home region. "Oh, that's interesting. . ." Mary says when I make that observation. "Um, I don't know. Yeah, if people don't have an affinity for the mountains, if they've not been to the mountains, they don't feel anything for the mountains, then they're not interested in mountain paintings, as a rule. And the same thing with the ocean or palm trees. What I find is that if people have been to places where I've painted then they'll like them."

"They like to buy what they've experienced anyway?" I say.

"Yeah. Exactly. As a rule, I think that's right, yeah. But now I don't even think about that so much. I try to paint those things that move me, and it's a wonderful thing if I make a connection with somebody who's also moved by that—if they see my work and say, 'Yes, I felt that,' and make that connection. . . . It feels like I'm creating a more creatively authentic art than when I was trying to manifest the visions of other people. . . . The irony is that my prices have quadrupled, at least, and I'm a lot faster painter."

I ask if there are other scenes in the immediate area she would like to paint, besides the spot she has stored in her mind as a good evening painting.

"I love down below the bridge, just down to the left of the bridge," Mary says. "There's a really neat sandbar, and I would very much like to paint that. Then I think I would just like to do different versions of this. You can emphasize different things in a painting. . . . I could probably do about four or five major paintings just from this hundred-yard stretch. I'm sure I could do more than that, but just the ones that would intrigue me."

She comments that when she was here earlier in the year the lily pads weren't as thick; the backwater had more open space. Since painting individual lily pads would be detrimental to the painting, she needs to figure out how to group them in such a way that they still will read like lily pads. She has noticed that the ones reflecting a lot of sunlight appear silvery while the pads tilting away from the sun "pick up a little more of their local actual color. So that's the kind of thing that I look for. And then: What is the value? What is the value of the color? What does it look like compared to the blue? How much lighter are the lily pads down here than the blue that they're sitting on top of? If I get the color and the value just right I shouldn't need much of the detail."

"You've been here two days in a row," I say. "Do you get a better sense of what you want, or what's here, when you come back like that?"

"Oh, yeah," she says. "That first time usually I'll just do kind of a simple sketch, but my intent is more to just soak up the atmosphere of the place, when I go to a new place. . . . Every place has its own feeling and spirit. And this is that way. I'm surprised this is still the river. But I can see that I'm really close, today, to capturing. . . It's not like a warm-up; today I really have it, and I have grabbed the essentials of what I was after, and the sense of place, I think. And so I feel like I could go home and do a finished painting from these notes that I've taken to myself."

Actually, because of the nature of painting on location, often Mary prefers the outdoor sketches to a finished painting. Good sketches have a freshness about them. It's difficult to maintain the sense of light and freshness in a finished painting done in a studio.

"Are you going to consider this a finished painting or not?" I ask.

"Well," she answers, "I'll probably tweak it a little in the studio, but not too much."

For all practical purposes, the canvas is now covered. Had Mary been alone and not speaking a lot while painting she would have reached this point forty minutes ago. Like members of a choir, all the elements of the painting know their parts. As with a musical composition, all of the desired notes are in place. "Now the fun part," Mary says. "The hard part is over."

Now comes the orchestration. While orchestrating all the parts is no small thing, that can be done in the studio. Sometimes the orchestration is done on location as well. "Now," she says, "I think the light has changed probably a little too much to orchestrate it, but I can do it in the studio. Or I can do it here just because it's a nice day and my paints are all here. But that's a fun part, when you just pull it all together now. And: How do I turn it into a nice finished work of art? It's just pulling things together, making them a little more seamless. But for all practical purposes, that's a really nice, complete statement." She declares herself pleased with it, then proceeds with some of the orchestration, explaining she will have to bear in mind that any changes she makes at this point need to agree with how things looked when the sun was at a different point in the sky an hour to ninety minutes ago. For instance, she points out, "there's a sheen on top of the grasses that when the grass is angled perpendicular to the source of the light will give kind of a bluish sheen. And the light is in a different place now, so I have to be sure that just because I see it in one place doesn't necessarily mean it was there when I first started."

Mary paints some more, explaining changes she makes that have to do with the value of light, chromacity, breadth, and other artistic concerns. She uses a certain brushwork technique to make it seem as though she has painted individual leaves against the sky. Her eyes sweep over the canvas to see if there is anything that doesn't belong or is disturbing, if any note is too jarring—if some area isn't as interesting as it should be or, conversely, attracting too much attention—a choir member trying to solo.

Suddenly she pronounces she is finished. "I'll maybe touch it up in the studio when I can see a little better," she says. "But I don't want to start taking notes from out here now because it's changed too much. But it really hangs together nicely, I think. When I get in the studio I'll still see little things—like this is a little bit too dark. And then I might do just a couple little touches of leaves. And then I noticed this [section] looks a little busy. But otherwise everything kind of does what it's supposed to and has a nice breadth."

As philosophical syndicated newspaper columnist Sydney J. Harris noted in one of his columns, pauses and spaces are important in art, for "all art is suggestion and implication." There is an "eloquent silence," as Mark Twain called it, that distinguishes great art. "The amateur is always *explicit;* he finishes every sentence, draws every line and plays every note with the same value," Harris wrote. "He leaves nothing to the imagination of the audience."

Mary believes in leaving something to the imagination, in "letting people kind of fill in the blanks. I've learned that lesson over and over. I'll take a painting (and think): *This one hangs together really well*, and go home and start putzing with it, and all of a sudden it's not engaging anymore because I said everything."

With this particular painting, she doubts she will spend more than ten minutes working on it in her studio, not wanting to spoil the freshness it has. She folds up her setup and packs away her paints. She thinks she will do another painting this evening, somewhere; she isn't sure where.

Postscript: Mary titled the painting The Other Side of the Tracks.

- 0000000 –

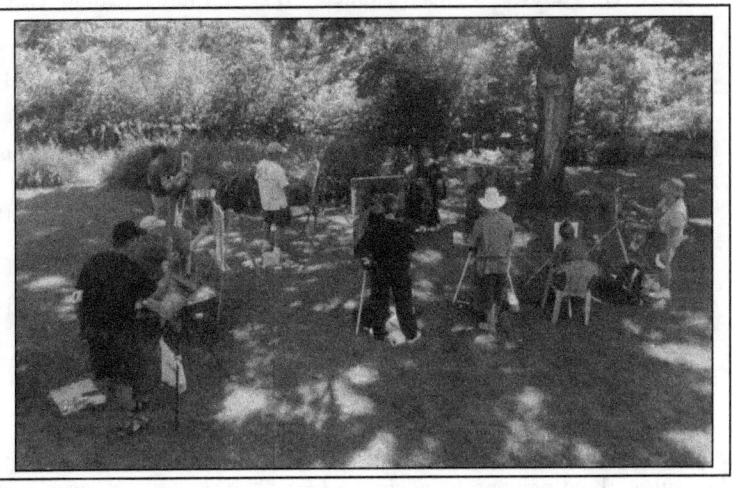

In the summer of 2008 Mary invited me to write an article about a painters group, made up of painters of varying ability, that painted together two afternoons a week, usually in Mary's yard. I attended the July 1st session.

Picture this: Eight painters have easels set up in the shade of a large maple tree in a large yard in Taylors Falls. All of them are fashioning a portrait of a young woman wearing a long black dress with red ruffles who is posing for them. For a three-hour period of the afternoon the artists paint for 25-minute stretches and take five- to 10-minute breaks.

While this may have the appearance of a painting class, it is not in fact a class. It is simply a group of professional and amateur painters from the area painting together, mainly for fun and practice.

"I kind of think that this is historic, what's happening here," says Mary Pettis, the nationally known artist who instigated this clustering of painters. "It isn't a class; I'm not teaching. These are just painters from the region that are coming in. I get 'em from the [Twin] Cities too, that drive up, and people that are in paint-outs in different areas. . . I just think it's kind of an interesting thing."

In fact, Pettis likens it to a "mini Giverny," alluding to how other artists painted with French Impressionist Claude Monet in Giverny, France.

Interestingly, the group of painters are painting where one of the St. Croix River Valley's pioneer painters, E.E. Edwards [Elijah Evan Edwards] lived. Pettis and her husband own the Angel Hill house Edwards and his family occupied for two short periods, first in the early 1860s and later in the mid-1880s.

"It's so incredible!" says Barb Young, a Taylors Falls resident who is one of the area's best-known amateur/semi-professional painters. "Here we are painting on his property. He was one of the first art teachers in the valley."

"And several artists have painted in the carriage house, I think," Pettis adds. "Unfortunately, it's full of my stuff from the farm, so I can't paint there.

The painting group, which has had painting sessions most Tuesday and Wednesday afternoons this summer, consists of a shifting membership. As few as three painters have shown up. "No one has committed to coming," Pettis says. "I just let 'em know where we'll be. . . . We keep in touch via e-mail when there's going to be a model, and then everyone just pays the model (directly)."

Most of the sessions have been held in Pettis's yard, a large yard framed by large trees and accentuated with flower beds. The group also has painted plein air style [in the open air] at such places as an iris garden near Forest Lake, MN, and a working pioneer farm near Elk River, MN.

"Marc Hanson is probably the most nationally recognized painter here," Pettis says during a break. "He's got a huge gallery down in

South Carolina. . . that advertises him nationally in all the national [art] magazines. And he lives next door to us. He's going to be in the history books. He travels all around the country teaching workshops, and in Europe and (other places)—like I do too. The bottom line is, most painters who are as good as I am, at least, in the country know about Marc Hanson. . . . He was a very prominent wildlife painter. Anyone who followed wildlife art knew of Marc."

Like Pettis, Hanson now mainly does plein air painting, primarily landscapes. "We both painted birds and animals for 20-some years," Hanson says. "But I think it's always been the connection to the land as much as the animals, which is why I ended up painting landscapes."

Stillwater, MN, resident Kami Polzin, who studied with Pettis, is another group participant with a national profile and paintings in far-flung galleries.

If Hanson's landscapes are in such demand, why is he spending time painting a portrait of a human model? Might he try to sell the painting? "Oh, no," he says dismissively. "This is exercise. This is like calisthenics. They hurt, but (they are) necessary. Anytime you take yourself out of what you're used to doing and do something different it's a whole new world. It just moves your brain over there and lets it work a little harder for a while. And then it helps you when you go back to what you're really all about. It really is calisthenics."

Pettis likes that analogy. "And working from the model makes us better landscape painters, and vice versa," she says. "Painting anything from life is tremendous."

"It's like in my workshops," Hanson says. "I make (students) do two days of black and white, no color. They're grumbling and mumbling. And then they're always just amazed at how much better they're seeing color after they've done the black and white work. So: the same thing—just getting out of the norm, breaking away a little bit."

Hanson says painting in a group takes him back to his art school experience, which he likes.

"Artists can be kind of reclusive by nature," Pettis points out, "so it's kind of nice to do this type of thing once in a while."

"Almost by necessity we're reclusive," Hanson adds. "How can you not like this?"

"Yeah, good people and a beautiful day and a great model," Pettis says. "I kind of think it's something that people are going to look back at, and look at these photos of this group of artists. I mean, I think it would be fabulous to see pictures of E.E. Edwards and the other painters that he painted with when he was painting in this region. Some of the Hudson River painters even came through up around here and painted with him. But there's no documentation of it."

Chris Young, a teacher who lives in Oregon who was visiting his mother, Barb Young, for a couple of weeks, feels "out of his league" with so many high profile painters, even though he has painted quite a few murals, including one of the Devil's Chair rock formation on the side of a building in downtown Taylors Falls. "I'm not a real artist like these people are," Young demurs.

The oldest painter present is Clarence Nelson, a Taylors Falls historian and environmental advocate whose art training goes back more than 40 years. The Brown & Bigelow art director taught one class he took. "I remember him saying, 'Don't paint an eye; paint the effect of an eye,' Nelson says. ". . . The tendency for beginners is to get too caught up in detail." He says he came to realize a person arrives as an artist "when you can learn to lay the brush down and take it [a painting] away and it says what needs to be said." Another teacher Nelson had would not make any judgment on his students' paintings, but rather get each student to talk about what he or she liked and disliked about his or her own painting. "And, by gosh, you'd go through that process and be thinking [while you were painting]," Nelson says.

Another former student of Mary Pettis, Joyce Staley, also is "liking painting with less detail" after making her mark by painting birds and other wildlife. She also likes the colors found outdoors. "There's just so much more outdoors," she says. ". . . I'm just excited to be part of this group."

While the painting sessions are not classes, Barb Young says "whenever you paint next to someone else you're always learning."

"I've taught workshops here, but this is different," Pettis says. "There's something very different about this collection of artists and kindred spirits that come together. . . . Painting outdoors is very difficult, especially on a model. Flesh tones are totally different in out-of-door light than they are in a studio. And not many people can do it well."

"I was noticing on my watch," Barb Young jumps in. "I'm saying: 'Now, what time was it that I loved the light in a particular way?' so tomorrow when I come back I can do the finishing touches at that time of day."

Pettis wanted to practice doing portraits of live models this summer as preparation for an exciting project with which she is involved. The second half of September will find her in China with a small, select group of artists who will sketch and paint in preparation for a United Nations exhibition. Having other artists join her was a way to hold down model costs.

This day the model is Jennifer Ramautar, a Balsam Lake resident who is a member of the Tribal Spirits Of The Sun dance and drum group. "It's interesting," she says of the modeling experience. "I really like seeing everybody's artwork. It's nice to see something come out of a blank canvas."

Like Marc Hanson, Kami Polzin was there just for practice, and to have fun. "Oh, I'm excited!" Polzin says to Pettis when she visits Pettis in her studio—a house two houses away from her residence—after the afternoon session has wrapped up. "That's addicting."

"Yeah, and it's different outside, isn't it?" Pettis says. "It's a totally different experience than having a studio model."

"Oh, the color was so exaggerated in my head," Polzin says.

"Yeah," Pettis responds. "But it wasn't exaggerated; it's really there—the colors are really there."

"It was such a rush," Polzin says. "It's just so fun."

"And it's changing," Pettis says. "You can't set anything up in a studio like that."

"It's so much more than life," Polzin says, "and yet it's so not a still life."

- 0000000 –

After the group painting session that day I interviewed Mary about her pending group trip to China, which would be led by noted artist Jove Wang, and the United Nations art project, with the hope that by the time she returned from the trip I could have interested a magazine in an article about the project and flesh out the article with a post-trip interview as well. Since no magazine expressed interest in such an article, I never did a follow-up, post-trip interview, so I will present the July 1st interview here in raw form. Mary told me Jove Wang sold large paintings for $100,000 and up.

He's done numerous historical paintings. . . . He lives in southern California [near Pasadena], and also in China. His family lives in China still, and so he goes back to China two or three times a year, at minimum.

So how large of a group is going to China?

Well, I think only ten people, including him. . . . I'll know more as the time approaches, and I'll know a lot when I get back. . . . We're going to be going way back into the villages that are still relatively unaffected by progress. And I think that might be one of the reasons he was asked to do the show at the United Nations. I'm blushing when he said this, but he had the chance to. . . pick nine other master painters, and he said that I'm a master painter and he wants me to show with him. And I was the only one from the Midwest, certainly, so I'm really honored about that.

That show at the U.N. will be focused on China, then?

Yeah, I think it will be. And we'll be doing large paintings—the size of the doorway almost. But large figures. He is trying to revive the art of doing large-figure compositions similar to what has been done in Russia and what used to be done salon style, but it's not French Academy kind of painting; it's more like the Russian large-figure composition.

Have you done anything that large?

Oh, no. I only did. . . I had one painting that I did. [*She points out an unfinished painting.*] This is the one that I did when I was down there with him [Jove Wang], and this is as far as I got. I did a little color study. . . It was from a bunch of different photographs. But what he liked was that this was a really complex composition. I was going to do it on a 30 by 40, but after he saw my color study he wanted me to do it large. And it was just five days that I worked on this and tried to employ the principles that he had taught in this large-figure composition workshop, which was by invitation only. But he had met me when I won a national scholarship from the Plein Air Painters of America about eight years ago, or something like that, for a fountain painting I had done in New York, in Central Park. So I won that award, and the award came in the form of a workshop in Scottsdale. But I couldn't find anybody I was really that interested in studying with at the time. But then about three years ago, right before my scholarship expired, I saw Jove Wang (would be) teaching a course, and I was really excited about the Russian painters at the time, and I know that the Chinese painters studied under Russian masters. That whole discipline is more Asian-influenced and Russian-influenced than it is French Academy-influenced, which is one of the strongest classical veins that we have, certainly, through classical realism.

But, anyway: Long story short, this was a painting that I had done. Everybody else was just copying a photograph, but I was composing and moving figures and having indirect light hit them. And this is from a real experience that I had. These are all my brother's kids, and I had told them I would paint the kids in the chicken coop when the little chickens came—you know, they come in a box of a hundred, just little chicks, and then they raise 'em for a couple months. . . . I always had that painting in the back of my head, that that was something that I really wanted to do. So I juggled all this various reference material and put the kids in there, but it was a real experience that I had, and a mood and feeling more than it is individual portraits. It's just a record of that experience, which is a different kind of art, kind of, than a lot of posed studio paintings. And Jove likes that kind of thing because he says that is real life. . . . There's a story where a guy commissions a Chinese painter to paint a tiger, and the Chinese painter said, "Well, it will take a year for me to do that. Contact me in a year." And so the client contacts the painter in a year, and the painter shows up with an empty canvas and his paints and sits down, and he says, "Come back tomorrow." And that evening he paints the tiger; he paints the painting of the tiger. And then the client, of course, wanted his money back because, he said, "I thought you said it was going to take you a year." And the painter said, "It has." He went and studied the tiger. He watched him move around, he studied the anatomy, and then he had it in his head, and then he could put it together and paint because he knew the tigers—I mean, the essence.

And what Jove is saying is: Go to these places; be a good enough painter that you sketch from life. You train your memory about the harmonics and the colors, and train your memory to those things that are contributing to the emotional experience—those abstract elements of line and shape, value, color, edge and texture. What are those things that we have to translate into paint, those abstract elements that give our viewers the same emotional response that we had when we were in front of that place or having that experience? And that's why he likes to work from life, but also from photographs, rather than pose people out, per se. He said posing people out and just painting them. . . most of the time is like theatre; it's not real life. You're painting theatre. You're painting the backdrops, and they're still-lifes. Everything is just carefully set in place. It's theatre. Unless you can get out in streets and experience the people, and how they move, and how they. . . and then try to memorize feeling, and then click the camera just for the structure and the details, and just the cold information, and then use that. So that's what we're going to be doing. But it's hard. Not everybody can do that. And this is the painting that I did that gave him the idea that maybe I would be the kind of person that could contribute to that show that he had.

What are the dimensions of this one?

This is 48 by 52 [inches], I think. When he first showed me that huge canvas I stared at that big white canvas and I thought: "There's no way I'm going to fill this canvas in a week." But working large is so good for getting the breadth; it's just amazing. It's really exciting. So I'm really eager to do a bunch more large ones like that.

How long will you be in China?

Ten days—ten or eleven. I think we maybe leave the eleventh day.

Will you travel around some?

Yeah. Yup, we're going to Shanghai, and then we're flying to the hub, so it's a ways yet. And it's in the province that's southeast of the one that had the earthquake in it. It's kind of south-central. And half the towns we're going to aren't even on Google, or they're not on maps. They're just little villages, I think, which will be fabulous because those are the ones that have the character, and that's the character that they want to record, I think.

But you'll be doing people more than landscapes?

The people in the landscapes. It's people in the landscapes doing their thing [such as working the land]. What I'm going to be trying to do, I think, is taking my land—my country—and my Midwest farm girl heritage. . . . I feel this kinship with the land. But now I feel a kinship with humanity too. I'm going to be a grandma, and you start getting moody and contemplative as life keeps going. I love humanity much more than I think I have in the past as I age. And I'm feeling compelled to tell people's stories. And moreover, I'm feeling like it might be my purpose to have gotten the kinds of training I have and trained with the artists that I've trained with over the years for the purpose of showing our common bonds that we have, that we share with people of all nationalities and colors and creeds around the world. And the world's become a smaller place, you know, and as an artist I want to demonstrate that through my work.

So, how many paintings do you think you might do for the U.N. show?

Well, for that it's only going to be a couple pieces. Everyone is going to do two or three, and it'll be up to Jove to determine the size and which paintings and which themes he thinks will contribute to having a good show. But I want to have a dozen paintings that we can choose among, so that's my goal. . . . That's the direction I'm going.

[Note: She will do the large paintings after she returns from China, after doing "numerous small paintings and studies there"—paintings in the 8 by 10 and 11 by 14 formats.]

From those color studies, you want to get the mood, the feeling of the day, the accurate color relationships that you can't pick up with a camera—and value too. . . . Cameras don't see the way the human eye sees, so by doing these little color studies, they're like notes to ourselves.

[The U.N. exhibit will be in Geneva, Switzerland, in September of 2009. Prior to that, Mary will be among a group of painters—likely the same group going to China—making a trip to Russia in April of 2009.]

We are very fortunate to have a Russian museum here in Minnesota. When I go out with my painter friends they say, "Oh, you're from Minnesota. You've got a Russian museum there." We're the only place in the United States that has an actual museum; there are a few galleries that handle the Russian art. But it's like Russian music: it's rich and colorful; strong, powerful painting. And they're usually very large compositions.

[Mary is particularly enamored with a style known as Soviet Impressionism.]

While we were going into modern art, and spent a hundred and ten or fifteen years really going into the totally abstract art, at the time the [Russian leaders] wouldn't let them do that; they had to paint within a context of themes that they [government officials] gave them. So they kept a strong academic training. It's interesting [to speculate about] what would have happened, like what would have happened to our art had we never been able to have the pendulum swing all the way to the abstract, which was a reaction—and rightfully so—to the French Academy and the really stodgy kind of Greek(?) stories and all that kind of thing. But on the other hand, they [Russian artists] weren't allowed to do that. . . . The paint is like Rembrandt's paint; it's just all thick; it's like cake frosting.

[When she began painting in the plein air style, Mary took in an exhibit of large Russian paintings in a Scottsdale, Arizona, art gallery, in the spring of 1998.]

I walked in the door and started looking at this art and the bottom just fell out of my stomach. I had never had a visceral experience looking at art before, and here I had dedicated my life to art, and I had been to the Metropolitan Museum and The Louvre and the Impressionist museums and all that, but I had never had it on just that visceral level. I appreciated the work from an academic standpoint, and I appreciated the technicalities and the sublime art, which they taught me at the atelier. And I had loved the transcendental painters and those guys—the Hudson River School. But I had never had an experience like walking through that museum with that show, those paintings. And I was trembling, and I was crying, and my stomach was. . . I can't describe it. I had just never had. . . It was like I had no idea that art could move people that way. And here I was an artist, and I just was never moved by the paint itself. It had nothing to do with the subject even; I was responding to the texture, to the alchemy of the paint, to the lusciousness. But even then, on top of that, the subjects. I mean, it had it all. But there was so much paint; I just couldn't believe it. I mean, thicker than cake frosting, just scooped on. And yet it all hung together, and it was all strong in structure and composition and all that. And I never looked back. I knew that was it for me; I was going to have to learn how they did that.

And so I started getting books and reading and doing stuff and trying to figure out how the. . . And copying, just from the books—trying to copy and just trying to get it. And then finally I found someone who has that training in Jove Wang, and Jove Wang teaching me how they did it. And it's such a thrill because now I feel like I'm on this exciting roller coaster of. . . Ah! It's just great to learn how to paint with. . . He would like it if I would paint everything with that sense of abandon and that bravura brush stroke. But I'm getting there.

But he [Jove Wang] doesn't want me to paint like him; he wants me to find my own voice within this style that I'm so excited about. And he wants to be my mentor; he's chosen to mentor me in this to help me find my voice in this particular style. So I'm so honored because, like I said, he gets forty to a hundred (and) forty thousand dollars for his paintings. I'm sure he sells some for just a few thousand too, but he is really up and (an) extremely successful painter who would not have to teach; he would not have to take the time to teach. But he wants part of his legacy, according to the letter that he sent out to those of us who were chosen, to be training a small group of master painters in America to do this—what he knows about the art of large-figure composition—salon-style paintings in this style. But we haven't been trained in America, really, to paint that way so much. That's what he says. And he wants to be one of the ones responsible for teaching a group of core people how to do these kinds of paintings. So, anyway, he probably just got a kick out of me 'cause I was a farm girl from the Midwest; I don't know. *[She laughs.]*

But everybody else is painting all these exotic things 'cause they had traveled with him and stuff before. And here I am painting kids and chickens in the chicken coop, you know. And he was just delighted. He didn't know why I was painting the straw all bumpy; he didn't understand. And then when I put in the little chicks, then he realized that: "Oh, it's chicks!" And this is like the third day in it. He didn't care; he just loved the painting. But then he realized that: "Oh, oh, oh, oh! These are chicks." But he thought: "Well, where's the mother?" He didn't understand that you get a box of chicks to raise, and that's what we do here. He was tickled by that. So we're going to Russia to study that. And then between Russia and that summer, in the following couple months, then we'll hone and work on the paintings. And then we go to Switzerland in September for the show opening.

So how long in Russia, for that trip?

I think it will be a two-week trip.

You will travel around some, then?

Yeah. Yeah. Yup. And that will be largely more research than painting; we'll be studying. We'll be going to the home of some of the great Russian painters, and some of the museums that only have the Russian art, of which there aren't many. And then he'll explain to us and help us translate what we're seeing.

Is this like a continuing thing they have there (at United Nations headquarters in Geneva), with different exhibits?

I don't know. I think so. I think the U.N. does have a gallery there. But I don't know how Jove was chosen, nor how big the time slot is [for the exhibit], or any of that. I just know that it really sounds good to be among them; I know it is a tremendous honor.

[Jove Wang's by-invitation-only large-figure workshop Mary attended in January of 2008 had about 12 students.]

He didn't want me to tell the others he was asking me to be a part of it [the U.N. exhibit]. Those, I thought, were the elite group of painters, and he didn't want me to tell the others. I think maybe one or two of them might be part of that. So I know it's something kind of special. So I've been painting like crazy with that wind beneath my wings now; I've been just buoyant. It's like I just can't paint subjects fast enough.

[Mary will pay her own way for the trip to China.]

Usually when something like this shows up on the radar, then the money will show up within one or two hundred dollars. If I decide to do something, then something falls in my lap, or some paintings that have been out there for years will sell, or I'll get a check from one of my galleries in Washington or Jackson Hole or someplace. But usually it's always just the amount allotted. So I just trust the universe that the universe will provide if my head's in the right place and (I'm) doing the right thing. Usually it shows up within ten or twenty dollars (of) the exact amount of what it is that I needed to do this or that thing. I swear it's happened seven or eight times like that—just like that. It's really uncanny. So I just have gotten to trust the universe. The Good Lord does a far better job of managing my life than I do, and I just turn it over and try to be a good artist and a good person.

Being part of a U.N. show really raises your visibility?

Yeah, yeah, yeah. That will be newsworthy in many ways. It's good for three or four ways. The first thing that I think is, I never feel like

I'm on this journey alone; I always, always, always feel like anybody who's ever spent ten bucks on a poster of mine is sharing it. I mean, I always feel that the people that have supported me throughout the years are part of this journey with me, and that it's their success too because they're the reason I was able to continue painting—people that have bought art and supported me throughout the years, people in the area that have been so good in so many ways. So that's the first thing I think of, is it will be really good so the people who have bought my paintings can say, "Wow, and I got her painting when she was selling it for three hundred dollars!," or two hundred dollars, or seventy-five dollars. "I got an original, and now look: she's selling them for twenty thousand."

And that's the thing too: The price will probably be (higher), just showing with Jove. And then they'll be large paintings, so they'll be expensive paintings. And that always sets a precedent when and if they sell. Collectors take notice of kind of whoever the people are that buy paintings like that. . . . So I'm hoping he [Jove Wang] will have one (priced at) $100,000, and then they'll look at mine and they'll say, "Oh, wow, look at that! That one's only $50,000!" So that's how we will hope to pay for the trip. That's the way it's supposed to work. Whenever my students sell a painting I say, "Yup, that's the way it's supposed to work."

☼

Eggtraordinarily Eggacting

Ernie Spinks ... eggshell carver

"When I say I carve scenes in eggshells, people just have no comprehension of what that entails," Ernie Spinks says. Spinks, who lives in the Hudson, Wisconsin, area, doesn't make etchings on eggshells, as many people may think he does. He cuts away parts of eggshells to form images and designs.

Using a pen-sized, dental-style drill with a bit that rotates at an astounding 480,000 revolutions-per-minute, he carves images of butterflies, birds, rustic cabins, flowers, and anything else that strikes his fancy into hollowed-out goose and turkey eggs—as well as chicken eggs occasionally. Chicken eggs being more fragile than the other two types, they are more difficult to carve. "Just about anything you can think of I can put on an egg," he says.

While he sells some of his delicate creations—they are available at a few exclusive gift shops in the Twin Cities and California for $150 to $350 each—his eggshell carving basically is a hobby.

"I don't want it to be a business because then I couldn't do it," says Spinks, who operates a TV repair shop in St. Paul with one of his brothers. "I've had the opportunity to make quite a few at different times for companies that wanted to give them away as an exclusive gift to some of their executives, but I just don't want to have to make 80 or 100 of them, and have a deadline. When you start putting them out like that all the fun goes out of it. Then it just becomes a job. Then I would need to look for a new hobby."

Most of the ones that are sold are encased in a dome display case and glued to a wooden base for stability. All carved shells are left unpainted.

Spinks carves about 50 eggshells each year, most of them "small" goose eggs that are two to three times larger than chicken eggs.

"They're a little tougher, and a little bigger, and you can do more with them than you can with chicken eggs," he says.

He became interested in the hobby about five years ago after a friend told him about a dentist who did some engravings on eggshells—"just little things," Spinks says. "I became fascinated and started to do some. Basically when I started I did nothing but chicken eggs." About 80 percent of them broke during the carving process.

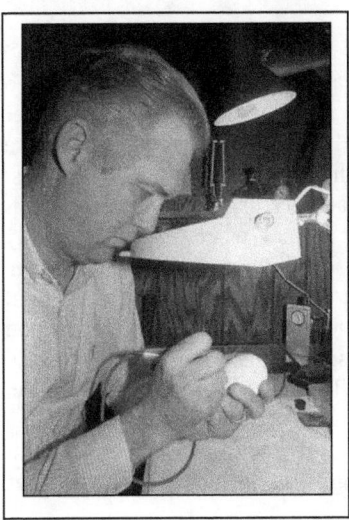
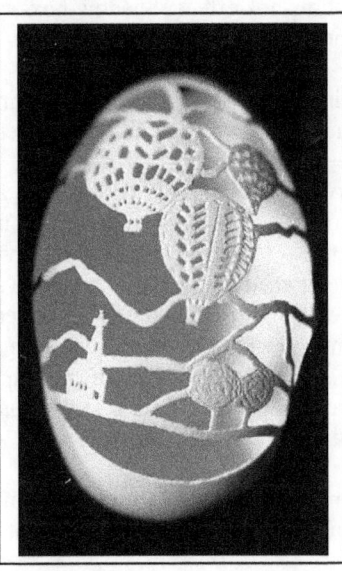

Through experimentation, he advanced from engraving to carving, which became easier after he acquired the super-high-speed drill he now uses.

"Over a period years I've been able to develop techniques that work, and learn where to cut first and where to cut last," he says. "That's the key. If you try to start where you should finish you're going to crush it."

Pointing to a particularly intricate carving featuring a hummingbird drawing sap from a flower, he explains: "It's obvious that with that hummingbird that's suspended by just its beak you wouldn't want to be cutting the eyes and the feathers in the wings after you got it hanging like that."

Even with his experience and improved facility, Spinks still breaks one eggshell out of every five he tries to carve. What makes that all the more disheartening is that nearly all of the ones that break into bits do so when at least 90 percent of the carving is completed. The more carving Spinks does on an eggshell, of course, the weaker it becomes. That's why the ones with lace-work design on all sides, which take the most time to carve—up to eight hours—are most apt to collapse. That's why he prefers to carve a design on only one side, producing a shadow box effect. Shadow-box-style shells can be carved in as short a time as two hours.

Spinks doesn't throw his drill against a wall, kick his desk and curse a blue streak when a shell "explodes," as many people might do under the circumstances. He admits he feels "a little heartbroken" when a carving he is pleased with breaks at the last stage, though. "You just throw it in the garbage and pick up another one," he says matter-of-factly. Obviously eggshell carving is not a craft for the easily discouraged person. Nor is it well-suited for the impatient person. Interestingly, Spinks says patience is not part of his natural temperament. "My kids say I have none," he says. "But it's relaxing to me. Everybody has an outlet, I suppose, and this seems like it's a very nice way for me to relax. I do it usually at night, when everybody's in bed. It's just a good outlet for me."

Spinks has had no formal art training. He feels that what he does requires more technique than talent.

"The thing about this that's so amazing, it seems, is that people see a guy my size and they see this work, and it sort of amazes them. They just can't connect the two together. They think some little old lady should be doing it."

He says the two most important, necessary qualities may be persistence and a steady hand. "Even though you know where you should cut and where you shouldn't cut, you still end up breaking eggs doing it the right way," he says. "But I realize when I start that the egg's completion is probably a 50 percent chance, and if it breaks it just breaks."

Spinks has heard about only four or five other eggshell carvers. "It's just amazing to people," he says. "And it is to me too. I look at them and laugh sometimes. Sometimes it's really hard to believe that you can do that to an egg. . . . I've had people just sit here and look, and (they) just could not believe that it can be done." - *March 4, 1986* ☼

Atavistically Haunting

Glen Riddle … found-object constructionist

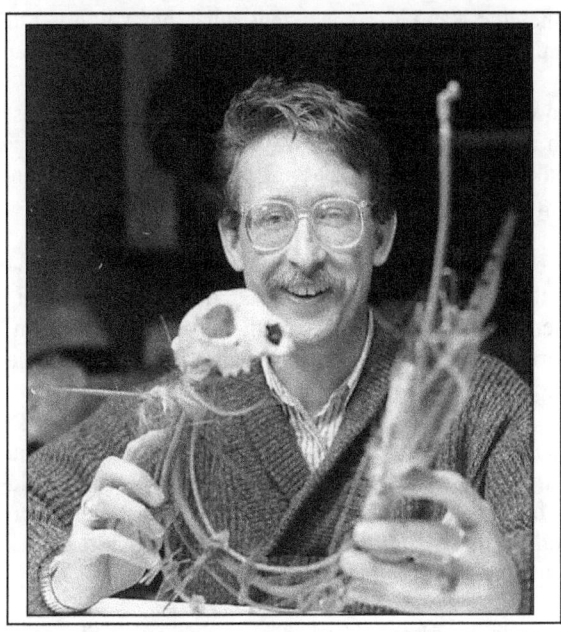

Glen Riddle harvested a good crop of beaver skulls from his garden this year—32, to be precise. "The neighbors probably think I'm pretty crazy," the Hudson, Wisconsin, artist and art teacher says. "They joke about it."

Riddle, a born-again Christian, husband, and father of two, buried beaver heads in his garden not as some satanic rite, but because he wanted to have the skulls to use in his art. Burying the heads, which he obtained from a fur buyer, sped up the decomposition process. He uses animal skulls, snake skins, thorny twigs, bird feathers, butterflies, turtle shells, mica, horsehair, and other natural objects in ritualistic-looking constructions he creates.

His work often is compared to traditional American Indian artwork. He says the similarity stems from his having grown up in South Dakota, "in an environment where the land and the natural materials were so conspicuous," with "just land and sky there," not from any effort on his part to copy or emulate Native American art.

"The pieces that I make are sort of spiritual, in a way," he says. "I wouldn't want people, though, to believe that I'm tied in with American Indian religion, because I'm not. I have a real appreciation for what they did—and, to some extent, what they still do. I think that I have a similar appreciation for the same materials. . . .

"I came to work with these things in the past few years because I like to work with materials in a primary way. I can do that with drawing, but drawing takes so much time. These I can make more spontaneously. I can make a piece in a couple of hours, maybe."

A typical construction is one or two feet long. It might have a small animal skull stuck on the end of a curved, thorny honey locust branch, a few feathers at the other end, a length of tattered snakeskin wrapped around part of the branch, pieces of paper-thin mica impaled on the branch, and horsehair dangling from it here and there.

Many of the creations have haunting, humanoid, skeletal shapes. *Kansas City Star* art critic Donald Hoffman wrote that Riddle's constructions have "a vaguely tribal look that hint at a time not our own." Joe Mackall of the *Washington Post* commented that the work "evokes the spiritual and the ancestral."

"An anthropologist dreams about discovering fetish-like combinations of wood, feathers, snakeskin, and handmade paper such as these," Deborah Lerme Goodman wrote in *Fiberarts*. "Even in a modern gallery, they are atavistically haunting."

In a statement about his work, Riddle wrote: "Such objects as snakeskins, thorns, and mica have come to serve as spiritual metaphors, particularly as arranged in new contexts. My work with them amounts to meditative acts of personal ritual." Transparent layers of mica, for example, serve as representations of truth. Snakeskin, on the other hand, is "linked to guile" in his symbolic code.

Riddle has collected "stuff" since his childhood on the South Dakota prairie. "I guess I figured that everybody had collections of bones and horsehair and stuff like that," he says. All of that collected stuff remained in boxes and bins while he studied art at Northern State University, in South Dakota, where he came to realize "painting wasn't that exciting" to him, "and that color really wasn't that important" either, then taught in a small South Dakota school system a few years before he felt compelled to resume his own studies for a master's degree.

"I realized that the land was so important to me at the time," he says, "that I wanted to study in another place that was flat. . . . So I applied to five MFA [Master of Fine Arts] programs in flat geographic areas." Indiana State University accepted him into its painting program. When he met with his "major" professor, though, Riddle revealed he didn't want to paint.

"It took me a while to kind of get my wits about me and figure out what I wanted to do in that master's program," he says. "I was there for three years; I was in my late 20s then. I started working with handmade paper, which was kind of nice because I used cotton rags, which I tore into small scraps, and then with the use of a special machine called a Hollander Beater I processed that cloth into a wet pulp that I fashioned into paper. I found that paper seemed a natural complement to this collection of stuff that I'd had for so long. I did have sort of a collage sort of mentality—juxtapositioning things, putting unlike things together in new contexts. Handmade paper seemed like kind of a natural way to do that. . . . It was in graduate school that I started to use this collection of stuff that I had. And people are always giving me stuff."

He also was a teaching assistant through part of that graduate school experience, during which he also did a lot of drawing. The university's anthropology and archeology departments hired him to do drawings. He "especially like(s) teaching drawing" to his 8th and 9th grade students in Hudson.

"In the past couple of years," he says, "I've started doing these constructions, with the twigs and the bones and so on, and they've been real satisfying to me. . . . I really don't try to market my work, in particular. I have sold some pieces now and again, but I have never taken my work to commercial galleries for representation. I send slides out quite often to university or college galleries that are soliciting proposals because it is exciting to show the stuff."

- November 5, 1990   ☼

Don't Spare The Rod

Tom Lovick, John Fox & Lewi May
... fishing rod builders

Spare the rod and spoil the child, an old adage has it. The opposite of that, however, is true in regard to fishing. Supply a fisherman with a finely tuned custom-built fishing rod and you spoil the fisherman. He will never again be satisfied with a factory-built, off-the-rack rod.

"You can build a lot better rod than you can buy," says Tom Lovick, who opened one of the most all-service, custom-oriented rod shops in the United States near Somerset, Wisconsin, less than three months ago. Lovick's spacious, cedar-paneled Two Rivers Rod Crafting shop is a place fisherman can have rods repaired, custom rods built, purchase rod components and rod-building equipment, or make their own custom rods on the premises, under the guidance of Lovick, his apprentice, Vern Yourchuck, or two other on-call rodsmiths.

"There's an art in building custom rods," Lovick says. "We like to call it an art because we put a lot more in than what the factories do."

"One thing we stress in the making of our rods is the quality. These rods are handled all the way through the making of them," Yourchuck says. "We're constantly bending on them, checking the blanks. Sometimes you will get what is called a checked blank from the manufacturer; it has a bad spot in it. So we bend them and put quite a bit of stress on them, because it's much better to have it break here than have somebody buy a brand new rod and have it break. So we're constantly beating on them, as I call it; checking them. We put a lot of pressure on the guides to check them. . . . We take the time to do stress checks on them, and the placement of our guides is quite a bit different than what you're going to get from a factory rod, because they don't have the time to sit there and measure where they're going to stick the guides. They get a certain sequence and they go with it. We put more guides on a rod than what the manufacturer will. Basically that helps with performance of the rod. In fact, that's the biggest part of it. If you have a rod that just doesn't have the guides in the right place it's not going to cast half as far as our rods will."

Another rod crafter, University of Wisconsin—River Falls agriculture professor Lewi May, says he "can buy a thousand blanks, all the same model, and every one of them would have to have the guides in a slightly different spot."

Locating a rod's "spine"—its stiffest side—is also important to rodsmiths. "There's a hard side and a soft side of every blank," Yourchuck explains. "We set that up so that when the rod is bent that hard side is right along the top of the ridge. If the spine is off to the side, when you have a fish on the line the rod will have a tendency to twist to the weakest point. If you're going for a 100-pound tarpon and you've got a rod that's twisting in your hand because it wants to go to the soft side of the rod, it causes a lot of problems."

The Two Rivers shop has blanks for all types of rods—spinning, baitcasting, fly, ice fishing, downrigger, and saltwater—with an in-shop inventory of 400 to 500 blanks.

Custom built rods are, of course, considerably more expensive than factory built rods. Excluding the ice fishing rods, prices at the Two Rivers shop range from about $45 to hundreds of dollars, depending on what materials are used and how ornamental the rod is.

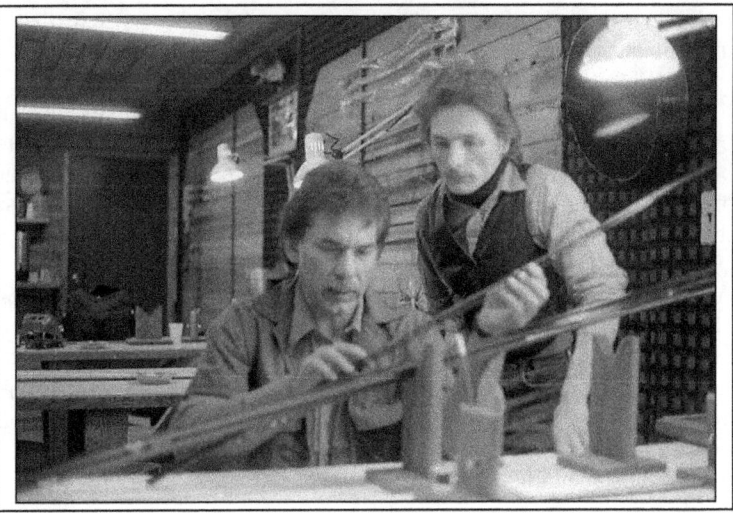

According to Lovick, custom rod building is "probably one of the fastest growing segments of the tackle industry right now. . . . I think this business is going to explode."

With 15 years of construction experience building farm and commercial buildings, Lovick "built everything" except the motors of the machines in his Two Rivers shop, which consists of an entrance area with a sales counter, an engineering room, a wrapping area, a finishing room, and a showroom. The wrapping area takes up about half the floor space.

"You get four people with eight-foot rods walking around and you need elbow room," Yourchuck says. "And Tom wanted to do it right. He wanted to be comfortable, because as much as anything we have people who just stop and sit and have coffee and talk rods for 30 minutes."

Sales have been strong so far as well, Lovick reports. He has been so busy helping customers build their own rods that he has built only about two rods a month, with Yourchuck responsible for the rest. "We try to encourage people to build their own rods," Lovick says. "A lot of people look at some of these rods and say, 'There's no way I could build one,' but after we walk them through a little bit they always come back and say, 'That's not hard.' . . . A lot of them go right into the trim wraps [decorative guide wrappings]. We let them practice on a blank for a while, and once they find out that they can do it, that it isn't that hard, they want to put trim wraps on right away. And why not, because we're here to help them. There isn't a rod that leaves here that's unsatisfactory."

Lovick says it takes the average customer six or seven hours, over a period of time, to build a six-and-one-half-foot spinning rod. He believes "it just adds to the fishing pleasure. Some of these guys go out and don't catch any fish, and they don't care. They made that rod, and they sit there and throw that rod."

At the same time he is teaching—he also lectures to many fishing clubs about rod building—Lovick remains an attuned student. "You learn so much from different people," he says. "I learn from everyone who walks through that door. Well, who else are you going to learn from? Those are the people that are going to give you their experiences. One little thing that comes out of their mouths could change the balance of the rod, or something like that."

While most of the rods are made of graphite, work sometimes also involves bamboo, fiberglass, boron and a fiberglass/graphite composite.

"My uncle started me on (making) bamboo [rods] when I was seven or eight years old," Lovick says. "He was building bamboo rods at the time, and that's what we started on. He showed me how to repair, and he built a few. Then when the fiberglass first came out he had to get into that, and started showing me about that."

Many of the reel seats on handles are made from such exotic woods as rosewood, teak, black walnut, and amethyst.

"We do just a tremendous amount of repair here," Lovick says. "We like to say we can fix 98 percent of whatever is brought in here. That other two percent would be bamboo that is so badly beaten up that we couldn't really afford to do it. . . .

"I haven't dug into it, but this is probably one of the few custom shops like this in the United States. Everybody has a little bit of everything, but I have a whole lot of the custom—the full line of rods, guides, handles, plus all the trim."

- February 15, 1989   – 0000000 –

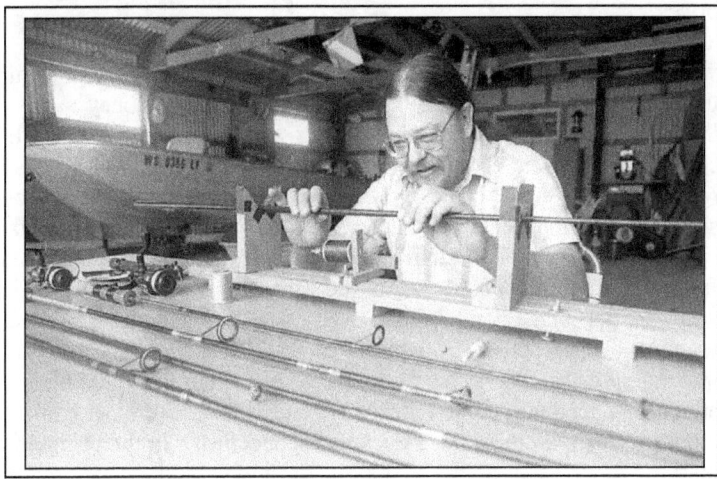

Once someone fishes with a custom built rod he regards mass-produced, off-the-rack fishing rods with the same disdain a man used to wearing custom-tailored suits has for off-the-rack suits. Just ask either John Fox [pictured above] or Lewi May. May, of River Falls, and Fox, of rural Birchwood, both fish with custom-built rods they made themselves. Both men also have customized rods for other fishermen, though the activity is pretty much of a hobby for both.

"When I first started doing it," Fox, 37, says, "I thought it would be kind of a handy thing to do around here, with all the resorts and fishermen and stuff. I must have built up about a dozen fiberglass rods—three or four fly rods, three or four ultralight spinning rods, and three or four heavier spinning rods—and carried them around to art shows, and had displays at a few places [sporting goods stores]. Nobody was interested." The major problem, as he sees it, "is that unless and until you've actually fished with a custom built rod you really don't realize the difference there can be between a rod you can buy off the shelf and one that's custom built for you. And the price-tag is outrageous; I'll admit it."

The high cost of rod components and the time required to make a rod drive up the price of custom fishing rods. It takes Fox 15 to 20 hours to build each rod. May, who teaches agricultural economics at the University of Wisconsin—River Falls, turns out each one in about 10 hours, since he has more experience and a more mechanized operation. An average rod May builds costs between $125 and $150. Ones with complicated thread patterns and other features cost as much as $300, or more. Still, he is able to find customers willing to pay those stiff prices.

"I find that for the most part people who come to me want something that is good, and they're willing to pay a little extra money to ensure that it's good," says May, who teaches an eight-session rod-crafting course twice a year through the adult education and UW—Extension route. ". . . People come in here frustrated because they've got a situation, and they know what they want to fit that situation, but they can't find it. So we start with a blank and start adding the components from there, and making it exactly the way they want. The smiles just seem to get bigger and bigger every week as the thing's coming together because this is it—this is perfect. But the thing is, you're making sure that that's the case. If the blank doesn't quite have the action you need we can trim it. And we probably have more choice of blanks to begin with, as far as action is concerned. In the commercial market they're not going to build a rod unless they can sell ten thousand of them. . . . I can build more varieties off Fenwick blanks alone than what Fenwick offers, just because they have blanks available in the components market that aren't available as rods, because it's not worth the time to set up and build a bunch of them and then not be able to sell them."

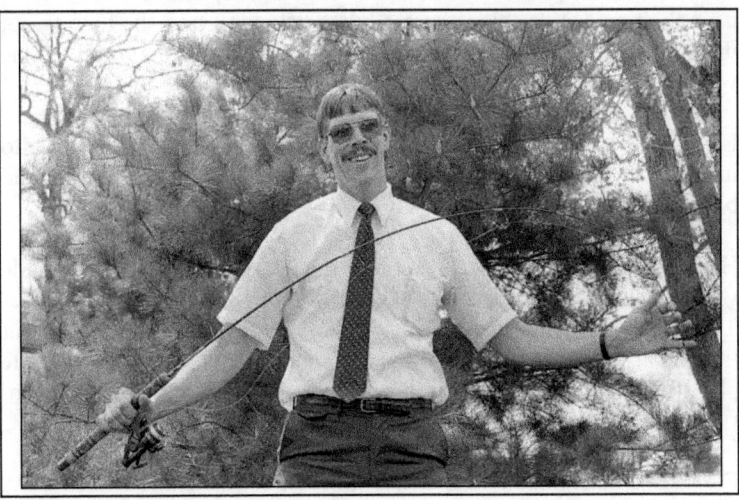

May [above], who has built rods for nine years, says most customers are more interested in rod performance than aesthetic flashiness. "The only reason I started," he says, "was that I was going to build myself the rod that would do everything. I learned through learning the craft that really what happens when you're custom building a rod is that you're custom building it for a certain situation."

Fox believes few fishermen understand the technical nature of fishing rod construction.

"Every blank, believe it or not, in cross section, is not round, like you think it is," he explains. "It's just slightly egg-shaped, which gives it what's called a spine, or a stiffer portion of the rod. Through the narrower part of that egg shape, the rod's got a little more stiffness. That's what gives you the snap when you cast, if the guides are lined up right. In other words, that rod is meant to bend in a certain direction. (If) you get one of those rods that for some odd reason develops a funny kink on the end, that's because the guides were put on in the wrong place, and after the thing's been under enough stress. . . it tends to want to start bending the way it was meant to bend, and the guides weren't put on it in the right place, so it doesn't bend along with the flow of the rod. . . .

"When they do machine built, or even hand-built, rods over in Taiwan or someplace, they don't care where the spine is. The whole idea there is to whip it out as fast as you can. So they grab a blank (and) feed it into a machine, or they grab a blank and start spinning. They don't have the time [to do things correctly]. They don't take the time to put the guides in the right place, even. Your odds of picking a rod off the wall and having it come out perfect are pretty small."

Fox is able to determine where the spine is located, and thus be able to understand where the line guides should be placed, by turning a rod blank with his fingers.

He wraps one color of thread around a graphite rod blank where a guide will be placed, then wraps on the guide with a different color of thread. The reason for using two different colors, he says, is "you don't want that metal, which is very sharp on the ends, to ever touch the graphite part of that rod. A small scratch is enough, when it's under tension, fighting a big fish, to snap that rod."

Fox uses a handmade thread-winding device for attaching guides—and "single-footed" guides rather than double-footed guides to give his rods more sensitivity—and a two-part epoxy-type finish to protect the rods from scratches.

"As far as I'm concerned, there aren't any two blanks that are one hundred percent alike," he says. "That only makes sense. No matter how careful they are, they cannot be exactly the same. So when I build a rod I either tape or rubber-band all the guides in the standard spacing. There are booklets and pamphlets and stuff that will give you the standard spacing for a six-and-a-half-foot spinning rod, let's say, and they'll tell you how far apart from the tip to the butt to put the guides to give you optimal action or whatever. I'll take those [guides] and tape them or rubber-band them on the blank, take it outside, put a reel on it with line on it, and lift a one-pound weight off the ground." If a one-pound weight seems pretty puny compared to a four- or five-pound fish, he says, consider "that fish is sitting in water, where it doesn't weigh a quarter of what it really weighs in the air." He lifts the weight "to make sure that the guides are in the right place so that the rod arcs evenly through its length. Then I take and put on a plastic practice plug, and I'll cast with (that)." If everything doesn't feel or look right as he casts, he "can move those guides back and forth and actually fine-tune the guide spacing to that (specific) blank, which can vary from one rod to another even on exactly the same blanks. I'll admit it doesn't vary a lot, but if you want something that's the ultimate in sensitivity that little bit might make a difference."

May, the "professor of poles," confirms that contention. "I can buy a thousand blanks, all the same model, and every one of them would have the guides in a slightly different spot," he says.

Both Fox and May make more graphite rods than fiberglass rods. While Fox uses his handmade thread-winding device for attaching line guides, May has a motorized thread-winding machine as well as a lathe machine for shaping cork and foam handles. "I know I'm going to continue to do this," May says, "so now when anything new comes out that will make the job easier I automatically buy it."

May belongs to the 15,000-member Rod Crafters organization, and organized a Rod Crafters chapter in River Falls.

"We get together once a month, October through April, and take turns basically putting on seminars," he says. "It's funny, because most of the guys have taken my class and they probably view me as knowing the most, and I'm probably the one who learns the most from them."

May started selling custom fishing rods before moving to River Falls (from the state of Washington) six years ago. "When I moved here," he says, "I didn't really have any contacts, and it's more word-of-mouth than anything else, so I decided to teach a class through our adult and continuing education and Extension courses. At the time I was kind of selfish because the only reason I decided to teach the course was because I didn't have any orders. What's happened is that since I've gotten so much exposure because of that course now it's [teaching others] actually a bigger portion of my business than actually selling them to other people. I sell components; I'm a distributor for a number of companies. Most of my students want to build a couple for friends and a couple for themselves every year, so it's really not worth going through all the hassles of getting a selling permit and all that kind of stuff."

May has turned out about 150 custom rods himself, about 15 of those for his own use. Fox, who also builds masterfully detailed, wooden model ships, and ships-in-bottles, has built 25 or 30 rods in 10 years' time, only a handful of those for other people.

"When I first got into rod building I thought: 'Hey, a guy could have a quality rod for a little cheaper price,'" Fox says. "But unfortunately, it didn't quite work out that way. . . . While it isn't too expensive to make your own rods, it can be pretty doggone expensive if you have to keep some sort of supply of parts and stuff around to fit just about any contingency that somebody might want to a custom built rod. You'd have to have thousands of dollars' worth of inventory, and I just wasn't ready to get into it like that. . . .

"If I build for myself, I build a bunch of rods that use the same guides and stuff like that, so I can get a little better deal on the price. Which would be okay commercially, except, again, you'd have to have thousands of dollars' worth of these things to cover every possible contingency. I tried for a while taking orders and then custom building a rod for someone, but I ended up with all kinds of problems. People wouldn't have the material when I would order it, then I'd have to tell the customer, 'Well, gee whiz, it's going to take another month or a month and a half for this part to be back-ordered.' It just went on and on and on. It ended up being so many problems that I don't do it commercially anymore."

May is content to keep custom rod building as essentially a hobby as well. He wants to build no more than one rod per month. He says his local Rod Crafters chapter may sell ice fishing rods. "Just about everybody who has ever had one of those in their hands will say to me, 'I want one,'" May says. "And I'll say, 'Well, we haven't talked about price.' 'It don't make any difference; I want one.' They're easy enough to build that I've encouraged everyone in the group to do these, and maybe we can go to some of these little shows on handcraft things or whatever."

One of the "little rules" Fox lives by is: Anything worth doing is worth doing well. "I do a lot of drift fishing with slip sinkers for walleyes, with either nightcrawlers or leeches or minnows or something, and you've gotta be able to feel that sinker slipping along the bottom, ticking off of rocks or sliding through mud or pulling through weeds," he says. "It gives you a good idea of what's down there, to begin with. And when a walleye picks something like that up, all it does is swim up and just go *swoooo!* You have to be able to feel that light little (pull) on the end of that rod because you fish with the bail open and the line just draped across your finger. When you feel that you've gotta let him have line instantly. The fish feels one slight little hesitation and he'll spit it out so fast it isn't funny, so it's gotta be very sensitive. When you're fishing that way it makes a world of difference to have a really good, well-made graphite rod—or boron, or some of the composites."

>- *I interviewed John Fox on May 6, 1988, and Lewi May four days later, on May 10th.*

☼

Taking Note Of Anita Beck

Anita Beck ... greeting and note card designer

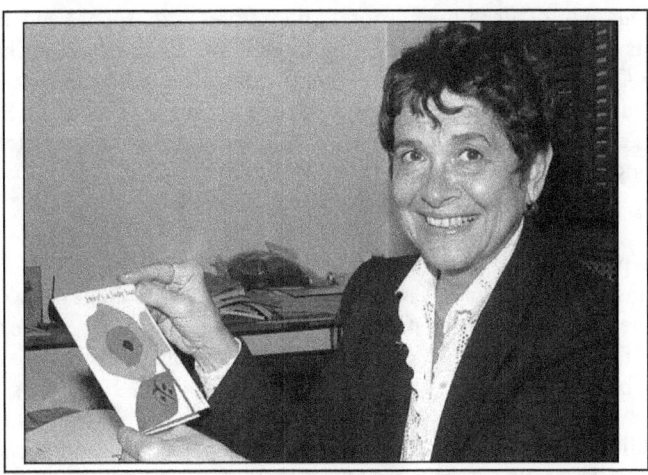

A *New Yorker* writer once commented that Anita Beck's card designs look like the work of either a modern abstract artist or a nursery school student. Perhaps it is that subtle combination of stylistic composition and childlike simplicity that has made her note cards, Christmas cards and other products so successful.

The energetic 63-year-old Minneapolis woman, who has precious little art training, and no plans to retire, uses bold, bright cutouts of flowers and animals on some cards while others employ spare, subdued watercolorings. All have a warm, happy aura about them, a sort of old-fashioned country-style charm that perhaps proves once again that you can take a girl out of a small town but you can't take the small town out of a woman.

Beck, whose married name is Bosiger, but who continues to use Beck as her business name, grew up on Minnesota's rugged northern Iron Range, in the town of Gilbert. Surprisingly, she didn't do much drawing and painting when she was young. She did do "a lot of dreaming—an awful lot of dreaming," she says. "I remember going to the store and loving patterns so that I would get a nickel or dime's worth of some little calico print and come home and fold it over a little book to make a pretty cover on the book. And my mother would say, 'Why don't you do something important with your time? That doesn't lead to anything.'"

Luckily, not all dreams are dampened by parental practicality.

Today Beck's creations are available through a mail order catalog and at thousands of department stores, bookstores, gift shops, and other outlets across the country, including three Reindeer House shops in the Twin Cities Beck co-owns with several women business partners. The original Reindeer House is part of Reindeer Square, a block of Santa Claus-red old buildings in southwest Minneapolis that house offices, a printing plant and a restaurant in addition to the gift shop, which features handcrafts and other items as well as cards.

"The product mix we have found successful," Beck says, "is local artisans' crafts, stationery—ours featured, but other card lines as well—and then a category called purchase goods. Purchase goods can be anything from dishes to placemats to books—anything that isn't possibly made by a local artist."

In addition to the flagship Reindeer House shop, there is another one on the Nicollet Mall in downtown Minneapolis and a third one in St. Paul. Busloads of tourists from as far away as Michigan's Upper Peninsula and Thunder Bay, Ontario, make Reindeer Square part of their Twin Cities itinerary. A room at the back of the printing plant allows them to watch the card-making process through plate-glass windows. Families and individuals from all over the United States and other countries visiting the Twin Cities make a point of stopping at Reindeer Square too. "What flatters me," Beck says, "is when they come in from California and say, 'There's nothing quite like this in California.' I love to hear it."

Anita Beck Cards & Such has some 30 fulltime employees. Women throughout the United States, who sell to stores on commission, comprise most of the sales force. Beck believes women have a better instinctual understanding of what other women want, and women buy most greeting and note cards, so it has always seemed natural to her that women should be pushing her products. That woman's touch on the creative side has unquestionably been a big part of her success too.

Beck began making cards commercially in 1946, working at her kitchen table, which she still does occasionally.

"I knew when I was in my early teens that somehow I wanted to work for myself," she says. "That was always a general decision. But I didn't know quite how. And it happened almost by accident. Some friends saw cards I designed for my own use and said, 'Gee, other people would like those.' So I began selling them to friends. I knew enough about printing because I was born in a small town where my father knew the newspaper publisher and got me a job." She later studied journalism at the University of Minnesota.

"Christmas cards were the first thing I ever did, and I still do them, and people tell me it's one of our greatest strengths. Christmas cards are what I did for nine years, entirely. And now I still do Christmas, but I had to expand into an everyday [line of cards] so I could keep the business going all year long. . . . The Christmas cards are sold to thousands of stores across the country. I don't ever tell the volume we do, but we sell millions of cards. I like the fact that we're a little company, because millions is not a lot in the card business today; billions is lots. But we are growing all the time. More and more people write and say, 'You express me.' And that's what it's all about."

Beck placed her Christmas cards, which had an unaffected handmade look that differed greatly from most others available, in such prestigious emporiums as Saks Fifth Avenue in New York and Dayton's department stores in Minneapolis and St. Paul. The cards sold so well at Dayton's that company executives asked her to design a shopping bag that would appeal to women, and then commissioned her to design other items when that shopping bag proved to be very popular. Before long Beck was a packaging design consultant to such other large Twin Cities businesses as 3M [Minnesota Mining & Manufacturing], General Mills and Munsingwear as well.

After concentrating on industrial design for 11 years she re-entered the card business, producing both boxed note cards and Christmas cards. Only this year has she begun making birthday, anniversary, wedding, and other "everyday" cards. While most of the note cards have no words either inside or outside, the everyday cards contain messages—though no syrupy poetry, Beck stresses. "I used to think that people could write their own greeting," she says, "but after all these years I've decided that if they want me to say it for them I will. It's no use bucking a trend. People like the help of wording it."

Besides cards, Beck also creates postcards, calendars, recipe cards, posters, market lists, party napkins, memo pads, and several other paper products.

The card line has more than 100 designs. Beck does most of the designing herself, though she does buy some artwork of others that conforms to her distinctive style.

"The techniques I use are fun—lots of paper cutouts, just like a child would do," she says. She also does some watercolor images. Someone else does the calligraphy.

Of some three-dozen new card designs introduced each year, five or six will prove popular enough to remain in the line for many years. One longtime bestseller has a spotted cover with the line: "Mercy, I'm slow with my merci!" "Lots of people relate to that," Beck says. "I guess we're all kind of careless." Another favorite Thank You card has a bunch of flowers and the words "Thanks a bunch" on the cover. One of Beck's many famous customers, Abigail Van Buren—Dear Abby—has used that one for years.

It's clear Beck enjoys being in "the happy business," as she likes to think of it.

- *May 10, 1984*

Come Out And Play

Suzanne Vadnais Monson ... collage & jewelry artist, painter & writer

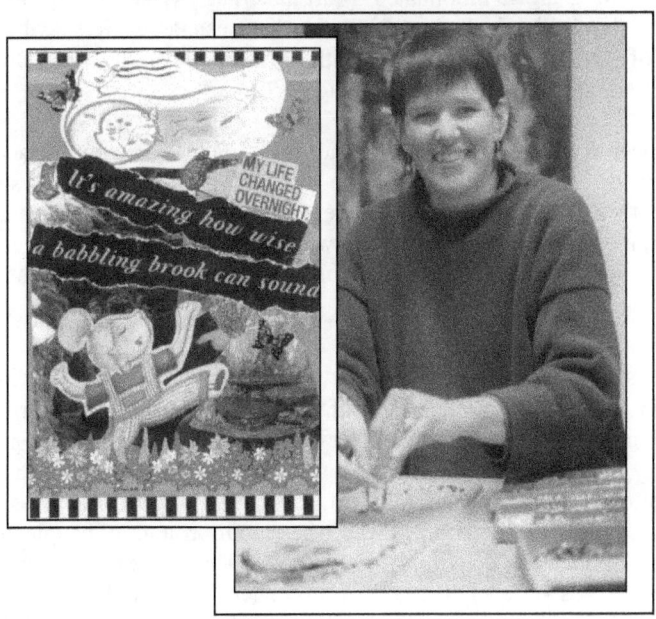

Collages epitomize the work of Suzanne Vadnais Monson. Collages are inherently playful, and she believes life should be full of play. They are inherently symbolic, and she sees a galaxy of symbols in the world. They are inherently surreal, and she is inspired by distorted dreams.

Monson's kaleidoscopic character is further evidenced by the fact most of her collages combine words and images, for she is both a writer and a visual artist. She plays with words as well as with paint and colored pencils. She crafts sentences as well as beaded bracelets and "magic toy boxes."

Come Out And Play, she invites people with her business name. "Something magical is waiting for you."

Monson, an Osceola, Wisconsin, resident, not only practices "creative expression," but teaches it to children and adults alike in after-school and community education classes.

"I find creative expression really helps people heal, move forward, (and) lead quality lives," she says. "All of the things that I've discovered in my life I hear from the students I work with, as they leave my class. . . . I always provide all the materials, so they don't have to buy anything to come to my classes. And that's usually what works, because people are so intimidated by art materials. What I do is, I say: 'This is what I think is the best. This is what I use, and here's a whole bunch of them you guys can play with.' And you can decide. 'Do I like this? Is it something I would do again?'"

Some people come to Monson's home for individual creativity coaching retreats. "I've had 12 people do this with me this summer," she says. "It's amazing to me that they've all been women, and they've all been women who want to start their own business—a creative business. They get excited that they can work one-on-one with somebody who's doing that."

There is a large measure of New Age mysticism in much of what Monson does. The spiritual element "seems to be a big part of why people relate to it," she says. "New Age-wise, who inspired me probably the most was Louise Hay, because she had this whole idea of affirmations, and how powerfully affirmations influenced our lives—what we think about determines who we are. Or, as a lot of people put it, what you focus on determines your reality. That's even a line out of *Star Wars*. It's such a hot idea now. . . . There I was, in high school, reading Joseph Campbell, *The Mask of Gods*, thinking he was the smartest man alive. And it just grew for me."

A presentation called "Killing Us Softly," given by a woman who studied advertising images of women, played into Monson's growing awareness. "She really made this young mind think: 'Wow! How is all of this stuff I look at affecting me?'" Monson says. ". . . I started seeing how visual things—what I looked at—had a profound impact on me." That led her to wonder what would happen if she "made stuff and put it out there" designed to have an effect she wanted it to have. The affect on her, she says, is she was putting attention on her dreams, desires, goals and hopes. "When you get into creative visualization and that whole world you start looking at self-care," she says. "That's really what it gets down to. So, yes, it's New Age, in that New Age is all about what your attention is on, and yoga and meditation and all of that. But it's really very Old Age in that how we take care of ourselves is how we do well."

Monson created a popular deck of 64 "Enrichuals" cards containing inspirational messages "for exploring your best life."

"I had so many of these decks of inspirational cards that I was using, and I just wasn't happy with them," she says. "They didn't go deep enough, was my thing. I wanted something that was deeper. When I set out to write them I did them for these kits I was making. I was making these little boxes that were like comfort kits. They had everything you needed for a fresh start or. . . . One of them was a soul-mates box; it was for two people. So every box had a theme, and I wrote 12 cards on this theme for the boxes, like a new beginning. When I got them all done I realized I had this awesome deck of cards. It was a magical thing. I said a prayer. I just said: 'Help me find the right words to bring this together, to bring this gift that I'm trying to get out into the world. Just help me do one powerful paragraph.' That's what I asked for. And in they came. I feel like, the truth is, I was a partner in creating that deck of cards. Something bigger than me came through me. What I know is that the people who use them tell me every time they pull a card it's powerful for them. They ask a question, they pull a card, and there's a powerful answer in that card. And I say: I wish I could take credit for that, but I know I'm just a part of it. I was just the part that sat at the keyboard and wrote it down. And then I did little collages for each one of them, just sort of on the theme of the card."

The Enrichuals cards have a collage, with both words and images, on one side and advice, instructions and probing questions on the reverse side. The collage for one, for example, includes such phrases as "Imagine joy," "Because there's an explorer in you," and "Something magical is waiting for you." "Invite your big dreams out to play!" the advice on the other side begins. "Visualize what prosperity is for you by doing this exercise. Close your eyes and imagine your way through an ideal day. . . How far away from your current reality was your ideal day?"

Having been inspired and influenced by both words and images, Monson combined them "early on" in her own creations. "When I was a young, starting out poet-artist," she says, "I would take my favorite poems, like Rilke poems or Adrian Rich poems, (and) I would paint these abstract backgrounds, and I'd make my own posters. I didn't have any money to buy the kind of art I wanted, so I made these huge poems, and I'd put 'em on my farmhouse walls. And—*ah!*—they were so inspiring to me. Just the parts I liked, you know; I'd put that on a big poster on my farmhouse wall. I remember this one I did that was huge. I took three sheets of tag-board and taped them together and did this really long poem that I just loved. It was called 'A Piece of Writing About The Parts,' by Susan Griffin. It was about what happens when you don't get nourished as an artist or a writer, and that part of you just dies. It was a piece of writing about the parts that die. And I wanted it in my face so that I remembered what I needed to do to stay in that groove of making art that inspired me."

Monson believes cosmic messages can crop up anywhere. Once she was walking on a beach, pondering her life, thinking *Am I on the right path, or should I just go out and get a job?* when she looked down and saw a hand-soap-size rock with a perfect white crystal heart embedded in it. "I feel wonderful, magical confirmation when that kind of thing shows up," she says.

Her Enrichuals cards are not her only handcrafted item with inspirational messages or stories. Her magic toy boxes, dream vision charms and spirited ceremony bracelets come with them as well. "I swear, the writing is half of why this stuff sells," she says. "And for writers, this is good to know. There is a way to make money writing that's not necessarily about publishing books, although publishing a book is nice."

Most of Monson's paintings derive from dreams. Her most popular painting, in print form, is of five brightly colored angels who came to her in her garden, in a dream. After a considerable period of silence, one of the angels finally spoke to her, saying simply, "Keep planting your seeds."

"This is an important message to get," Monson says, "but I thought it was going to be like the meaning of life coming to me in the garden."

Her Come Out And Play gifts are available at a number of Twin Cities art galleries and gift shops, including The Bibelot Shops, some of the toniest emporiums in the region. This past year she also managed to make it into her ideal national market, Femail Creations, a Las Vegas-based company considered "sort of *the* national business for gifts and products that inspire women," according to Monson. Her products also are found at the comfortqueen.com website of self-care maven Jennifer Louden, along with Monson's weekly *Instant Soothing* ideas, which she describes as dollops of insight and inspiration. Longer personal essays appear in *The Edge*, a Twin Cities New Age monthly newspaper focusing on the human potential movement. In those, Monson shares stories of her experiences as an abused child and the steps it took to gain self-empowerment and understand the process of "personal reinvention."

"I took three classes at The Loft [a literary arts center in Minneapolis], working with some of my favorite writers, to get to the point where I could tell those stories," she relates. "They're difficult stories, a lot of the things I'm talking about. And I started talking about my background as an abused child, which, for me, it had to be, because there's sort of this saying: It's what on top that comes out first. That was on top. So until I told it, until I actually got it on paper, I couldn't say anything else. I tried; it wouldn't happen. I would just get frustrated, and I would have to stop. So I kept writing 'em, and I would give them to my friends to read. That was the safe thing for me to do. My best friend, my husband, my sister. And I would say, 'What do you think?' And they would all just be like: 'Wow! These are powerful.' And my best friend happened to be the production editor for *The Edge*, and after she had read probably 25 of these things she said, 'Sue, I would really like you to submit some of this stuff to *The Edge*, because I think there's a real need for storytelling in *The Edge*, as opposed to people standing on a podium telling you, "You should do it like this," preaching to people, trying to convert them.' . . . So I thought: I'll give it a try. The very first one I wrote was very simple and fun. That's how I broke the ice. It was a story about meeting my husband and taking a walk with him. From there, the themes were what helped me decide which of my stories to tell. . . . Then I started getting feedback from people. I started getting phone calls, e-mails, letters from people saying, 'Thank you for talking about this. Thank you for telling me what you're doing, because it helps me.' (Some of these were from) psychologists, professionals in the Twin Cities. I mean, it was just phenomenal. I still get them, saying: 'You don't know what a service you're doing, to be writing about this in this format.' It's not a self help book; it's a story, and it's a very different sort of genre to put this stuff out in."

Monson also finds gratification in the instant feedback she receives from students of all ages she teaches in elementary school after-school art programs and adult community education programs. She teaches introductory, single-session classes on everything from sketching to soft pastels to oil painting, paper collage, polymer clay, and journaling. "Almost everything is around creative expression," she says. "It may not be specifically an art class; it might be journaling. But when I'm teaching journaling it's about using journals creatively, and sort of illustrating your life story." One of the things she loves to do is show people how to make collage covers for their journals. "Really what I'm noticing is that there's a real resurgence in homemade, handcrafted things you can do at home, with your family."

Currently, the polymer clay classes are among her most popular. "Everybody wants to use it, and work with it," she says, "because you don't need a kiln and all the special equipment you need for working with (most) clay. And it's colored. This clay has 36 bright colors, and they can blend and mix. You can make everything from cool Christmas ornaments to jewelry with it. People are blown away that this is something they can do in their kitchen, bake in their oven, and have beautiful finished art an hour later. You can take a picture of anything, rub it onto an unbaked piece of clay, pull it off, and you've got a perfect copy. So people make little pins, or refrigerator magnets, of their grandchildren, or things they care about."

Aside from the good money she makes teaching, Monson loves teaching community education classes for the opportunities it gives her to touch people's lives. "You get to come in and teach something powerful," she says. "You don't have to grade anybody, which was always a struggle for me [as a college teacher], because I felt that if they were trying it should matter. Of course, schools don't work that way. So it works better for me to do art programming, and programming that people think of as enrichment—fun stuff."

More than a dozen women interested in attaining their heart's desire—as mentioned, most have wanted to start their own creative business—have taken the one-on-one creativity coaching retreats Monson offers. "They work with me for two four-hour sessions," she explains. "We do whatever they want to do. They've got a palette of options they can pick from." Those options include Deepening Your Intuitive Wisdom, Drawing Your Dreams To Life, and Putting The Pieces Together ("the world of transformational collage"). "Every one of them is a little different; they want to do something a little different. And I've learned so much doing that. It's great for me to get to do this as a business, but for me as an artist to learn what people want to know more about, that's what I find, I think, the most exciting."

The coaching continues with four 45-minute follow-up telephone conversations.

"Normally you do a retreat and then you go home," Monson says. "And what happens for most of us is: we go home and we lose it. We lose that magical, wonderful whatever it was we captured at that wonderful retreat. So what I decided was to tailor this retreat the way I would want a retreat, and that was to have a continued relationship with these people after they got home, so that when they ran into roadblocks or problems we could blast 'em apart. We could work on it together and look at what came up that was a challenge and start to help them find a way to begin their dream again, regardless of whatever happened, whatever showed up."

Monson believes people discover, re-discover, or keep in touch with their true spirit when they create art, that we can reinvent and reinvigorate ourselves with play, that we can realize both our hearts' and souls' desires and make choices that move us toward the lives of our dreams.

- *October 15th and October 29th, 2002*

☼

A Person Of Characters

Terry Scott ... cartoonist

Not every artist making a living drawing cartoons has his or her work published on newspaper comic strip pages or in slick, mass circulation magazines. In fact, the drawings of most cartoonists are more likely to be found on promotional caps and pencils than on the pages of the *Saturday Evening Post*.

"I think probably at least sixty percent of all cartoonists are involved in advertising cartoons where you're going to make, like, fifty dollars a crack and you know you're going to make it," says Terry Scott. "Then they freelance their cartooning on the side to magazines, like I'm doing, and try to do a lot of things all together to make it work."

Scott, who is in his mid-20s, lives about 25 miles southeast of Superior, near the village of Lake Nebagamon. To make a go of things in his chosen profession, he is involved in cartooning in a number of ways— as a commercial artist, a freelance cartoonist, a retail businessman, and a teacher. He says that after three years in business "things are starting to really go well."

He derives the largest percentage of his income from advertising and promotional jobs he does for businesses within a 50-mile radius of Lake Nebagamon. That involves everything from painting signs and designing restaurant menus to creating trademark cartoon characters such as the Mad Stamper character he came up with for a Superior-based rubber-stamp business.

Less than a year after that rubber-stamp business was created Scott suggested to the owner that a goofy character called the Mad Stamper could attract attention. "He didn't really say much about it at that time," Scott says, "but after a month or two I was in his place and he said, 'Terry, you know, I was thinking; I really should have kind of a goofy character made up, the Mad Stamper or something,' like it was his own idea."

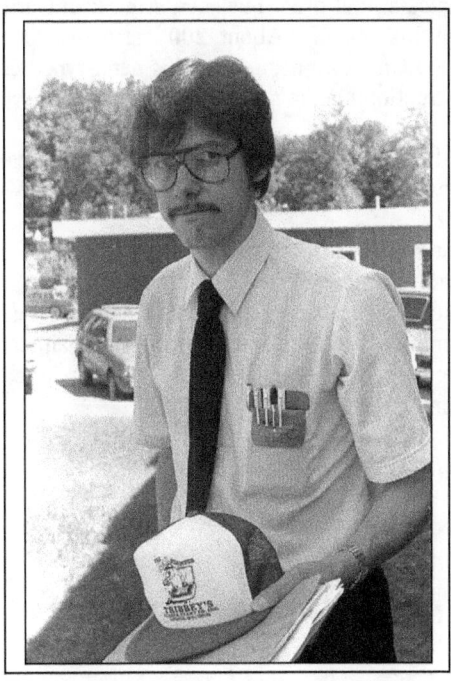

Scott has created "about a dozen" such trademark cartoon characters, including a Coho salmon for a Superior charter service and Bobby Blueberry for the village of Iron River.

While Scott is still on the road a lot soliciting new clients, he is now known well enough that some businesses contact him first and others hire him for several different projects. AMSOIL, a national company based in Superior, recently commissioned him to draw cartoons for its monthly newsletter.

Because of his busy schedule of commercial work, he has sent out few single-panel cartoons to major magazines in the last year or two, that being more of a gamble than contracted commercial jobs. While none of his cartoons have yet appeared in well known general interest magazines, several have been published in trade and technical journals.

Like most cartoonists, Scott's nirvana goal is to have a comic strip syndicated nationwide. "I haven't really set on an idea that I think is universal and that is going to be really appealing," he says. "So what I want to do first is self-syndicate some things [statewide] and be successful at that and then show the syndicates some ideas that way."

Scott also operates a mail order business, American Cartoonist Supply Company, from his home. About 200 cartoonists and gag [joke] writers around the United States receive his hand-typed catalogs listing art supplies, instruction manuals, market guides and other products.

"It seems like there's a real move now towards more cartooning, and there's a scarcity of good cartoon materials," he says.

Scott has taught classes in both cartooning and advertising/promotion at vocational and technical schools in both Duluth and Superior. This fall he will teach 10-week courses in both subjects—cartooning and advertising/promotion—at the Wisconsin Indianhead Technical Institute in Superior. He would like to develop a correspondence course in cartooning sometime in the future.

- *July 31, 1985*

Shelf Life

Mark Wardean ... mushroom carver

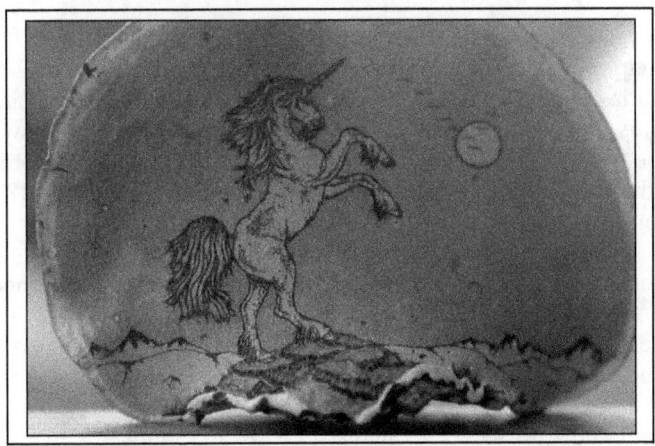

Mark Wardean likes to call shelf mushrooms "nature's own canvases." While most mushrooms are as perishable as carved pumpkins, shelf mushrooms are nearly as dense as wood, which allows Wardean to use woodburning tools to decorate the smooth, creamy undersides of them with nature scenes, drawings of animals, and other images.

The popularity of the Centuria, Wisconsin, artist's mushroom art has, well, mushroomed since a member of country music singer Travis Tritt's fan club saw some of Wardean's creations in a Twin Cities area gift shop in 1993 and commissioned Wardean to wood-burn a shelf mushroom for Tritt.

"Everybody wants something on a mushroom," Wardean says. "It seems to be pretty impressive that Travis Tritt has one. That's fine. It's fun to do. There's a lot of other carving and stuff I'd like to be doing, but people want the mushrooms done, so I can't get away from doing that."

Wardean likes to keep things natural with his art by concentrating on woodburning both wood and leather. "I try to stay away from paint," he says, "because it's not that natural, unless I make it out of berries or something like that." He has played around with mushrooms for more than 10 years.

"I had seen other people work on them," he says. "At that time I did a lot of ink drawings, and carving."

Although skeptical that decorated mushrooms would fare well in the marketplace, he tried doing one and sold it. After working for a Centuria-based lawn care/landscaping service much of this year, he recently dropped that job to focus on creating art fulltime. He now has all the work he can handle with mushroom art orders through word-of-mouth alone. "Why not do this when I have the calling for it?" he reasons.

A moose he put on one mushroom led to three more orders for moose. One of a Wisconsin Point lighthouse led to three more orders for light-houses. One person wanted the identical lighthouse, two others any lighthouse.

"I don't know if I'll ever get into a store," Wardean jokes. "Every day somebody sees a piece and I've gotta re-do my list, and add a couple, and move them around. The list is growing."

Before this recent burst of activity most of his sales were made in Minnesota, at gift shops and art fairs.

For Wardean, finding mushrooms to work on is as much fun as the actual woodburning. He finds the shelf mushrooms all year long, "just about anywhere" he walks in Wisconsin's woods. Shelf mushrooms grow on the lower portion of tree trunks, with most of them in the eight- to twelve-inch size range.

"I'm kind of picky on which ones to use," he says. "If I don't want to use it I don't want to knock it off a tree. The moisture content has to be just right." Some shelf mushrooms "are kind of a nesting ground for larvae of some kind," so he inspects each mushroom before removing it from a tree. "If I see there's a family of something living in there, I can't have that. . . . I find them pretty easily. I've got a pretty good eye looking through the woods for them because I've been doing that for years."

Wardean cleans the bottom and bark side of the mushrooms, by hand, and often cleans the smooth side with bleach, which also sanitizes them to a degree. Generally a mushroom must dry for two or three days before it is ready to accept wood-burning, although in autumn some of the mushrooms are dry enough to work on immediately.

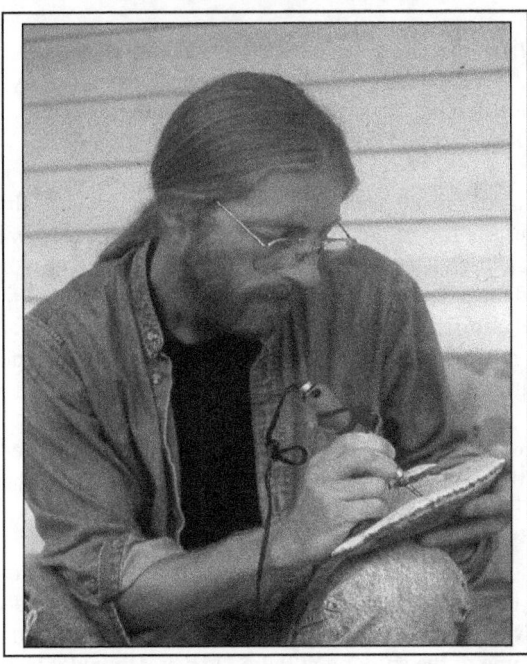

Wardean uses a sharp tool of some sort to draw on the smooth side before beginning to burn the image with two woodburning tools that are as well-worn as Willie Nelson's battered guitar. Each mushroom's particular shape helps him decide what image would work well with that mushroom. "Sometimes," he says, "you can see if there's something in there naturally...."

"Once I've got all the foreground and background—I go at it pretty heavily on the detail—I might want to break up the scenery, the foreground from the background. I'll go in there and shade just to try to break it up." He uses coffee, soy sauce, and other substances to achieve shadings of brown. Another shading technique is to scrape away the white outer skin to reveal a medium-brown, velvety layer beneath. Subtle heat control of the woodburning tools produces a range of shading as well. "With one of my woodburners," he says, "I can control the heat in such a way that I don't have to go in and shade with something like coffee. I would say there are probably a dozen different colors with just the one woodburner, depending on how hard or light you're doing it. It burns anywhere from light brown to black. There are a lot of colors in there." If a mushroom canvas has a blemish that cannot be removed he will create a design that hides the blemish by working it into the design.

Wardean likes that each piece of mushroom art is different. "I can do the same piece on three different mushrooms and they're all still amazingly different," he says. "I've had people say to me, 'Do this one again.' 'Okay, but you know the mushroom's different.'"

Wardean also carves pieces of driftwood that suggest shapes to his artistic eye. He recently carved an eagle into a relatively small piece of driftwood a friend found along the Cimarron River in Colorado. "It almost had the shape of the eagle," he says. "That's why I like working with a piece of driftwood—to see the shape it's got in it and go from there and make it happen. It's more like an abstract type thing, the shape of the wood."

He uses his woodburning skills on carvings and on stretched leather he frames with Native American-style crossed-corner frames he constructs himself.

"There's so much that I can do, and I'm just not taking enough time to do it all," he says. "I find myself doing what other people want more, which is where you want to go as far as turning it into a business, but you lose some of the enjoyment there. I try not to, but it happens."

He has found a "do nothing" approach to be the best preservation method for his mushroom creations. He says some of the first decorated mushrooms he did are still in the same condition as when he worked on them.

"I've tried a lot of different things and nothing has really worked better than just leaving them natural," he says.

That must please him, for natural is his style.

- *September 2nd and October 23rd, 2000*

The Bird Knows The Words

David DeMattia ... animatronics designer

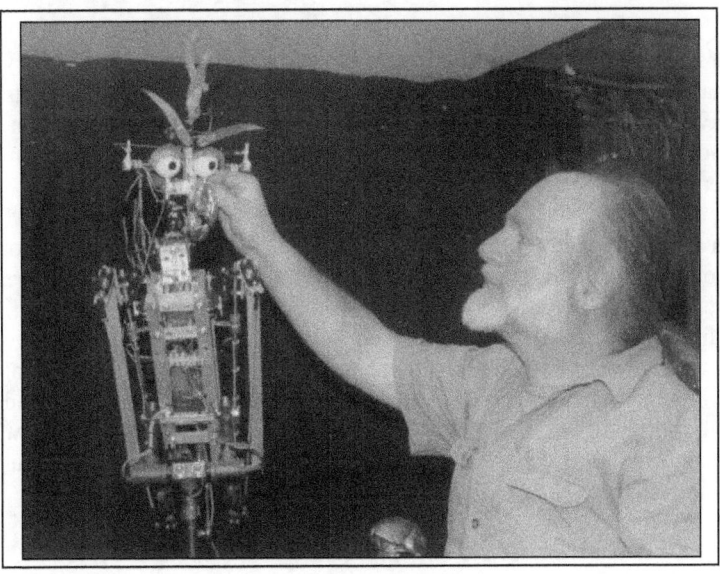

I interviewed David DeMattia about his Robobird II creation Feb. 22, 2008. This profile also includes information taken from an August 16, 2012 interview, by which time he had moved to north of St. Croix Falls.

With a background in sculpture, theater and engineering, it seems logical to David DeMattia that he would come up with a creation such as Robobird II, a two-foot-tall Erector Set-like mechanical bird—an "animatronic" character—he programmed to lip-sync and dance through a two-and-a-half or three-minute recorded song. Actually, the programmed bird speaks the verses of a song rather than sing them.

DeMattia, a Lindstrom, Minnesota, area resident who was Festival Theatre's sound designer for four years, will debut Robobird II at Gallery 135 in downtown St. Croix Falls this Saturday, March 15. The featured bird, as well as other examples of DeMattia's "strange sculpture and other odd things," will be on display from 10 a.m. to 4 p.m. DeMattia will be on hand for a wine and cheese reception from 4 to 5 p.m., then spend an hour talking about how the history of his work led to Robobird II, putting Robobird II through its performance routine a time or two, and answering audience questions.

"I've been wanting to experiment a little bit more with shape and form and character," DeMattia says, noting that animatronic technology is "just light years ahead" of where it was in the 1990s.

When most people think of their life being made into a movie they imagine what actor or actress they would want to portray them. In David DeMattia's case, his first thought is not of an actor but a director. Hands-down, he would want offbeat, audacious, quirky filmmaker Tim Burton to direct a movie about his life.

As a Rorschach test reveals personality traits, that preference says a lot about DeMattia's makeup. The odd, the strange and the whimsical are commonplace in the work of this multi-media artist. Indeed, his informal appearance and loose, easygoing, somewhat impish demeanor give him something of a whimsical aura, as though he possesses the spirit of a blithe fairyland being. Given that he made many visits to Disneyland while growing up in southern California's Simi Valley, that somehow seems apt. Inspired by those visits, DeMattia was filled with fanciful notions from an early age.

"I was probably one of the only kids that would bring a drawing pad," he says. "I would go there and watch their shows. . . and I would plot out movements and sketch."

Later, study of and experience in sculpture, theater and engineering led DeMattia to his own smaller scale animatronics/robotic projects.

"That's still my love—the sculpture, the animatronics, the robotics—bringing that to a performance, which is always my thing," he says. "It's always about the performance and the love of the character."

Inspired by "a combination of robots, the theater and the immersiveness of the story" on his boyhood visits to Disneyland, DeMattia started making puppets, and then marionettes, at a young age. He built his first rudimentary animatronic character while in fifth grade. Beginning in junior high school, his involvement in speech, debate and theater pushed him toward performance. At age 17 his family moved to Wichita, Kansas, where he completed high school. He studied theater at Wichita State University, then moved to Texas to study electronics and industrial engineering at the University of North Texas, where he minored in radio, television and film. A Dallas-Ft. Worth-based company called Ecolab hired him as a designer. While employed there he created a nine-foot-tall talking Christmas tree for a shopping center and "different kinds of creatures" for a Dallas science museum, designed animatronics for a children's television program called *J.J. The Jet Plane*, and did lighting and sound design for the Dallas Children's Theatre and a couple of smaller theater companies.

When Ecolab offered him a job at its research center in the Minneapolis-St. Paul area in 1996 he jumped at the opportunity and moved to Minnesota. Eventually he grew disillusioned with the corporate culture and left Ecolab in 2003, after 11 years with the company, to start his home-based Sleeping Dragon Studios business, which originally had both an arts side and a consulting engineering side.

As sound designer for the St. Croix Festival Theatre, he designed and built (mainly out of Styrofoam) four different-sized man-eating plants for Festival's 2004 production of *Little Shop of Horrors*. Robobird II is his biggest animatronics project since then.

The "II" designation suggests there was a Robobird I, as indeed there was. DeMattia created that one for an animatronic stage show in Texas in the mid-1990s. He could program it to perform only very simple movements, though. Even so, that creation marked a milestone for him because it was the first time he used a computer to edit sound.

Robobird II is financed partly by a $1,000 grant from the East Central (Minnesota) Arts Council. DeMattia approached the arts council with a loose concept, was approved, decided that his animatronic character would be a bird, then "hit the hardware store" in search of construction materials. After deciding he would use ping-pong balls for eyes, he scaled the rest of the body in proportion.

"The technique I used was a lot like I sculpt," he says. "I get some things together, attach 'em, see how it looks, and then move on from there. This is all free-form."

He couldn't be quite as cavalier when it came to the computer programming involved, however. "It takes forever to program this because I can only program one movement at a time," he says. ". . . I'm thinking that for every 30 seconds of movement I have in excess of 10 hours of programming."

Robobird II is capable of more sophisticated movements than was Robobird I. The new metal bird also has two much smaller backup singers, Peep 1 and Peep 2, who perform pretty much the same role as Gladys Knight's Pips did.

Someday Demattia would like to create an immersive, half-hour musical variety show featuring North Woods creatures and pre-recorded music. He already has done some sketching for it. Now, he says, "it's a matter of sketching it off, figuring how much it's going to cost (and) where I'm going to put it."

Because of the mechanics involved, it would be a challenge to stage such a show in more than one location. "To make it portable would ramp the cost up a little bit," he says, "because you would have to make sure that things can break apart (and that) you can get them through a three-foot doorway, that your robots don't break when you try to move them."

Clearly, DeMattia has a clear idea of what he wants. "I've had this idea for years, to do this show," he says. "And now that I've gotten to know a lot more musicians it makes the idea a little more feasible for original music, or public domain music."

"Follow your bliss" has become something of a mantra for the modern age. In David DeMattia's case, he pursues whimsy and bliss naturally follows.

The Light Stuff

Cork Marcheschi ... light artist

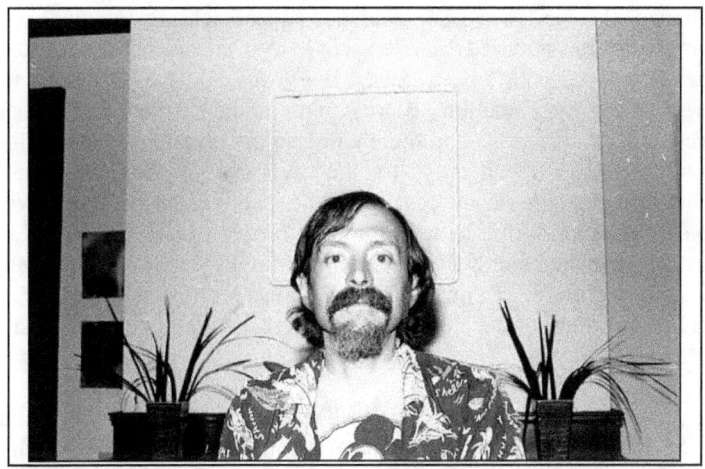

Having turned on Minneapolis, avant-garde artist Cork Marcheschi, like an apostle of light whose mission has been accomplished, feels it is time to return home. Where's home? I ask him, knowing nothing of his background, knowing only what little I have read about him in a *Minneapolis Tribune* article about neon art, that he is *"the* neon expert in this country as well as Europe." San Francisco, he answers, and there is an immediate click in my mind at the suitableness—the obviousness, even—of this fact.

San Francisco. Of course. It couldn't be much more apparent if he wore a sign stating such. Where else could this gauntly slender, goateed, doughy-complexioned, stringy-haired 38-year-old man with an effeminate edge to his voice wearing an irreverent—Walt Disney no doubt would have thought it blasphemous—"Mickey Rat" T-shirt, unbuttoned, loud, black silk Hawaiian shirt and a laid-back demeanor be from but San Francisco? Add a pair of cool shades, as he does later when we walk across the street from his home to his studio-office at the Minneapolis College of Art and Design, and you have a consummate beatnik—a prosperous one, to be sure, which seems almost a contradiction, but the spirit and the style are there, nonetheless—a holdout from the Beat Generation subculture depicted in the novels of Jack Kerouac, a child of San Francisco's bubbling Fifties ferment who has kept his youthful faith by transforming his purple Victorian house in south Minneapolis into a beatnik's heaven where he can stay Forever Hip, for while he came of age in the Sixties, Marcheschi has more of the sensibility of the beatnik than of the hippie. One thing is certain: Seventies flash and glitter never invaded his dim chambers.

"Minneapolis has been just a fabulous place for me to live," says Marcheschi [pronounced Mar-*kess*-key], who moved here in 1970 to teach at MCAD. "It's been great. I've loved it. I've developed my career here—my reputation. But it's getting time for me to move back. I've been lots of places, and there's just no place that turns me on like San Francisco." Specifically, it is the city's famous North Beach area he finds so enamoring—"the old fatherland bohemia of the West Coast," as Tom Wolfe called it in *The Electric Kool-Aid Acid Test*. Despite the name, North Beach is not next to the Pacific Ocean. Marcheschi describes it as a mixed Chinese/Italian section "with a lot of the old literary flavor of the city still on the street. And it just feels good to be there," he says.

He acquired his unusual nickname when he was a baby. A non-Italian friend of the family heard everyone else calling him "carino," which is an Italian word meaning, roughly, "cute," and shortened that to Corky. The *Gasoline Alley* comic strip character Corky was popular in 1945, so soon everyone was calling the baby Corky.

Largely because of the disciples Marcheschi has attracted, Minneapolis has become one of the neon centers of the nation in recent years, in terms of both how much there is on display and the quality of the craftsmanship. In the past couple of years, particularly, there has been a resurgence of interest in neon, which was long disdained as gaudy and vulgar, for indoor decoration as well as outdoor signs and advertising.

"When I came to Minneapolis in 1970 there was no neon really happening here," Marcheschi recounts. "There were a couple of commercial shops. I knew I wanted to work with it for my artwork, so I was able to get a plant together, and the college let me put it in the college so students could use it and it would be at my disposal. We were the first ones to really set up a shop that operated that gave young people an opportunity to learn the craft of neon. And some of these people had to make a living, so they started doing little sign jobs around here, and my artwork started to attract more attention locally because it's very accessible. . . . And it just sort of happened that way. So when I drive around town and see all the neon all over the place I feel secretly rather pleased to know that I've had an influence, at least on the surface of the city. My students have gone on to put up most of the signs in town."

While he is sometimes classified as a neon artist, Marcheschi rejects that label. "I don't do neon art," he says. "There's art, and that's it. You don't separate the material from art. That's a craft. I'm interested in light, and not particularly neon. It just so happens that neon gives me the kind of light that I can use, or expresses what it is that I'm interested in, the best. I've been playing with light since I was 14."

He says playing with light means "exactly what it sound like. . . . It's not a calculated activity. . . . I go in with very little in the way of a preconception and just kind of take it from that point. That's how I work the best. I just really fly by the seat of my pants. And I like it. That's one of the activities of art that I enjoy very much for myself. I'm not saying that that is a typical art activity. But speaking purely for myself, I like that not knowing."

If he will accept any label more specific than artist it is "a sculptor of energy." He considers energy his true medium, with light an incarnation of that energy. "My work with light, art, and life draws from the richness of history and the energy that has been passed on from artists, musicians, and people who have touched my life," he wrote in a statement about his work included in a recent exhibition catalog. "It is this energy, life energy, that I attempt to capture. The mysteries of light and life are very close, and I enjoy the practice of dealing with a material that both is and isn't there."

He lists as major influences scientists Nikola Tesla and Werner Heisenberg, writers Jack Kerouac and Allen Ginsberg, comedian Lenny Bruce, jazz and blues musicians, artists such as Kasimir Malevich and Jackson Pollack, and other unconventional luminaries of both past and present.

Most of his works consist of "non-referential" geometric shapes—squares, rectangles, triangles, and other basic forms. Probably his trademark design, in fact—his Campbell's soup can—is a simple square. By the use of block-out paint to direct the light, a frame made of parallel neon-filled tubes produces one solid, vivid color inside the square and a diffusing halo of another color outside the square.

Marcheschi has created many of these 24-inch squares, which sell for $3,200, in different eye-popping, mesmerizing color combinations.

In the same vein, a 1982 work entitled *But No-o-o-o-o-o Memorial*, in memory of John Belushi, consists of a pink oblong shape remindful of a rear-view mirror surrounded by an intense blue halo.

Marcheschi doesn't make neon signs, or swans, or rainbows, or anything of that sort. He says such things are not art, but pieces of craft. "Art's not better than craft; they're just different—cats and dogs," he makes clear.

"You put a tree in a painting, or you put a tree in a photograph or something, and when people look at it it's not necessarily the tree that the artist put there; it's a tree that people have seen before. So if you do a painting of someone's face in a real dreamy mood or something there's a *déjà vu* attitude that the viewer has. And it also allows the viewer to have fantasy about the artist being a person that has hand-eye coordination, and that's what separates this person from the artist. That may be what separates that person from a craftsperson, but not from an artist. An artist's tool is his or her will—it's their choice. And you basically will pieces into existence. When the thing is done, or when you find it, when you choose it, when you pick it, it becomes art, because you've said so. It's an act of will."

He believes an artist should have something of the outlaw about him, in the sense that outlaws, as Tom Robbins observed in his novel *Still Life with Woodpecker*, through the point of view of the main character, "raise the exhilaration content of the universe" even when they fail. Marcheschi feels artists should embody that same sort of walk-on-the-edge existential intensity.

He uses non-referential shapes because he doesn't want to "muddy up the composition with things that people recognize." He wants people to have unique experiences with his light sculptures. "If you have an experience you understand," he says with a mystical obscurity that sounds so like the psychobabble of so many self-proclaimed self-help gurus that it has a suspiciously pretentious ring to it. That doesn't necessarily make it a bogus claim in this case, of course; it's just that overuse of the metaphysical promise automatically raises skepticism. "The understanding is the experience," Marcheschi continues. "There's no explanation. Not 'What does it mean?' What does it mean to be in love? What does it mean to see a fabulous sunset? If you feel awe when the sun goes down, when you want to sort of disappear into the ocean, you've understood the meaning."

Even each one of his 24-inch squares, he says, should offer a viewer a unique experience. "If you can't find differences within each piece and with the subtleties of the colors then the technological society that you were born into has blinded you, it has numbed you, and you need stimulus."

People throughout a large part of the Western World have had the opportunity to experience Marcheschi's artwork, at well over a hundred individual and group exhibitions in such cities as New York, Toronto, San Francisco, Montreal, Bonn, Copenhagen, Caracas, Tokyo, and others great and small. He probably is better known in Europe than in the United States since light art has a longer, more honorable tradition there than here. He says he is one of three artists in the United States doing what he is doing with light; the two others are in Los Angeles. German Public Broadcasting produced a half-hour documentary film about him in 1975. Three years later he spent a year in West Germany on a fellowship. In recent years he has done more private commissions, cutting back on the number of gallery showings because "the thrill is sort of gone" from that.

A few of his pieces are on permanent public display. The largest is a $65,000 commission on the side of a building 80 feet above ground level in Seattle. The 1,300 feet of neon tubing glows in 17 different patterns. Originally the pattern changed daily; now it does so at more frequent intervals. In Minneapolis there is a green neon line 75 feet long and one foot high stretched along the side of the skyway connecting Pillsbury Center and First Bank Place. In St. Paul there is a work of his on display in the Minnesota Mutual Life Insurance Company building. The Minneapolis Art Institute purchased one of his pieces for eventual permanent installation.

He also has created several set designs for stage plays in the Twin Cities and West Germany, and for a Canadian television special starring magician Doug Henning.

As mentioned, Marcheschi has been playing with light since he was 14, which means he has been at it for 25 years. He started in the summer of 1959 by creating "a very dim but colorful teenage vision of a beatnik nocturnal pad" in the basement of his family's house, where he and his friends could retreat from parents and middle class mundaneness. As Marcheschi describes it, "beer cans with holes in them became lanterns and [whiskey] bottles with colored water filtered Xmas lights." Dubbed "Casa Loco," this surreal sanctuary of light and music turned out to be an on-going project that occupied Marcheschi until he entered the College of San Mateo in 1963. When a friend from that period whom Marcheschi hadn't seen since high school visited him in Minneapolis in 1982 it struck him that Marcheschi's house is merely a larger version of Casa Loco, decorated as it is with six or seven of his own light sculptures and other funky furnishings.

"It made a good impression on me and helped me in my belief that my relationship to my material is a very natural and long-lived one," Marcheschi wrote in the exhibition catalog.

As natural as it might be, though, it wasn't inevitable that Marcheschi would become a professional artist. His first love—the passionate, abiding object of his devotion—is music, "specifically blues." For seven years, from 1963 to 1970, he played bass and—the last couple years of that period—synthesizer in rock and blues bands. The synthesizer was not the type of keyboard instrument common today, but an early pure-tone Mad Scientist model whose electronic undulations were controlled with dials and knobs. One of his bands, The Fifty Foot Hose, had "a real strange reputation" on the West Coast, recorded an album for Mercury Records, performed at all the major Bay Area venues such as the Fillmore and Avalon ballrooms, and toured as part of the Flying Bears Medicine Show and Musical Experience, a Mercury Records revue headlined by such acts as the Buddy Miles Express, Leon Russell and Chuck Berry. "I loved it," Marcheschi says of that experience. "And I still prefer the company of musicians to artists."

All this is not to imply that Marcheschi abandoned art during that period. After studying at the College of San Mateo from 1963 to 1966, he transferred to California State College—Hayward, then went on to graduate school at the California College of Arts and Crafts in Oakland, where he earned a Master of Fine Arts degree in sculpture in 1969.

When the Minneapolis College of Art and Design offered him a teaching position it was time to decide between a career in art and further adventures in music. Since he felt freer and more creative being an artist, he made the move to Minneapolis.

"I've relegated myself to (being) sort of a musical historian," he says. He has a valuable collection of records, as well as impressive collections of ceramic glass and books. "And now I'm starting to get close to producing some music, in terms of other people's music, and production for record companies." Besides teaching sculpture, he also teaches a course on the relationship between blues and fine arts. "The soul of black music and the position of the artist in contemporary culture are very close to the same," he believes.

Usually he is enveloped by music when he works, either in his studio/office at MCAD, where he considers the stereo system the most important equipment in the long, narrow room, or at the large, high, Command Central desk in a small open room just inside the front door of his house, where he sketches out most of his sculptural designs.

He begins a project by doodling, basically—putting shapes down on graph paper with colored pencils. "The most important thing is just to get started," he says. "Once you're started the process sort of takes over." The pencils are not exactly the same colors as the neon, but similar enough for his purposes. His neon palette holds more than 50 hues. A phosphorus coating inside the glass tubing produces color, by the way. When electricity passes through the tube in the form of an excited gas it, in turn, excites the phosphorus, creating a radiation.

Marcheschi leaves most of the actual construction to two colleagues, Norm Anderson and Brad Jirka, who are more proficient technicians than he is. "I do the installation," he says, "but I'm not skilled at bending neon tubes. I make straight tubes, and I like certain aspects of it, but I'm not very skilled at it, and I really don't have any interest in becoming skilled at it. . . . The idea of being an artist is that you create. . . . The thing would not exist without me. Norm and Brad could be replaced. They really couldn't be replaced, as far as I'm concerned, but I could find other people who have the skill to bend that tube. But there obviously hadn't been another person that had the idea until I came along to do that particular piece. It doesn't make me special; it's just my idea. So I think when you're looking at art it's never really any concern who has done the work, it's who had the idea."

While saying that an artist creates, Marcheschi actually is speaking, to a degree, in shorthand. He regards art as more a process of selection and perception than it is pure creation. "When the thing is done, or when you find it, when you choose it, when you pick it, it becomes art, because you've said so."

Some neon crafters believe neon's renewed popularity is connected to the rise of high tech, a theory Marcheschi tears into like a hawk attacking a field mouse. "Neon doesn't relate to technology in any way, shape or form," he states flatly. "It's primitive. It's in exactly the same place that a 1917 automobile is; that's the technology that it's still at today. Light's a finite material. It's just 'stuff.'"

Light is a phantasmagoric entity which exists as energized particles of air—"the incarnation of visible energy," as one person [Otto Piene] put it. It has a limited—perhaps illusory—life. When its electrical line is severed light ceases to be. This mystical material—if, indeed, light truly is a material—is not a standard art medium, for most artists, like most people, are tactile types who like to be able to touch something tangible, to feel what they create, and as they create. Light art is channeling amorphous light energy into pieces of plug-in sculpture.

Jack Burnham offered this viewpoint in *Beyond Modern Sculpture*: "The controlled use of light is the most flexible visual art form yet devised, and its enormous variety of uses is far from exhausted. At its present stage emitted light best demonstrates one of the primary qualities of *systems*: the tendency to fuse art object and environment into a perceptual whole. In fact, the trend of Light Art is to eliminate the specific art object and to transform the environment into a light-modulating system sensitive to responses from organisms which invade its presence."

Inherent in light is the quality of fire, that primal natural element that entranced and terrified our earliest ancestors with its mystical flaring force. Early in his career Marcheschi put together assemblages of glass tubes, wires, transformers, switches, and other electrical components that flowed and hummed and sparked in random fashion, pulsating with bolts of energy that made most viewers as skittish as thunderstorms no doubt did Early Man.

"The material was so powerful and beyond the traditional art experience that when the works were activated the response was either fear, awe, or possibly some primordial response to fire or lightning," Marcheschi laments. "I was very happy to see people respond beyond the formal, but in many cases the power of the material did not allow for the work to be viewed as art but rather as some type of fantastic display."

If light in a kinetic form, as fire, can cause awe and anxiety, though, in a static state it can sooth and comfort. Light symbolizes enlightenment, hope, and life itself. Burnham wrote that "luminosity acts as an emotional stimulant: primeval man's response was to be drawn toward the life-giving energy sources of heat and light." Marcheschi's oeuvre includes pieces with board-mounted lightbulbs that look like experiments from Thomas Edison's laboratory. The bulbs have soft, wavering glows that give them an ephemeral, wispy glimmer. Intuitively putting into practice Marshall McLuhan's dictum, in *Understanding Media,* that "The electric light is pure information... a medium without a message," Marcheschi began, in 1977, producing primarily static pieces—or seemingly static pieces; actually they flicker on and off 60 times per second—hoping they would have a meditative affect on viewers. He doesn't want the technical materials to be the focus of attention; he wants his pieces to "resonate with an enigmatic quality" so that viewers will ask themselves cosmic questions and perhaps come to a greater understanding of what it is they are doing with their lives. Burnham: "Increasingly, pure energy and information seem to be the essences of art." McLuhan: "The electric light escapes attention as a communication medium just because it has no 'content.' ... Electric light and power are separate from their uses, yet they eliminate time and space factors in human association exactly as do radio, telegraph, telephone, and TV, creating involvement in depth."

"Art, like medicine and technology, has changed," Marcheschi says. "A lot of people don't like the idea that it's changed, but everything changes. If they don't want it to change then they shouldn't take penicillin when they get sick; they should go back to wearing a little garlic around their neck. Then we'll go back to just painting faces. People used to paint faces [portraits], and paint buildings, and paint landscapes because there weren't cameras. The only reality trap we had was the artist. The person was sort of like a visual recorder of history, and that's how we know a lot about things before the development of the camera in the 1850s.... The moment you had the camera, which is an excellent reality trap, the artist (was) free from visual reality, and with the Impressionists you start to see sort of a technological attitude in terms of this technology—this camera—frees the artist to start to look at other realities. So, scientifically: the way light was broken up in Impressionist paintings, the way... the eyes mixed these colors from a distance. When you get close to them there's no composition. With a little distance there is a composition. And you see it going from that to questions that artists are asking today in their work, which are very basic and very human questions. They don't ask them directly; they ask them through your ability to interact.... My pieces are always about *a* question. They're always asking what it is that you're seeing, and hopefully that just becomes a metaphor for everything: What is it that you're doing with your life?"

Marcheschi believes people are less intimidated by his abstract light sculptures than by abstract paintings or other abstract sculpture because they are intrigued by the ethereal action.

"The works are not passive; indeed, the subtle pulsings of the gas make for a vivacity unequaled by paint," art critic William Hegeman wrote in an exhibition review in an arts magazine. "In part they are friendly tributes to the history of color field painting, but the differences in medium and conception make them new and pleasurable visual experiences."

In a basic sense, artists have always used light in paintings. "With growing sophistication, artists have analyzed and reinterpreted every aspect of indoor and outdoor illumination for the canvas," Jack Burnham wrote. Colors are but representations of light. The luminous nature of real light, though, opens unexplored avenues of creative expression.

Marcheschi says he never thinks about his light sculptures as anything other than his work. "This is what I do," he says. "The way that I work is much more the way that a sculptor works, simply because a painter normally works with paint, and I definitely don't work with paint. So, I mean, just as a process of elimination the work is more sculpture than it is painting. It also exists in real time, which frustrates a lot of things because a piece has a life expectancy. The time that it's on relates to your clock time."

Although many of Marcheschi's pieces look two-dimensionally flat when viewed in their activated state, they still must be classified as sculptures if for no other reason than that shaping something into a work of art is, by definition, what a *sculptor* does. Marcheschi, in fact, perceives his work not as two-dimensional, or even three-dimensional, but four-dimensional, with time the fourth dimension. For one thing, his aeriform art exists only as long as its electrical lifeline is connected. It has a limited, measurable life. For another thing, the fact that his works flicker on and off 60 times a second gives them an animate quality that painting and traditional sculpture do not have. "As you stare at the work it goes through a lot of changes, even though it seemingly is static," Marcheschi says.

Just as fireworks are little more than noise and smoke in daylight, Marcheschi's light sculptures also need a dark setting to be most effective. The contrast between the life energy of light and the deathlike nothingness of darkness is metaphorically significant.

One of Marcheschi's most personally meaningful and satisfying works, *Frog Urn Crate*, deals with the issues of life and death, existence and non-existence, and continuity and impermanence in a startlingly direct manner. The piece centers around an urn containing the ashes of one of his closest friends, who asked Marcheschi to create such a commemorative piece before his mystically-anticipated death in April of 1982. The urn rests inside a silicone rubber-covered crate, entrapped by several clear glass tubes and thick copper wires, giving the crate/casket the stark appearance of a jail cell. Bare electrical apparatuses within the box give one the eerie impression an execution is about to take place. And, in fact, something of the sort could be said to happen, for every 20 minutes an electrical charge zaps the urn. In another sense, however—and this no doubt is Marcheschi's main intention—this electrical charge is the antithesis of an execution. It is an enerization, an infusion of life energy, an affirmation, to quote a George Harrison song, that life flows on within us and without us.

- *September 1, 1983*

☼

Computer Clash

Don Miller ... computer art artist

To people who think of computers as cold and technological and art as warm and visually sensual, computer art may sound like a contradiction in terms. University of Wisconsin—River Falls art professor Don Miller likes to play on those diametrical forces and perceptions in his computer-composed "paintings."

Starting with an organic photographic image—usually a human form, face or body part—Miller uses a computer to distort, reduce, enlarge, copy and in other ways manipulate that image, or parts of the image.

"The tension between opposites is central to my art-making," he says, referring to the integration of organic images and the geometric elements the computer contributes. "... I would say that what I'm real interested in is an integration of a more technological medium with more primitive technology, if you want to call painting a more primitive technology. I'm interested in the kind of lines and shapes and forms that a machine makes. I think those things are easily transferred into this final image. There's a sense of geometry and a machine-like quality that I really like."

Miller, who has been concentrating on creating artworks with a computer for four years, likes the freedom to experiment and the flexibility a computer allows him to have. "I'm able to do things with visual images that I couldn't do working with older technologies such as pencils or paintbrushes and canvas," he says. "... I don't think that the computer is necessarily better than more traditional technology; it's just different. It has a lot of advantages and disadvantages. A lot of people don't like the computer because they can't get their hands into the application of the color. There's a certain distance that you have between your hand and what's happening inside the computer."

For Miller, that distance quickly dissipates as he works.

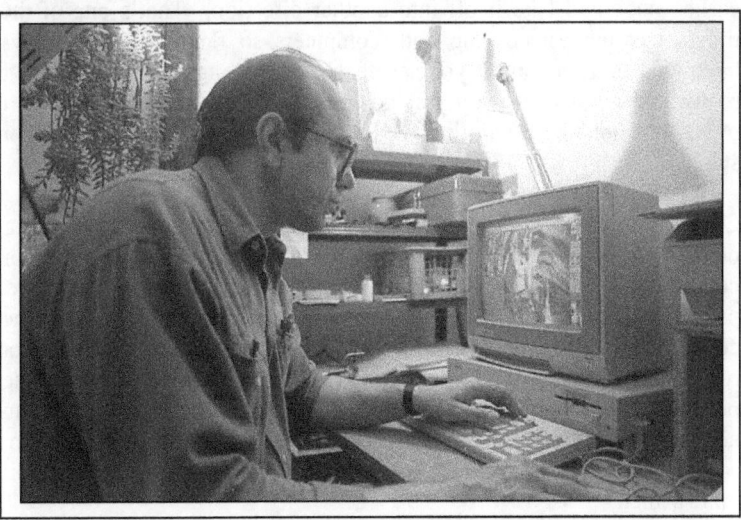

"After I've been working with the computer for 10 or 15 minutes I become totally absorbed and I don't see the rest of the room; all I see is what's happening on the screen," he says. "It's like going to a movie, going to sit down, and all of a sudden the theater vanishes and you're in the image, you're part of it."

Miller is able to play with a basic image in a wide range of ways by selecting program options he wants and moving a mouse around as he views the evolving image on the computer screen. He may "define" a certain part of the image and drag that part around the screen, or use it like a rubber stamp to duplicate it. He may enlarge a section to several times its original size, or reduce the size of a defined area. He might distort an image as funhouse mirrors would. Color manipulation has almost endless possibilities. "I can do lots of things with color very rapidly," he says. "I can work with 32 colors at one time. I can go in and change any one color in innumerable ways. I can change the value—the intensity, or saturation. I can add bits of one hue to another hue, so I can regulate my color very subtly. Actually, the enlarged palette is 4,096 colors; I can use 32 of those at any one time. There are other ways of using more color on the computer, but right now that's all I need."

Some of his computer paintings take 20 to 30 hours to complete.

"I keep editing and editing," he says. "I might reach a certain point where I feel that I'm not really getting anyplace and go back to an earlier stage and take it off into another direction. That's one of the things that makes working with computers so flexible—you always have your original, and if you save each stage along the way you can't really make mistakes; you just go back to an earlier stage and start over. It's not like a painting where you can't go back to that earlier stage."

Once Miller has something he likes he prints it out on high-grade paper, on an ink-jet printer. "Most of the printers that are available for computers are dot-matrix printers," he explains. "But I use an ink-jet printer because it puts out vibrant colors, and they're more like the colors on the computer screen." Even so, he says, the printer does not reproduce the screen colors exactly. "Usually what I do is print out the palette and look at the palette so that as I'm working on the image I can adjust my color, or I can at least know what's going to happen when, say, a certain red and a certain green prints out; it might print a little bit more violet."

When using "rag" paper in a dot-matrix printer he previously used, Miller frequently added to the printout image with pencils and/or paint. The brilliant, clay-coated paper he uses in the ink-jet printer makes such mixed-media creations more difficult.

Given that the printouts are limited to 10 inches in width, Miller must print one section at a time and piece together the sections if he wants to make large paintings.

In the "advantage" column, Miller likes the fact it is possible to store about 25 computer paintings on one disk. "It's real efficient," he says. "You can work in a small space and accumulate quite a few paintings."

He believes there is a misconception about computer art in that most people think a computer artist must be "very knowledgeable about programming language and that kind of thing. . . . In the beginning I think it was a necessity, that people had to know how to program, because there was very little software available. But now it's very, very rich, in terms of the amount of software available to the artist."

He believes another misconception is that "a lot of people think that doing computer art is real expensive, that you have to invest $50,000 in order to be able to do it. You could buy some real exciting equipment—some real elaborate equipment—for that price, but you can set up for a lot cheaper than that. There are many computers now around the $1,000 range that are fairly sophisticated. It's not prohibitive, like it was five or ten years ago."

Miller uses the computer in a painting class he teaches "as a means to get the students to explore all kinds of composition possibilities. A real important part of painting is composition, and the computer, I think, is a real valuable tool in that respect."

While Miller exhibits his work in gallery shows throughout the United States, and sells a few of his digital paintings, teaching comes first for him.

"I think it's necessary for me to do artwork in order to teach," he says. "One activity feeds the other. But I'm not making my living as an artist. I think there's a good kind of freedom in being able to teach, which I enjoy, and being able to do my artwork. It's a nice balance for me."

While "a lot of people don't like the geometric patterns and so forth that comprise the image, I really like that," Miller says. "I like the fact that when you look at a resulting image that you feel that the computer was used somehow in the creation of it. . . . I think there is that thing that occurs with a computer that is really exciting. There are things that sometimes happen by accident that can be utilized. And I like the idea of working with random things and going back and selecting out of that random range. So I think that one can use an accident. I don't think that it's something that always works, obviously, but sometimes things happen that are random that can be exciting."

- *May 1, 1987*

www.ingramcontent.com/pod-product-compliance
Lightning Source LLC
Chambersburg PA
CBHW051632170526
45167CB00001B/162